Susan Sheridan is Adjunct Professor of English and Women's Studies at Flinders University, South Australia. She was instrumental in the development of Women's Studies as a discipline, taught in that area for much of her career, and was Reviews Editor of *Australian Feminist Studies* from its inception in 1985 until 2005. She has published widely on women's writing, feminist cultural studies and Australian cultural history.

Also by Susan Sheridan

Christina Stead (1988)

Grafts: Feminist Cultural Criticism (editor, 1988)

Debutante Nation: Feminism Contests the 1890s (co-editor, with Sue Rowley and Susan Magarey, 1993)

Along the Faultlines: Sex, race, and nation in Australian women's writing, 1880s to 1930s (1995)

Who Was That Woman? The Australian Women's Weekly *in the postwar years* (with Barbara Baird, Kate Borrett and Lyndall Ryan, 2002)

Thea Astley's Fictional Worlds (co-editor, with Paul Genoni, 2006)

NINE LIVES

SUSAN SHERIDAN

UQP

First published 2011 by University of Queensland Press
PO Box 6042, St Lucia, Queensland 4067 Australia

www.uqp.com.au

Typeset in 12/16 pt Bembo by Post Pre-press Group, Brisbane
Printed in Australia by McPherson's Printing Group
Author photograph taken by Michael Bradley

Cataloguing-in-Publication Data
National Library of Australia

Sheridan, Susan, 1944–

Nine Lives: Postwar women writers making their mark

ISBN 9780702238680 (pbk)

Includes bibliographical references and index.

Women authors, Australian – 20th century.
Australian literature – Women authors – History and criticism.
Australian literature – 20th century – History and criticism.

A820.99287

University of Queensland Press uses papers that are natural, renewable and recyclable products made from wood grown in sustainable forests. The logging and manufacturing processes conform to the environmental regulations of the country of origin.

Contents

Introduction

The scene is Australia 1959. Gwen Harwood starts a guerilla war on literary editors by submitting her poems under male pseudonyms, whose poetry is accepted where the efforts of a housewife from Hobart have been rejected. Dorothy Hewett, silent for the previous decade, publishes *Bobbin Up*, a successful novel but one that allows little scope for her poetic gifts or her theatrical ambitions. Elizabeth Jolley arrives in Perth from England and begins to send out stories, but must wait until 1976 to publish a book.

At the same time, Judith Wright and Rosemary Dobson, who have been publishing since the 1940s, are lauded as key voices in the postwar blooming of Australian poetry. Thea Astley successfully publishes her first novel, a modernist study of emotions.

Alongside these success stories, three other women writers are working away in obscurity – self-critical Amy Witting and Dorothy Green hesitate to send out their poetry and stories, while Jessica Anderson enjoys for the first time the freedom to write novels rather than money-earning journalism.

These nine women, the subjects of this book, are part of a generation of Australian women writers born between 1915 and 1930. They emerged in the wake of an earlier generation of women, including Christina Stead, Eleanor Dark and Katharine Susannah Prichard, who had come to dominate serious fiction writing in the 1930s and 1940s.[1] Unlike those heroic predecessors, however, they were not readily visible in the lively literary scene of the postwar years. Most published writers, not to mention reviewers, editors, publishers and university teachers of literature, were men. Popular wisdom has it that after the war women were removed from the public sphere and imprisoned in domesticity, but this was not entirely true. Significant numbers of women were writing, and painting, too, combining the artistic life with the domestic. On the whole, their achievements did not attract much notice, although they were there, creatively responding to the challenges of the postwar world.[2] Our picture of the Australian literary scene from the late 1940s to the mid 1960s as strongly male dominated is far from accurate. It is a picture that needs to be reconfigured by including the women in it.

I have chosen a handful of the most interesting writers, whose early careers during the postwar decades took various roads to success, some much longer and more winding than others. Judith Wright and Thea Astley were published regularly and gained critical recognition almost from the time they started writing. The work of other women appeared fitfully, if at all, during the 1950s and 1960s.

A number of talented poets made a strong early start in the 1940s – Rosemary Dobson, Dorothy Hewett and Dorothy Auchterlonie (Green) – but over the next decade Hewett was silent and Auchterlonie published very little. Dobson continued with a reduced output, however, and in the 1960s Hewett resumed publishing poetry, and Gwen Harwood's first two volumes appeared.

So too did Oodgeroo/Kath Walker's *We Are Going* (1964), the first book by an Aboriginal woman to appear in print.

In fiction the situation was more complicated. Kylie Tennant, Ruth Park, Nancy Keesing and Nancy Cato had, from the 1940s onwards, gained popular success in writing novels, children's stories and radio plays. Joan Phipson, Patricia Wrightson and others transformed Australian children's literature. Yet their work attracted little critical attention at a time of growing separation between literary and popular fiction, when Australian literature began to be taught in the universities and a canon of significant works was built around Patrick White's modernist novels. Thea Astley's novels were among the few by women to be admitted into this canon.

Another group of women fiction writers of this generation would not see their work published in book form at all during the 1950s and 1960s – Elizabeth Jolley, Amy Witting, Olga Masters and Jessica Anderson. Jolley's stories attracted only rejection slips for years, and she had to wait until the mid 1970s to have a book published. Amy Witting, too, despite having published several stories in magazines during the 1960s, including the prestigious *New Yorker*, did not see her name on the cover of a book until 1977. Olga Masters raised a family of seven children and worked as a journalist before gaining success as a fiction writer when she was in her sixties, beginning with *The Home Girls* in 1982. Jessica Anderson was the first of this group to publish a novel, in 1963, when she made the transition from writing for money – pseudonymous magazine stories and radio scripts – to publishing serious fiction under her own name.

Because of these delayed starts, this study of the early careers of nine women who began writing in the postwar decades necessarily ranges from the 1940s to the 1970s. The context of their individual stories is the period of Australian cultural history that saw a cultural renaissance over the years between 1945 and 1965. During this time the work of AD Hope, Judith Wright and Patrick White won international recognition. James McAuley, David Campbell, John Blight, Francis Webb and Vincent Buckley joined the ranks of established male poets with Kenneth Slessor, RD FitzGerald and Douglas Stewart. The modernist fiction of Hal Porter and Randolph Stow was set alongside that of Patrick White. It was a high point for local publishing enterprises, with Lansdowne, Rigby, Sun Books and University of Queensland Press starting up, and Penguin and Macmillan establishing Australian editorial offices.[3] It was the period when *Quadrant*, *Overland*, *Australian Letters*, *Australian Literary Studies*, *Westerly* and *Australian Book Review* joined *Meanjin* and *Southerly* to establish an array of literary magazines, most of which still occupy the field today. Annual anthologies of poetry and short fiction had been initiated in the 1940s by Angus & Robertson, to be followed by the journal *Australian Letters* in the late 1950s with their annual *Verse in Australia*.[4]

The Commonwealth Literary Fund began a subsidy scheme that underwrote the publication of 'outstanding Australian works which have a limited audience', including poetry.[5] Serious literature had more cultural clout than at any previous time, as Australian literature began to be taught in schools and universities. As well as the emergence of new poets and novelists, this period saw the burgeoning of modernist painting from internationally acclaimed artists such as Sidney Nolan, Arthur Boyd and Charles Blackman. There was an explosion of iconoclastic energy in theatre, ballet and music, encouraged by government subsidies and the formation of new bodies including the Australian Ballet and the Elizabethan Theatre Trust.

At first women's participation in this cultural renaissance was limited: Judith Wright and Rosemary Dobson were seen as brilliant exceptions. But as the 1960s moved into the 1970s, many women shared the benefits of increased support for literary enterprises, not only government subsidies for publications and writers' fellowships through the Literature Board of the Australia Council (formed in 1975) but also the spread of literary prizes, writers' festivals and the like. There were expanding opportunities to write for radio and television. Changes in the publishing industry, which made it more possible for local publishers to risk taking on new writers, especially authors of innovative fiction, contributed to an increase in the writing and publication of books by women. During the 1980s when an expansive literary scene met an expanding audience for women's writing, inspired by the second wave of feminism, women writers came into their own. But the story told in this book is the prelude to this 'decade of the women'.

Literature was a particularly unwelcoming and uncertain profession for women in the 1950s and 1960s. To account for that uncertainty requires a complex set of interlocking explanations, in terms of the social, political and cultural climate of the times – the ideologically driven ousting of women from public life in the postwar period, the dominance of Cold War cultural politics that few of these writers participated in, current literary tastes and whether the kind of writing they were attempting was understood or valued, and finally their distinctively feminine commitments to marriage and family. As writers, they entered the literary scene in a small nation during a key period of its social and cultural development, yet their fortunes varied greatly. The differences among them depend partly on the genre they chose, partly on their personal circumstances (whether they had to earn a living, for instance) and partly on their literary connections, or lack of them. All were passionately committed to the art of writing, but while some maintained intense literary friendships with their male peers, others lived in relative isolation from the literary scene.

A focus on writers' careers, examining their creative development and reputations alongside one another, makes it possible to identify gendered patterns of cultural production and reception.[6] Rachel Blau DuPlessis's concept of the 'nexus' formed by artists of a particular time and place, who have 'shared meditations but not necessarily shared conclusions or even practices', invites us not only to (re)discover each writer as an exceptional woman, but to read them together and place them centrally in a picture that includes their male peers.[7] To do this is to produce fresh configurations of that literary scene, and consequently of literary history.

While the present study takes gender as a central category of analysis, it incorporates significant disagreements with some earlier feminist approaches to gender and literary production. Women in a patriarchal world have been characterised as rank outsiders (Virginia Woolf), as lacking an authentic speech of their own (Luce Irigaray), as eclipsed by male culture (Tillie Olsen).[8] These are all memorable zero-sum metaphors, figuring women's complete exclusion from men's power.

But if this were absolutely the case no women's voices would ever be heard. Not all women are equally excluded from the exercise of cultural power. Female voices are heard, female visions are seen, though fitfully. If we explore Olson's visual metaphor of eclipse, we could say that an eclipse is a momentary event – it does not last – and this would better describe the periods of invisibility in individual careers. But an eclipse is also a recurrent event, and this would better describe the varying degree of visibility that educated women as a group have experienced in the worlds of cultural production, at least over the past two hundred years. Finally, if we consider that an eclipse is caused by the passing of one planetary body in the path of another, we could suggest that it is the varying relationship between male and female artists, as two distinct groups, that accounts for the intermittent obscuring of women's creativity. Certainly, when women did appear to dominate the Australian literary scene in the 1980s, there were distinct rumblings that men were being edged out – a complaint illustrating the zero-sum game perceived by feminists, but in reverse.

Of course male and female writers and artists rarely experience themselves as part of a gendered group. They are more likely, if they are conscious of any group identity at all, to acknowledge an affinity of artistic aims, for example, in the case of the modernists, or to concede some significance in their generation's historical experience or their national identity as Australian writers. To consider writers of a particular generation and place as part of a gendered group is not to impose a feminist (or anti-feminist) consciousness on them. Nor is it an attempt to share their self-perceptions. Rather, it is to stand back and look for patterns in their lives and careers, similarities and differences that may be explicable by considering the interaction of gender with class, race and other social structures of power.

Feminist ideas about women as cultural outsiders, striking though they are, prove unsatisfactory means of explaining these patterns. Subtler instruments are needed to analyse the varying degrees of recognition that this cohort of women experienced when they began writing. Literary sociologist Pierre Bourdieu's conceptual framework of cultural capital offers a more finely calibrated account of both individual writers and the literary milieu in which they operate. It can include considerations of class and other advantages that at times may outweigh the disadvantage of gender, and it can help identify the specific conditions of literary publishing in Australia in the decades immediately following World War II.

Bourdieu's concept of cultural capital refers to the various non-economic resources that people may accumulate, which give them a competitive advantage over other players in whatever game they join – in this case, the literary game. Cultural capital is made up of intellectual capital gained from one's education, social capital in the form of networks of family, friends and contacts, and symbolic capital in the form of recognition, influence and authority.[9] Women, members of the working class, ethnic and sexual minorities, all find access to these resources more difficult than ruling-class men do. However, their access is not categorically denied, and the challenge when considering women in the writing profession is to estimate how they managed access to various kinds of cultural capital.

A writer's access to economic resources is a crucial issue. Most subjects of this book were engaged in non-profitable cultural production in the form of poetry, drama and literary fiction. Bourdieu points out the inverse relationship between material and symbolic success in the literary field. Indeed, poetry as a sub-field of literary production is marked by its distance from the possibility of generating profits, which does not prevent it occupying a high position in the symbolic hierarchy of literary forms.[10] A corollary of this inverse relationship between profitability and symbolic capital is that writing for money – journalism, genre fiction, children's books, magazine and radio work – carries lower status and its practitioners have not generally been considered serious contenders in the literary stakes. This was particularly the case in the postwar period, though not so much today. Jessica Anderson, for instance, drew a veil of obscurity over her early journalistic writing, published under unknown names. Yet even here there are anomalies – Judith Wright was not seen to have compromised her established reputation as a leading poet when she published children's stories and material for radio and magazines.

The high-status field of poetry was flourishing in 1940s Australia when Judith Wright and Rosemary Dobson began to publish.[11] During the war years there was a flurry of energy invested in little magazines, in annual anthologies and some more ephemeral literary publications. In 1939 the Commonwealth Literary Fund was established, and it subsidised literary publications, including poetry. Between those years and the new flowering of little magazines in the 1950s, poetry was well served by the *Bulletin*'s 'Red Page', *Meanjin Papers* (founded in 1938), and the English Association magazine, *Southerly*, founded in 1939. Poetry was regularly published in newspapers, as well.

In these multiple outlets for the publication of individual poems, critical evaluation and gatekeeping activities were exercised by specialist editors rather than by commercial publishing houses. As well, over this whole period of the 1940s and 1950s, poetry was not subjected to the appalling degree of censorship that blighted fiction, both local and imported.[12] In such a context, it was easier for a new poet to see her work in print than for a fiction writer. This meant that the literary milieu into which young women poets entered was open to new voices, and poetry enjoyed high prestige among literary forms. By the time Gwen Harwood began sending out poems in the late 1950s, the number of Australian literary magazines available to choose from had expanded greatly. Book publication for poets, always subsidised, was encouraged during the 1960s by the expansion of teaching Australian literature in schools and universities.[13] Virginia Woolf's prediction that the twentieth century would see the emergence of women poets seemed to have been vindicated.[14]

Women fiction writers, whether published and overlooked, like Anderson, or not published at all until they were middle-aged, like Witting and Jolley, were disadvantaged by comparison with their contemporaries who wrote poetry. Until the late 1970s, looking for a publisher for an Australian novel almost inevitably meant looking to London. The only significant Australian publisher of quality fiction titles during the period was Angus & Robertson. Patrick White, Kylie Tennant, George Johnston, Charmian Clift, Barbara Jefferis and Elizabeth Harrower, as well as more commercial writers such as Jon Cleary and Morris West were published in London (and often in the US as well).[15] Few local publishers were willing to make an investment in new novelists during the years when hardback publication was standard and paperback reprints rare. This made the publisher's investment in a new fiction author an expensive risk, until Australian offices of British publishers expanded and paperback originals became more common for literary fiction – an innovation initially promoted during the 1970s by Brian Johns at Penguin.[16]

As well as limited publishing opportunities for fiction in the postwar years, there were stronger disagreements about what kinds of fiction were desirable. It is no accident that Astley, the only woman novelist to have been accorded the highest accolades for her novels during the 1960s, was working in the modernist style, with a definite leaning to satire, as was Patrick White.[17] Her early work was seen as part of the new kind of Australian writing, 'loaded with poetic imagery and symbolism'.[18] For new writers who eschewed such experimental, 'poetic' fiction, it was difficult to get a serious hearing. Beatrice Davis, Astley's editor, rejected novels by Jessica Anderson, Elizabeth Jolley, and Amy Witting.

Among proliferating literary magazines, publishing enterprises, state support for writers and the spread of Australian literature as a subject for study in schools and universities, most of the influential protagonists were men. What roles did they play, with their friendships and enmities, their political predilections, and their relations with their female contemporaries? The names of several editors and academics recur in the stories told in this book. Douglas Stewart's editorship of the *Bulletin*'s literary Red Page from 1940 until 1960 made him a highly influential presence, both as a reviewer and a selector of poetry and stories. Through his friendship with Beatrice Davis, his taste also informed decisions made about poetry publishing at Angus & Robertson. Some of his peers such as Alec

Hope considered his taste in poetry rather commonplace, but he was a great encourager of new writers, and was an important mentor for the young Rosemary Dobson, Nan McDonald and Nancy Keesing; Elizabeth Riddell also regularly published poems in the *Bulletin*.

Southerly, based at Sydney University and published by Angus & Robertson, was edited first by academic RG Howarth and then, at the suggestion of Beatrice Davis and Alec Bolton, by poet Kenneth Slessor. The two men were close friends and their successive stewardships of *Southerly* provide a vivid example of the way the literary profession in Australia in the 1940s, 1950s and early 1960s was 'based on male homo-sociality – in all its richness, and with all its exclusions'.[19] Women were not well represented in *Southerly*, although Howarth published some early poems by Judith Wright and Rosemary Dobson, and Kenneth Slessor published poetry by Nancy Cato and Nan McDonald, and, in the late 1950s, Amy Witting's first stories.

Clem Christesen, editor of *Meanjin*, was more of a loner, who started out in Brisbane without close links to either the Sydney literary world or the academy. *Meanjin* rapidly became a force to be reckoned with, and most ambitious new writers submitted work to him. He formed strong but combative relationships with several of the women writers in this book, including Judith Wright and Gwen Harwood. He published the teenage Dorothy Hewett, but not her later work, although they carried on a friendly correspondence. He was a lifelong friend to Dorothy Auchterlonie Green, but both she and Judith Wright found it hard to forgive him for what they perceived as his cavalier treatment of their husbands' work.

Among the new journals starting up in the 1950s, *Australian Letters*, edited by Geoffrey Dutton and Max Harris, included women among its published writers and featured both Dobson and Wright in its 'poets and painters' series. Dutton and Harris were also influential publishers, establishing Sun Books and *Australian Book Review*, and Dutton edited important early critical works on Australian writers. Stephen Murray-Smith, editor of *Overland*, became a mentor for Dorothy Hewett, though he was critical of her poetry and preferred her less adventurous short stories. Alec Hope and James McAuley (founding editor of *Quadrant*) were highly influential poet-professors throughout the 1960s. They were important mentors for Gwen Harwood, admired Wright's and Dobson's work from a distance, and both had stormy friendships with Dorothy Green.

The only woman who wielded comparable literary influence during this period was Beatrice Davis at Angus & Robertson. She was determined that the company should be the 'literary hub of Australia' and, with Douglas Stewart, initiated the annual anthologies *Australian Poetry* and *Coast to Coast*.[20] Yet like all literary editors, she had her pets and her prejudices and while she proved to be an inspired mentor for Thea Astley, she rejected Amy Witting's best work, as well as early manuscripts from both Elizabeth Jolley and Jessica Anderson. Kylie Tennant, as a reviewer and, later, member of the Literature Board, supported many new writers, as did Nancy Keesing. Thelma Forshaw, by contrast, could be devastating in her reviews. Rival critics Dorothy Green and Leonie Kramer both devoted their scholarly energies to the work of Henry Handel Richardson, but neither saw it as her responsibility to support women writers in particular.

Women appeared in noticeable numbers in professional associations such as the Fellowship of Australian Writers and the English Association. The formation of the Australian Society of Authors in 1963 called forth the talents of women like Jill Hellyer, Nancy Keesing and Barbara Jefferis, yet such necessary organisational work brought with it little power and prestige.

★

This book aims to create a group biography of nine out of the generational cohort of Australian women writers born between 1915 and 1930. Among Australian precedents for this kind of feminist group literary biography are Drusilla Modjeska's *Exiles at Home* (1981), about the 1920s–1930s generation of women novelists, linked through their correspondence with Nettie Palmer, and Ann Vickery's *Stressing the Modern* (2007), which deals with the poets of two generational cohorts, born in the 1860s and the 1890s. It was a feature of the period in which all these writers flourished that they were politically active at some stage of their lives in feminist or socialist causes, and such activism emerges as a central theme in both these group biographies.

The women writers who emerged in the 1950s and 1960s for the most part did not know one another. They had no comparable network of friendship, nor did they have any common political concerns until later, in the 1980s, in relation to the anti-war and conservation movements. Only Dorothy Hewett had both radical political commitments and also a commitment to experimentation in living as well as writing, while the others mostly led lives of apparently conventional heterosexuality.

What commonalities they had were not chosen affiliations, but rather derived from the social and cultural experience shared by that generation of women. They grew up in the shadow of the Great War and lived though the Depression, World War II and post-war reconstruction. Because of these events, few of them travelled outside Australia, unlike Stead, Richardson, Prichard and Franklin before them. Yet they shared a different and more urgent sense of connectedness to the wider world, in their acute awareness of the legacy of past wars. As well, they shared a commitment to making a life and a career in Australia: cultural life was to be established here, not sought elsewhere – and this was as true for immigrant Elizabeth Jolley as for fifth-generation settler Australian Judith Wright.

All nine women came from middle- or upper-class families and, unlike most of their predecessors, nearly all had some form of post-secondary education. While they all undertook income-earning work at some time during their lives, only Astley, Witting and Green pursued careers in teaching (both secondary and tertiary) from youth until retirement age. These three came from more modest families and had completed degrees and teaching qualifications, with the intention of earning their own livings. None of the others seems to have been driven by the desire for a professional career: education at private girls' schools in the 1930s was 'academic' in the subjects taught, but failure rates were high: girls were not generally expected to be keen on matriculating and going to university.[21] Professions considered appropriate for women were few – nursing, teaching and librarianship – and career opportunities within these professions were severely limited (especially after marriage). For girls with a literary bent, the available jobs in publishing or journalism required no further education at all. Dorothy Green's venture into the literary academy shows how slowly the major social institutions moved towards accepting women as equals. While her contemporaries Thea Astley, Dorothy Hewett and Elizabeth Jolley all taught at universities for significant periods of their lives, none of them saw teaching as her primary vocation.

Like the great majority of women in the larger cohort, all these nine writers married and had children – demographically speaking, they participated in the great postwar marriage and baby boom. These personal circumstances affected their literary productivity, and had a more marked impact on their professional lives than those of their male peers. To mention a few of the best-known of these men: Patrick White inherited a sufficiently large income to be able to live independently during the early part of his career; Alec Hope and James McAuley were both appointed to chairs of English, even though neither of them held postgraduate qualifications higher than a Master of Arts degree. All three had domestic partners who devoted themselves exclusively to providing the writers with a secure home and social life. None had major child-raising responsibilities. Such considerations do not usually enter into accounts of the careers of male writers, but they are crucial in the lives of their female counterparts, as we shall see in the chapters that follow.

All nine subjects of this book had domestic responsibilities – homes that they managed single-handedly, and children whose needs frequently competed with their creative desires. Wright, Green and Hewett were effectively principal breadwinners in their families, yet they also looked after the daily round of home, children and social life. All did their own typing and correspondence (a role often taken on by male writers' wives). Judith Wright expressed the dilemma this way:

> I've always had to do a lot of hack work: writing school plays for the ABC, and doing children's books, generally doing the housewife jobs in literature, you might say. I don't think anyone in Australia, unless they've got an academic job, can support themselves with this kind of really serious writing which you can in Europe, for instance. And certainly no woman could. It would be very difficult. Trivialisation of life is a real problem for women, dealing so much with what's regarded as trivial, and trying to find your own value system and live by the values of a serious writer is very difficult when you haven't got what you might call a support base.[22]

Writing as a profession for women in this period was a contradiction in terms: the predominant images of women in postwar modernity as domestic or erotic goddesses did not encompass the role of artist or intellectual. How did women who ventured into such roles see themselves? Was there an inevitable disjuncture between 'woman' and 'writer'? Their predecessors often envisaged their professional lives as requiring a choice between love and autonomy, or simply found marriage and a profession incompatible, as did so many of Vickery's and Modjeska's subjects. Yet of the next generation, the vast majority of women writers married and raised children. How did they manage the balancing act of marriage, family and writing? Above all, why did a handful of women writers succeed where so many others failed? What measures of success and failure predominated in the 1950s and 1960s, which perhaps no longer apply to literary reputations?

Was this kind of eclipsing a distinctively Australian phenomenon, or did postwar women writers in other Anglophone cultures face it too? How did the professional experiences of Australian women writers compare with those of their peers in other places?

Despite the prominence of a few female intellectuals such as Simone de Beauvoir in France and Iris Murdoch in Britain, women writers on the whole were poorly represented in the literatures of Europe and North America in the postwar decades. Indeed, Sylvia Plath's brief and tragic life has become an icon of the constraints within which creative women lived. Women artists across the Western world shared to some extent a contradictory position. On the one hand, they were women caught up in the massive changes that took place in everyday life brought about by the spread of postwar consumerism and media culture. On the other, they were intellectuals who shared with others concerns about communism versus capitalism, nationalism versus internationalism, artistic modernism versus realism and the political responsibilities of artists in a post-holocaust and post-Hiroshima world. If 'postwar modernity' is understood in terms of both everyday life and the war of ideas, women writers of the time were positioned on the fulcrum of these two forces.

In Australia specific versions of those cultural conflicts between the political Left and Right and the aesthetics of modernism and realism were exacerbated by strict literary and artistic censorship. Two major controversies in cultural politics in the 1940s set the tone for the following decades. In 1943 there was uproar over William Dobell's Archibald Prize–winning portrait of Joshua Smith. And the following year poetry under the name of Ern Malley was published in the magazine *Angry Penguins*, whose editor Max Harris hailed the author as a modernist genius: the authors turned out to be James McAuley and Harold Stewart; to add insult to injury, Harris was prosecuted for publishing obscene material. Both incidents involved violent reactions against modernist experimentation, which forced both writers and artists into taking strong positions for and against.[23]

The conflict over modernism affected fiction writers even more than poets, as was seen in negative responses to White's early fiction. Notable among these was poet AD Hope's review of *The Tree of Man*, calling it 'illiterate verbal sludge'.[24] This was a daunting context for new writers like Astley. Censorship of sexual material, which had a long history in Australia, added to the problems for novelists: in the late 1940s Christina Stead's American novel *Letty Fox: Her Luck*, was banned on the grounds of obscenity.[25] Such censorship influenced Jessica Anderson to seek a publisher in Britain rather than closer to home, a choice that delayed her recognition in Australia.

The Cold War political polarisation of the period profoundly affected the literary scene. Little magazines were generally sympathetic to the Left, except for *Quadrant*, which was specifically established as an anti-communist enterprise. The funding of *Meanjin* and *Overland* was reduced or refused on several occasions. Government grants to individual writers were also affected. Kylie Tennant experienced this kind of political wrangling when in 1952 she was attacked in parliament as a 'communist' recipient of Commonwealth funding, and again ten years later when, as a member of the Commonwealth Literary Fund's Board, she was lobbied by her friends, editors Clem Christesen and Stephen Murray-Smith, to support their applications.[26] There was some overlap between political alignments and the controversies over modernism: as a communist Dorothy Hewett felt she had to deny her admiration for Ezra Pound and Edith Sitwell, denouncing their influence on the 'Angry Penguins'[27] – but at the same time cutting herself off from sources of poetic inspiration.

Most of the women were wary of being drawn into such taking of sides. The young Judith Wright was suspicious of all groups and coteries, as she wrote in 1952 to Barbara Blackman: 'What's lacking is the creative stillness; refusal to impose oneself on events, refusal to be imposed upon.'[28] Rosemary Dobson declined James McAuley's urgent invitation to join *Quadrant*'s editorial board, for 'one must write as an individual'.[29]

When their children were young, these women had insufficient time for politics or writing. Furthermore, their sense of the social responsibility of writers in most cases did not match that of their male contemporaries. They tended to direct their energies to such causes as Aboriginal rights, refugees, conservation and peace, without aligning themselves to political parties. Their critical responses to postwar gender, race and class relations, deeply influenced by their wartime experiences, were marked by a certain detachment from 'national' questions and political independence from traditional Left–Right oppositions. Because of this, they rarely appear in cultural histories of the Cold War period, yet most of them held strong political convictions and were to varying degrees literary activists by their own lights.

I chose each writer featured in this book because she did, finally, make her mark as a serious writer, however long it took. The nine lives outlined here are not by any means full biographies, even of each writer's professional life, but in all cases the story of her apprenticeship in writing and publishing reveals significant aspects of the place of women in the postwar literary scene. In every story the focus is on the individual woman and her work, but the questions asked are common ones – How did she come to see herself as a writer? How did she get started? What resources did she have at her disposal? What uses did she make of them? Who and what helped or hindered her? How did she achieve that 'creative stillness' that Judith Wright recommended? What were the conditions of possibility of her getting published and having her achievement recognised?

To answer these questions I have made extensive use of unpublished correspondence, both personal and professional, which I have used to illuminate the writers' professional concerns. Letters offer insights into a writer's literary relationships, into the various aspects of themselves that they project to different correspondents, and the way those correspondents regard them. The AustLit online database has been invaluable in locating contemporary reviews of published work, as well as information about the place and date of early publications. This resource has made it possible to find out quickly and accurately how often a poet published in the *Bulletin*, say, or *Meanjin*, or the *Sydney Morning Herald*. It enabled me to check when short stories published in later collections had first appeared, and where.

The availability of published material about these nine writers varies considerably. To date, only Judith Wright, Dorothy Green and Elizabeth Jolley have been the subjects of published biographies, although there are several more in the making. A good deal of the voluminous correspondence of Judith Wright and Gwen Harwood has been published, with useful context-setting and explanatory notes by the editors. Many writers of this generation were interviewed about their lives and work, and these interviews, published and unpublished (notably the oral history collection at the Australian National Library) have proved invaluable. Only Dorothy Hewett and Judith Wright published full-length autobiographical works during their lifetimes, although others published short pieces: I have used these extensively, though always conscious of the hindsight on which autobiography depends. I have used critical analyses of their works sparingly, since my focus has been principally on the production and reception of their earliest published work, rather than on the themes and strategies of their writing.

Notes

1 Drusilla Modjeska's study of these writers, *Exiles at Home*, Sirius/Angus & Robertson, Sydney, 1981, is a key precedent for the present study. Katherine Bode's recent empirical study of publication figures complicates this picture, showing that, despite their dominance in serious fiction, women's titles were outnumbered by men's for most of the first half of the century: 'Along Gender Lines: Reassessing relationships between Australian novels, gender and genre from 1930 to 2006', *Australian Literary Studies*, 24(3–4), 2009, pp. 79–95.

2 Susan Sheridan, 'Cold War, Home Front: Australian women writers and artists in the 1950s', *Australian Literary Studies*, 20(3), 2002, pp. 155–66.

3 Patrick Buckridge, 'Clearing a Space for Australian Literature, 1940–1965', in *The Oxford Literary History of Australia*, eds Bruce Bennett and Jennifer Strauss, OUP, Melbourne, 1998, pp. 184–5. After 1965 most of these local companies were bought out by British publishers.

4 The nationalist poets, Jindyworobaks, also produced annual anthologies for several years.

5 Angus & Robertson published a lot of poetry under this scheme: Neil James and Elizabeth Webby, 'Canon around the hub: Angus and

Robertson and the post-war literary canon', *Southerly*, 57(3), 1997, pp. 51–66.

6 As Ann Vickery shows in her recent book, *Stressing the Modern: Cultural politics in Australian women's poetry*, Salt, Cambridge, UK, 2007, p. 5.

7 Rachel Blau DuPlessis and Peter Quartermain, *The Objectivist Nexus: Cultural poetics*, University of Alabama Press, Tuscaloosa, AL, 1999, p. 22; quoted in DuPlessis, *Blue Studios: Poetry and its cultural work*, University of Alabama Press, Tuscaloosa, AL, 2006, p. 66.

8 Virginia Woolf, *A Room of One's Own*, Hogarth Press, London, 1928; Luce Irigaray, *This Sex Which Is Not One* [1977] trans. Catherine Porter, Cornell University Press, Ithaca, NY, 1985; Tillie Olsen, *Silences: When Writers Don't Write*, Virago, London, 1980.

9 Pierre Bourdieu, *The Field of Cultural Production*, edited and introduced by Randal Johnson, Polity, Cambridge, UK, 1993, Editor's Introduction, pp. 6–7.

10 Bourdieu, pp. 47–8.

11 Rosemary Dobson, *A World of Difference: Australian poetry and painting in the 1940s*, 3rd Blaiklock Lecture, Wentworth Press, Sydney, 1973. Chris Wallace-Crabbe, 'Poetry and Modernism', *The Oxford Literary History of Australia*, pp. 217–35.

12 Nicole Moore, *The Censor's Library*, Melbourne University Press, forthcoming.

13 Angus & Robertson and (later) University of Queensland Press took on volumes of verse, and small independent presses maintained a steady output of verse monographs.

14 Woolf.

15 Information from AustLit database.

16 Bruce Sims, presentation at 'Resourceful reading' Conference, Sydney University, December 2008; on publishing in general, Patrick Buckridge, 'Clearing a Space for Australian Literature, 1940–1965', *The Oxford Literary History of Australia*, pp. 169–92.

17 Susan Sheridan, 'Thea Astley: A woman among the satirists of post-war modernity', *Australian Feminist Studies*, 29(3) 2003, pp. 261–71.
18 Sidney J Baker, 'Australian Novels and Our Prose Poets', *Sydney Morning Herald*, 23 August 1958, p. 13.
19 Susan Sheridan, 'Gentlemen's Agreements: *Southerly*'s first editors', *Southerly*, 67(1 & 2), 2007, pp. 333–47.
20 Jacqueline Kent, *A Certain Style: Beatrice Davis, a literary life*, Penguin, Ringwood, Vic, 2001, pp. 73–5.
21 Janet McCalman, *Journeyings: The biography of a middle-class generation 1920–1990*, Melbourne University Press, Melbourne, 1993, p. 127.
22 Judith Wright, interview with Jim Davidson, *Sideways from the Page: The Meanjin interviews*, Fontana, Sydney, 1983, p. 403.
23 Dobson, *A World of Difference*; Michael Heyward, *The Ern Malley Affair*, UQP, St Lucia, 1993.
24 AD Hope on *The Tree of Man*: 'The Bunyip Stages a Comeback', *Sydney Morning Herald*, 16 June 1956, repr. in *AD Hope: Selected poetry and prose*, ed. David Brooks, Halstead, Sydney, 2000, pp. 213–15.
25 Nicole Moore, 'The Totally Incredible Obscenity of *Letty Fox*', *Journal of the Association for Australian Literature*, 2, 2003, pp. 67–79.
26 Jane Grant, *Kylie Tennant: A life*, National Library of Australia, Canberra, 2006, pp. 74–6 and 95–8.
27 Dorothy Hewett, *Wild Card: An autobiography 1923–1958*, McPhee Gribble, Melbourne, 1990, pp. 90, 113.
28 JW to BB, 15 May 1952, in Bryony Cosgrove, ed., *Portrait of a Friendship: The letters of Barbara Blackman and Judith Wright, 1950–2000*, The Miegunyah Press, Melbourne, 2007, p. 8.
29 RD to JMcA (draft) 23 February 1956, Rosemary Dobson Papers, National Library of Australia, MS 4955, Folder 16.

CHAPTER ONE

Judith Wright in the mid 1960s

Judith Wright sets her course

Judith Wright's early poetry, when it began to appear in magazines during World War II, struck readers as the work of a mature poet, with its unselfconscious acceptance of Australian history and landscape as its inevitable and natural milieu. Poet and critic Bob Brissenden described her as 'the typical poet of the forties: the decade in which Australian poetry came of age and learned to forget that it was adolescent and antipodean'.[1]

Yet this apparent confidence in herself and in her place in the world was hard won. Recalling herself as she was in 1937, a young woman of twenty-two, Judith Wright wrote in her autobiography, *Half a Lifetime*: 'my year in Europe had thrown any hopes I had for the future either of my writing or of the world itself into confusion'. It was clear to her that war was inevitable, 'a fact that had not dawned on most Australians':

> Remembering the posters in Munich, the hushed apprehension in Vienna, the rally in Nuremburg, the Blackshirts in London, I wondered how long it would be before the Spanish war experience

> overtook those of my friends who had labour sympathies, let alone socialist views.[2]

Before this trip she had spent several years at the University of Sydney, attending classes in English, philosophy and anything else she thought would prepare her to be a poet. This was her ambition: the fact that she could not enrol formally, because her failure in mathematics had prevented her from matriculating, did not faze her. An inheritance from her grandmother enabled her to live independently in Sydney, first in a boarding house run by a distant relative then in rented rooms near the university. She avoided the Women's College, where she feared her new freedoms would be curtailed. She read voraciously. Auden, Eliot, Yeats and Dylan Thomas became her favourite writers.[3]

Returning to Sydney after her year in Europe, out of touch with her old university friends and gripped by despondency, Wright looked in vain for direction from other Australian poets. Slessor's poetry she thought 'masculine, tough or glittering or self-absorbed, and I did not want to write in the least like that.' She visited Mary Gilmore, another possible mentor, but 'she seemed a little too everyday, too homely', and Judith thought her work 'too simple, too Georgian, a new damn-word picked up in England'.[4]

Over the next four years, working at a series of inconsequential jobs in the city, and discovering to her dismay that she was going deaf, she wrote little. The war broke out. She had 'one or two irrelevant love affairs; uniforms are a potent concealer of realities and an incitement to sex, as indeed is war itself'.[5] In one poem from this time, 'The Company of Lovers', she depicted wartime affairs in a more sombre light:

> Death marshals up his armies round us now.
> Their footsteps crowd too near.

Lock your warm hand above the chilling heart
and for a time I live without my fear.
Grope in the night to find me and embrace,
for the dark preludes of the drums begin,
and round us, round the company of lovers,
Death draws his cordons in.[6]

Her despondency only began to lift as the train carried her back to New England in early 1942 to help her father on the family property, Wallamumbi, while her two younger brothers were serving in the armed forces: 'I found myself suddenly and sharply aware of "my country." These hills and valleys were – not mine, but me; the threat of Japanese invasion hung over them as over me; I felt it under my own ribs'. Now she was 'on a different track. Such poems as I had written came of a new identification with the land and its inhabitants'.[7] 'Dust', written at this time, begins:

This sick dust, spiralling with the wind,
is harsh as grief's taste in our mouths
and has eclipsed the small sun.
The remnant earth turns evil,
the steel-shocked earth has turned against the plough . . .

The final stanza underlines the concurrence of this new consciousness of the country and her urgent desire for a different future after the war:

. . . Our dream was the wrong dream,
Our strength was the wrong strength.
. . .
We must prepare the land for a difficult sowing,

> a long and hazardous growth of a strange bread
> that our sons' sons may harvest and be fed.[8]

By the end of a second freezing winter at Wallamumbi she was anxious to move on again. This time she looked north to Brisbane, which had become a hub of the Pacific war effort and, as a consequence, focal point for the new cultural turn towards the Pacific and to the United States rather than Britain.[9]

When 'The Company of Lovers' and three other Judith Wright poems arrived on his Brisbane desk in July 1942, Clem Christesen, editor of the new literary journal, *Meanjin Papers*, must have been delighted. Here was a war poem by a woman responding with clear-eyed intensity to the heady concurrence of sexual passion and fear of death. This was the first of a series of her poems that would appear in his journal and help to make its name as the leading Australian literary magazine of the 1940s. In turn, it was Christesen who in 1946 published her first volume of verse, *The Moving Image*, which brought her the attention of wider audiences and the praise of influential reviewers. This book, soon to be followed by *Woman to Man* (1949), quickly established Judith Wright as a leading poet of her generation.

The relationship between Judith Wright and Clem Christesen was important for both of them, but it had its difficulties, and they reveal conflicts below the surface of their mutual successes. Their association began well. Judith wrote from New England, sending poems and praise for *Meanjin Papers* which, she wrote, was providing poets with a means of reaching the public, so vitally important 'if the regimentation and mental brutalization of war are not to overcome us altogether'.[10] And indeed, by the time 'The Company of Lovers' was published in the magazine's eleventh issue, most of the established names in Australian literature had appeared in *Meanjin*, including Mary Gilmore, Miles Franklin, Vance and

Nettie Palmer, Rex Ingamells and RD FitzGerald. So too had several of Wright's contemporaries who would soon become well known – John Blight, Rosemary Dobson, Dorothy Hewett. As well as poetry, the magazine published debates about nationalism and the future and reviews of recent Australian books. But it was struggling financially, as Christesen told Judith in the course of their correspondence. She sent a donation of three pounds and later, when she had secured a job in the Universities Commission in Brisbane, wrote offering her services to *Meanjin* as an unpaid assistant editor in her spare time.[11]

Clem Christesen and his wife Nina helped Judith find a place to live in the war-crowded city. It was a small room in the riverside suburb of New Farm, recently vacated by Dorothy Auchterlonie, another poet who had been Judith's fellow student at the University of Sydney in the 1930s and had been sent to Brisbane to run the ABC news service. She and Judith had not become close friends at university because Dorothy had been an evening student, and here again their paths diverged as Dorothy was leaving Brisbane for Sydney and marriage.[12] Despite their many common interests, it was not until the 1960s in Canberra that the two women formed a strong friendship.

As if freed up by the warmth and squalor of wartime Brisbane, Judith wrote poems that looked back on her New England years, poems such as 'South of My Days', which would become a landmark in Australian poetry for its expression of intense love for country, here imagined as a sensitive creature, 'delicate', 'wincing', 'hungry':

> South of my day's circle, part of my blood's country,
> rises that tableland, high delicate outline
> of bony slopes wincing under the winter,
> low trees blue-leaved and olive, outcropping granite –
> clean, lean, hungry country . . . [13]

Unlike New England, Brisbane also offered a lively literary scene. Barrett Reid, leader of the Barjai group of young writers and artists opposed to social and aesthetic conservatism, invited Judith to speak about poetry and the New World Order which, they hoped, would transform the postwar world. Here she met Barbara Patterson, who later married the painter Charles Blackman and became a lifelong friend.[14] At the *Meanjin* office, which was located in the Christesens' house, she met such Brisbane writers as James Devaney and Paul Grano, and visiting American poets Harry Roskolenko and Karl Shapiro.[15] At about this time she probably also met poet John Blight, who remained one of her few literary correspondents.

Most importantly, it was in the *Meanjin* office that she met Jack McKinney, the man who became her life's partner. Clem Christesen had asked her to read McKinney's manuscript, 'Towards the Future', because he was considering publishing it but did not know what to make of this 'wild philosopher' who had no degree or academic position. Judith was drawn to, and puzzled by, this work, which 'looked farther afield than anything I had read for new ways of thinking'. And then she met the man himself, 'a small slender man with white hair and remarkable blue eyes', who left his conversation with Clem to follow her into the kitchen and help with the washing up. He had read her poems and asked to meet her. Unlike other men of her acquaintance, Judith said, Jack 'shared his enthusiasms and ideas as though I was an authority'. His ideas excited her because he was taking on the task of rethinking basic concepts of Western culture, something that she also believed must be done 'if we were ever to break free of nationalism, wars, money worship and the domination of material possessions'. To accept the challenge to become Jack's 'helper and adviser' would, she felt, give her poetry the philosophical grounding it needed.[16]

Yet the more convinced she became of the rightness of Jack's direction, the more reluctant Clem was to commit himself to publishing 'Towards the Future'. Judith had no doubt where her loyalties lay, even though she said that for her nothing was simple. 'A practically penniless wayside philosopher twenty-three years older than myself was the man I wanted and he, in his calm, decisive manner, had chosen me as helper and companion.'[17]

She had become deeply disillusioned with Clem. Her letters from her *Meanjin* period stress her fondness for Nina, while she compared 'gradually waking up to what C really is' to Christina Stead's heroine realising the perfidy of her former lover in the novel *For Love Alone*.[18] At first she might have felt a degree of hero-worship from a distance, but, if so, it did not survive the face-to-face relationship in Brisbane. The two writers shared a common commitment to forging a new literature for the postwar world, but she soon discovered that Clem would not treat her – a woman only a few years his junior, whom he acknowledged to be a fine poet – as an equal. Judith was not used to the offhandedness he displayed.

She became more critical, thinking Clem too impressed by people with university degrees or power. She thought his judgments uncertain, even while acknowledging that he kept the journal open to new ideas. She could see that Clem was insecure and irascible, that his commitment to the journal overrode all other considerations. He was forever falling out with its backers and his former co-editors.[19]

In 1945 the Christesens left Brisbane for the University of Melbourne, where *Meanjin* seemed assured of a more financially secure future. As the war retreated, Brisbane looked like falling back into its former dullness and distance from the centres of power, and Clem wanted to build *Meanjin*'s status as a national journal. Judith refused his invitation to move to Melbourne with *Meanjin* as its paid editorial assistant, preferring to stay in Brisbane with Jack McKinney and devote herself seriously to her writing.

She offered Clem the manuscript of her first book of poems, *The Moving Image*, and he undertook to publish it. The process was beset by what seemed to her unconscionable delays, and by the time the book saw the light of day fifteen months later, relations between poet and publisher were chilly. When Judith wrote several times requesting some kind of contract that would put their arrangement on a businesslike basis, he took umbrage, interpreting her request as a slur on his integrity.[20] The written agreement finally appeared in October 1946, along with the book.[21]

There was a further misunderstanding: Clem was told that Judith had criticised the price of the book, and wrote that he was deeply hurt. Her reply began, 'Tut, man, don't take it to heart.' She explained her comment (that five shillings was a lot of money for someone like her, earning as she did no more than the basic wage) but did not apologise. She told him that she had applied for a grant to write a novel about Hunter River history and named him as a referee: 'Is that all right with you, or not?'[22] The brisk tone of this letter (and of an earlier one that began, 'So you want an Index, do you?'[23]) indicates that she was by no means intimidated. Although in *Half a Lifetime* she claimed that she was a mere female in Clem's eyes, the young Judith clearly knew how to crack the verbal whip when necessary.[24]

Continuing demand over the years for permission to reprint poems from *The Moving Image* – 'South of My Days', 'Bullocky' and others – kept the correspondence between Wright and Christesen alive, but they never maintained their early friendship, or even a literary partnership.

The Moving Image, containing twenty-three poems, was dedicated to Judith's father and featured an epigraph from Plato that explains its title: 'Time is the moving image of eternity.' The long title poem in three parts announced this philosophical, even cosmic, dimension of the book and no doubt reflected the influence of

Jack McKinney's ideas. The other shorter poems, written between 1940 and 1944, variously allude to the opposition of life and death, and many carry a reminder of the war during which they were written, as in 'Waiting':

> Day's crystal hemisphere travels the land.
> From starfrost to starfrost the folded hills lie bare
> and the sheep move grazing or stand.
> How can the sirens of danger pierce this air?
> Only the parrots exploding in green and scarlet
> shatter its glass for their shrill moment's flight.[25]

The underpinning ideas give new depth to Wright's fresh perceptions of Australian landscape, creatures and people.

The Moving Image was reviewed enthusiastically by many of the leading names in Australian literature, both established (James Devaney, Marjorie Barnard, critic AR Chisholm, poet and *Bulletin* literary editor Douglas Stewart) and emerging (poets Rosemary Dobson, Nan McDonald). It was reviewed in the *Age* and the Adelaide *Advertiser* as well as the Sydney and Brisbane papers and journals. Books of poetry were widely reviewed at the time, but in this case reviewers were unanimous about the maturity and polish of the verse. An article on contemporary Australian verse in the British journal *Poetry Review* singled Wright out for praise, based on this book.[26]

Mary Gilmore and Vance Palmer, among others, welcomed it warmly. Palmer commented that although Wright used traditional forms, 'she is modern in that she gives new shapes to things,' and concluded, 'I think she is the most richly gifted poet this country has produced for years.' Although Marie Pitt reported that she did not like the 'sense of failure and lack of magic', Mary Gilmore praised her as 'the outstanding girl or woman poet in Australian today', adding: 'She has wrung my heart so many times . . . she is not over-driven by emotion. Emotion is controlled and suggested; it is subterranean.'[27]

Among Wright's contemporaries, the book won plaudits for its rich imagery, masterly handling of rhythm and fresh vision of Australian landscape and characters. Although its serious philosophical bent was not entirely to Douglas Stewart's taste,[28] Nan McDonald's response was positive. Her review pointed out that the dominance of the war in these poems only emphasised the darkness that was always there: Wright's consciousness of peril and death 'inevitably breeds an intense awareness of life'.[29] Rosemary Dobson called the poems 'sure and beautiful', 'a harmonious fusion of mind and eye'; she also remarked on the design of the book.[30]

Judith Wright's 'equality of heart and mind'[31] with Jack McKinney brought her, she wrote, beyond happiness, a faith in the future – in 'the human capacity to create and affirm life' – that enabled her to go on writing: it was 'enough to provide me with a step-ladder out of my solipsistic despairs about the nature of life and meaning'.

> Moreover, there was no doubt about it, I was in love – in love with a man and a mind, even though I had renounced any idea of ever marrying with my deafness and the warnings my surgeon had given me about the doubtful chances of bearing a child after my pelvis had been crushed [by a fall from her horse when she was a teenager].[32]

Such a relationship without the seal of marriage (for Jack was still married to his first wife), was not readily accepted at the time, and Judith was aware that her father, whom she loved dearly, was at first grieved by it. The difficulties of her early life – her mother's death after a long illness when Judith was only eleven, and an unhappy relationship with her stepmother – had made Judith strongly independent. Besides, as she reported wryly in *Half a Lifetime*, her recognition as a poet, as well as her physical disabilities, 'somehow put me out of consideration as a normal daughter of the rural aristocracy'.[33]

Judith's relationship with Jack was eventually accepted by the family, and the lovers settled in together in a cottage, 'Quantum', at Tamborine Mountain. She resigned from her Brisbane job and applied for a Commonwealth Literary Fund Fellowship to write a book based on her family's diaries from the early days of 'pastoral movements (I would soon learn to call them invasions)'.[34] This became *The Generations of Men*, but it was not published until 1959. For their first five years together, until their daughter Meredith was born, the couple lived frugally on Jack's small World War I pension and Judith's fellowship, her shares in the family firm, and her earnings from writing poetry and stories.[35]

Judith's output of poetry was steady, and by late 1947 she had another collection of almost forty poems ready. She offered them first to Clem Christesen, under the provisional title 'The Burning Glass'.[36] This phrase comes from 'The Maker', a poem about the power of the poet:

All things that glow and move
All things that change and pass
I gather their delight
As in a burning-glass; . . .[37]

Christesen did not respond to her offer, and the collection eventually came out two years later under the title *Woman to Man*, published by Angus & Robertson. This title, and the three powerful love poems with which it began – the title poem, 'Woman's Song' and 'Woman to Child' – meant that some influential critics passed over its theme of creativity, emphasising the novelty of love poetry in a distinctively female voice, and readily assuming that it was autobiographical.[38] Yet the book was complete before Judith became pregnant with her only child.

Consistent with her earlier poetry's philosophical bent, the love invoked in the epigraph from Francis Bacon is that love which produces 'all the variety in the universe'. This impersonal *eros* and its relationship to the creative process, rather than individual sexual passion, is the subject of most of the poems.[39] In 'Woman to Man', the product of love is imaged as a child ('the selfless, shapeless seed I hold') and yet 'This is no child with a child's face . . . /This is our hunter and our chase,/the third who lay in our embrace.'[40] It is metaphysical poetry, where the seen and the unseen world fuse in images; and, like the great metaphysical poets of the seventeenth century, Wright often dramatises this meeting in the encounter of 'you' and 'I'. Like Yeats's 'Crazy Jane' poems, Wright also embodies irreconcilable conflicts in some outcast figure, an old man or an old woman.

As Judith had predicted, her second book was never as popular as *The Moving Image*, but it sold well 'though critics were clearly uneasy with the "feminine" emphasis'.[41] Some critics, however, were enthusiastic. Elizabeth Vassilieff's review in *Meanjin* claimed that Wright's feminine sensibility and skill made her poetry distinctive and that male reviewers failed to recognise that only a woman could have made such a world.[42] Philip Lindsay's essay on Wright in the London *Poetry Review* praised her as 'the first woman to honestly unbare [sic] her lover's heart in verse'. He went on:

> She offers the open cup of love to any of us unafraid to look into the naked heart that is both the possessed and possessing, that is both courageous and timid, both demanding and submissive, of a woman above the cowardly evasions of so many of her sex, one

> honest and proud of her strong womanhood that can excite and satisfy love.[43]

Such enthusiasm underplayed the range of poetic subjects in this book. By comparison Douglas Stewart's review was more attentive to Wright's distinctive qualities. He wrote that *Woman to Man* had the same unique vision as *The Moving Image*, the same masterly translation of vision into art, and the same admirably plain style. Yet on the very first page, 'the book moves into midnight', which is 'at once creative and destructive, the primal midnight of the universe'. Here is 'a tragic intensity surpassing anything she has previously written' – although Stewart noted regretfully that the 'Australian' poems here 'do not create the legendary effect of "Bullocky" and "South of My Days"'.[44] It was precisely the 'legendary effect' that Wright was now resolved to move beyond.

Mary Gilmore's letter to Judith delighted in the concentration of the verse:

> Such simple verse; but what inclusions! All the suns in a drop of water; eternity in a little smile; nothing, everything. Might in an atom. Well, we have the atom bomb, but yours is not explosive & cruel – yours is life out of death, & the long evolution of time. I could wish I were as big as you! . . . But you will have to write one long poem or the future will not hold you for bigness . . .'[45]

Her reference to the atom bomb points to the crucial cause of Wright's passionate urgency: as her biographer Veronica Brady has commented, feeding into these poems is a post-Hiroshima consciousness that the human mind has released 'energies which can destroy the world as they have contributed to making it'.[46]

Mary Gilmore's prediction about Wright needing to write a long poem to be noticed was wrong. However, her long prose project, *The Generations of Men*, caused Wright some anguish. It was rejected by Angus & Robertson, which had invited her to edit the annual anthology, *Australian Poetry*, in 1948, and had welcomed the opportunity to publish *Woman to Man* – editor Beatrice Davis was keen to establish the company as the leading publisher of serious Australian writing.[47] But they wanted fiction, whereas the university presses that Wright tried wanted history.[48] The manuscript, the result of long hours in the archives researching a subject that the professional historians had barely begun to approach, lay in a box for nine years until 1958, when Frank Eyre, Oxford University Press's Australian editor, seized upon it, along with a children's story for which Wright had also unsuccessfully sought a publisher, and published them both.[49]

During the 1950s, Angus & Robertson, with Rosemary Dobson and Nan McDonald as its poetry editors, continued to publish Wright's volumes of poetry, *The Gateway* in 1953 and *The Two Fires* in 1955. *The Gateway* was the first of her books to be published in London, where Angus & Robertson now had an office as well as in Sydney. A review in the *Times Literary Supplement* described Wright as 'one of the most distinguished of the younger Australian poets', 'a poet of great imaginative power, passionate and grave'; but the reviewer thought *The Gateway* uneven, 'suggesting a time of pause and experiment'.[50] Elyne Mitchell in *Southerly* welcomed this further journey into philosophical poetry: here, again, love was the informing principle of life, but this book leaned less towards 'the dark gods'. Mitchell noted the appearance of Jungian symbols of integration, for example in 'The Lost Man', yet she wished Wright would more often use the imagery of the country where she grew up, for 'landscape made particular can give great strength to the philosophical content'.[51]

Certainly, images in *The Gateway* consistently tended towards symbolic abstraction: the observed natural world that predominated in *The Moving Image* was now more likely to furnish symbols or allegories. This tendency was already visible in *Woman to Man*, and here Wright took it further. The task she shared with Jack of changing the human world view involved reaching towards elusive realities in the unconscious (hence their interest in Jung). For Wright as a poet, this meant doing new things with language: as she wrote to her poet friend, Jack Blight, at about this time, 'I'm trying to simplify more and more; to strengthen the image by ceasing to obscure it with words. Difficult in English. The Chinese can do it in an ideogram or two.'[52] Both the pared-back language and the Jungian symbolism can be seen in the title poem, a symbolic narrative of self loss that concludes the book. It ends:

All ended there;
yet all began.
All sank in dissolution
and rose renewed.

And the bright smoke
out of the pit of chaos
is the flowing and furious world.

And the mind's nightmare
is the world's sweet wellspring
(the traveller said).[53]

This image of death and renewal pointed the way to the next volume, with its epigraph of the Heraclitean fire, 'an ever-living Fire, with measures of it kindling, and measures going out'. *The Two Fires* continued the major theme of creative and destructive forces with an intense focus on living things and the rush towards death, as in:

> The word the board holds up is Sanctuary
> and the road knows that notice-boards make sense
>
> but has no time to pray. Only, up there,
> morning sets doves upon the power-line.
> Swung on that fatal voltage like a sign
> and meaning love, perhaps they are a prayer.[54]

The poet's particular responsibility was to speak with precision, an ethical as well as an aesthetic imperative:

> . . . Speaking with a pure voice,
> and that the gull's sole note like a steel nail
> that driven through cloud, sky, and irrelevant seas,
> joins all, gives all a meaning, makes all whole.[55]

With these titles bringing her total to four books of poetry within the decade, Judith Wright was established as one of Australia's preeminent poets. 'This brought her more fame than she had ever expected, and often rather more than she enjoyed.'[56] Or, as Judith put it graphically in a letter to her friend Barbara Blackman, 'all I want to do is stick my tongue out at being a Poet and Writing Poetry. I refuse to have labels stuck on me and as for that Judith Wright, she turns me up. (However if I can make a bit of money out of her, I don't mind).'[57] She treasured her life with Jack and their small daughter Meredith and the isolation of Tamborine Mountain, and kept her distance from the literary world, attempting to achieve that 'creative stillness; refusal to impose oneself on events, refusal to be imposed upon'.[58] Yet both desire and necessity drove her to write prolifically, not only poetry but lectures, stories and radio scripts.[59]

The extra income was crucial in keeping the household going, and it pushed her out into public view: what she wrote was noticed and admired. She was invited to deliver a Commonwealth Literary Fund lecture at the new Canberra University College in September 1954, and poet-academic Alec Hope came to visit, presumably to convey the invitation.[60] She chose as her subject 'William Baylebridge and the Modern Problem', and, reflecting perhaps on her own position, presented him as a man whose desire to be 'an acknowledged prophet and leader of thought' conflicted with his desire to be a great poet. Baylebridge was one of a number of Australian poets she had discovered in her research for *A Book of Australian Verse* (1956), an anthology commissioned by Oxford University Press. In 1955 she gave a series of ten lectures on Australian poets (eventually published as *Preoccupations in Australian Poetry*) at the University of Queensland, where she had been awarded an honorary doctorate.[61] A lecture delivered at the University of Sydney in 1958, 'Romanticism and the last frontier', explored the Romantic inheritance of nineteenth-century Australian poets Charles Harpur, Henry Kendall and Christopher Brennan. On this trip to Sydney she took the opportunity to continue research in the Mitchell Library on Harpur,[62] on whose neglected work she later wrote a monograph.[63] The groundwork of her important contribution as a literary scholar was done in these years. As Brigid Rooney has pointed out, her literary scholarship was recovering an Australian poetic tradition in which her own work belonged, albeit in 'a line of literary fathers'.[64]

This impressive list accounts only for her professional life as a writer in the 1950s. 'It was happiness, as well as need, that kept me writing and working,' she wrote later. Judith was also kept busy as a conscientious mother (this included running the Red Cross juniors at the local school) and housewife (making clothes, growing vegetables and keeping hens, as well as the usual round of housework). Jack's health was not robust and he often needed looking after; but he, too, worked constantly, and Judith typed his essays and discussed them with him. During these crowded years she also wrote letters prolifically, to friends such as John Blight, Barbara Blackman and Kathleen Macarthur, as well as to literary contacts. In the mid 1950s she experienced a traumatic event in her personal life – an ectopic pregnancy, as a result of which, she was told, she could have no more children.[65] After this she was unable to write poetry for a long time.[66]

The 1960s brought 'new loads of work and sorrow – but at least, miraculous as it seemed, without further use of the bomb, that monster whose gaze had transfixed us for years'.[67] During this decade Judith Wright kept up her demanding pace of literary work. She wrote for children a lovely series of bird poems,[68] and two novels.[69] Her essays appeared as *Preoccupations in Australian Poetry*, and her short stories as *The Nature of Love*.[70]

Publishing a volume of 'selected poems' is a high point in a poet's career. Wright achieved this in 1963, when Angus & Robertson brought out not one but two selections. *Five Senses* contained twenty-eight new poems as well as some chosen from her previous books, and *Judith Wright*, in the Australian Poets series intended for use in schools, had a smaller selection from the same range of work. Wright's next new book, *The Other Half* (1966), was the occasion for numerous retrospectives on her poetic development. *Preoccupations in Australian Poetry* was even more widely reviewed, reflecting a growing commitment to teaching Australian literature in the universities. Certainly Wright was one of the few non-academics (and one of only two women, the other being Leonie Kramer) to write a chapter for *The Literature of Australia*, an important collection aimed at an academic readership, edited by Geoffrey Dutton and published by Penguin in 1964.

Judith Wright was now an important name in the emerging canon of postwar literature. She was one of the few Australian poets to achieve international recognition, winning the Britannica-Australia Literary Award in 1964 and the Poetry Society of Great Britain annual award in 1967. Also in 1967 she was the only Australian invited to the World Poetry Conference in Montreal. An outbreak of publicity stories in the press greeted these honours. Like it or not, she was now a household name, as well as a literary one, and would remain so for the rest of her long life.

Becoming a writer, for her, had been a matter of finding a direction in life that would take her beyond the popular early poems and would sustain her spiritually, emotionally and intellectually. This, 'my survival as a poet and as a person', had been the gift of Jack McKinney, as she recorded late in her life.[71] Her life was changed forever by his death in 1966, and her energies would thereafter be more and more committed to political work for conservation and Aboriginal rights. Both areas of political activism had already been established: she had co-founded the Wildlife Preservation Society of Queensland in 1962 with her friend Kathleen Macarthur and others, and in 1964 had met Kath Walker (Oodgeroo) for the first time, after being invited to read the manuscript of *We Are Going*. This political work, and her move to live outside Canberra, eventually led to her meeting HC 'Nugget' Coombs, with whom she formed a close and long-lasting relationship that had to remain hidden from public knowledge.[72]

Despite her demanding life of activism, Judith Wright continued to write until her death in 2000. She contributed in myriad ways to literary culture in postwar Australia, all the while asserting her independence from literary and academic circles. Her contribution to the reshaping of national culture more broadly continues to reverberate in the current Indigenous rights and ecology movements, and in ongoing reconsiderations of the history of settler Australia. She never shrank from the demands of public advocacy for the causes she espoused, literary and otherwise, but she also fiercely guarded her privacy. Her deafness made social life difficult except with close friends and family – she joked with her blind friend Barbara Blackman, 'All in all I am thankful to be deaf and curmudgeonly rather than blind and sociable'[73] – but it no doubt also helped her to maintain that necessary 'creative stillness'. Poetry continued to be central for her and her preoccupations remained remarkably constant. One of her last poems, 'Patterns', begins with an allusion to the atomic blast, effortlessly moving that image of fire into wider dimensions, using the clear, passionate language that was always her hallmark:

> 'Brighter than a thousand suns' – that blinding glare
> circled the world and settled in our bones.
>
> Human eyes impose a human pattern,
> decipher constellations against featureless dark.
>
> All's fire, said Heraclitus; measures of it
> kindle as others fade. All changes yet all's one.
>
> We are born of ethereal fire and we return there.
> Understand the Logos; reconcile opposing principles.
>
> Perhaps the dark itself is the source of meaning,
> the fires of the galaxy its visible destruction . . . [74]

Notes

1 RF Brissenden, 'The poetry of Judith Wright' in *Critical Essays on Judith Wright*, ed. AK Thomson, Jacaranda Press, Brisbane, 1968, p. 42.

2 Judith Wright, *Half a Lifetime*, ed. Patricia Clarke, Text Publishing, Melbourne, 2001, p. 143.

3 *With Love & Fury: Selected letters of Judith Wright*, eds Patricia Clarke and Meredith McKinney, National Library of Australia, Canberra, 2006, p. 11.
4 *Half a Lifetime*, p. 148.
5 *Half a Lifetime*, pp.153, 156.
6 Judith Wright, *A Human Pattern: Selected poems*, ETT Imprint, Sydney, 1996, p. 2.
7 *Half a Lifetime*, pp. 158, 164.
8 Judith Wright, *Collected Poems 1942–1970*, Angus & Robertson, Sydney, 1971, pp. 23–4.
9 Judith Wright recalled the flattering interest in Australian writing from some American troops, and the new confidence it generated among poets, in 'Australian Poetry after Pearl Harbour' in Wright, *Because I Was Invited*, Oxford University Press, Melbourne, 1975, pp. 129–30.
10 Quoted in *With Love & Fury*, p. 10. Her words echo those of Christesen's editorial in *Meanjin* 8, 1942: 'Military victory alone will not save us, if we lose the intellectual battle . . . Let it be emphasised that there is sufficient reason to speak of a crisis of modern thought and knowledge so violent and so far-reaching as can hardly be found in any known period of history'.
11 In *Half a Lifetime* Wright gives the date of her arrival as the spring of 1943 (p. 168) but a letter to Christesen dated January 1944 announces her imminent arrival (*With Love & Fury*, pp. 12–13).
12 *Half a Lifetime*, p. 168.
13 *A Human Pattern*, p. 11.
14 See Bryony Cosgrove, ed., *Portrait of a Friendship: The letters of Barbara Blackman and Judith Wright, 1950–2000*, The Miegunyah Press, Melbourne, 2007.
15 *Half a Lifetime*, p. 171.
16 *Half a Lifetime*, pp. 188, 191.
17 *Half a Lifetime*, p. 209.

18 Wright papers, NLA MS 5781, box 105, folder 747: notes for *Half a Lifetime*. In *The Equal Heart and Mind: Letters between Judith Wright and Jack McKinney*, eds Patricia Clarke and Meredith McKinney, University of Queensland Press, St Lucia, 2004, there is a similar comment in a letter to Jack (pp. 143–4), which Clarke and McKinney take (wrongly, I think) to be a reference to *The Man who Loved Children*.
19 Wright, 'Brisbane in Wartime', *Overland*, 1985, pp. 66–7; *Half a Lifetime*, pp. 186, 206.
20 Veronica Brady, *South of My Days, A biography of Judith Wright*, Angus & Robertson, Sydney, 1998, pp.132–3.
21 *With Love & Fury*, p. 28.
22 *Meanjin* archive, Melbourne University Library Special Collections, Wright file: CC to JW 7 March 1947 and JW to CC 13 March 1947.
23 *With Love & Fury*, p. 13.
24 Brigid Rooney puts this well when she notes that Wright's 'characteristic fearlessness and principled certainty of view are legible as signs of a born-to-rule patrician outlook . . .' in *Literary Activists*, University of Queensland Press, 2009, p. 10.
25 Repr. in *Collected Poems*, p. 9
26 WJ Harvey, 'Poets of the Antipodes', *Poetry Review*, 39, 1949: pp. 425–8. In this journal *The Moving Image* had a brief but positive notice in an anonymous general review in 38(2) 1947, pp. 126–7.
27 Wright Papers NLA MS 5781, Folder 230.
28 *Bulletin*, 16 October 1946, p. 2.
29 *Southerly*, 8(3) 1947, p. 184.
30 *Australian Book News & Library Journal*, December 1946, pp. 255, 257.
31 'The equal heart and mind/ that answer love in kind' is from the Dedication to 'The Forest' in *Five Senses*, Angus & Robertson, Sydney, 1963.
32 *Half a Lifetime*, pp. 210–11, 209.
33 *Half a Lifetime*, pp. 234–5.

34 *Half a Lifetime*, p. 249.

35 *Half a Lifetime*, p. 258.

36 *With Love & Fury*, p. 33.

37 *Collected Poems*, p. 32.

38 Vincent Buckley in his *Essays in Poetry, Mainly Australian* (1957), repr. in *Critical Essays on Judith Wright*; also Douglas Stewart, note on 'The Author' in *Five Senses*.

39 Cf. Brady's discussion of this dimension of the book, *South of My Days*, pp.136–7, and more extensive discussions of Wright's thought in Shirley Walker, *The Poetry of Judith Wright*, Edward Arnold, Melbourne, 1980 and Jennifer Strauss, *Judith Wright*, OUP, Melbourne, 1995.

40 *A Human Pattern*, p. 20.

41 *Half a Lifetime* pp. 260–61.

42 *Meanjin*, 9(1), 1950, pp. 69–73.

43 *Poetry Review*, 41(4), 1950, pp. 207–11.

44 *Bulletin*, 14 December 1949, pp. 2 and 43.

45 MG to JW 22 July 1950, Wright Papers NLA 5781, Folder 230.

46 *South of My Days*, p. 136

47 Neil James and Elizabeth Webby, 'Canon around the hub: Angus & Robertson and the post-war literary canon', *Southerly* 57(3), 1997, p. 51.

48 Judith Wright papers NLA MS 5781, folders 748 and 749. ts 'Chapter 2: the 1950s', p. 1; permission to quote from transcriber, Patricia Clarke.

49 *Half a Lifetime* pp. 278–9.

50 TLS review reprinted in *Bulletin*, 3 March 1954, p. 2.

51 'The Vision and the Way', *Southerly*, 16(1), 1955, pp. 32–5. Mitchell's own writing about the land would have interested Judith, and there is a reference to buying her 1945 book, *Speak to the Earth*, in *The Equal Heart and Mind*, p. 82.

52 *With Love & Fury* p. 78.

53 *Collected Poems*, p. 117.
54 'Sanctuary', *A Human Pattern*, p. 82.
55 'For Precision', *A Human Pattern*, p. 73.
56 Editors' note, *With Love & Fury*, p. 59.
57 *With Love & Fury*, p. 109.
58 JW to BB, 15 May 1952, in Bryony Cosgrove, ed., *Portrait of a Friendship: The Letters of Barbara Blackman and Judith Wright, 1950–2000*, The Miegunyah Press, Melbourne, 2007, p. 8.
59 Some stories went to women's magazines but she claims not to have used her own name.
60 *With Love & Fury*, pp. 88–9.
61 *South of My Days*, pp. 196–7.
62 JW to Barbara Blackman, *With Love & Fury*, p. 107.
63 *Charles Harpur*, Australian Writers and their Work series. Lansdowne, Melbourne, 1963; Canberra and Sydney lectures reprinted in Wright, *Because I Was Invited*.
64 *Literary Activists*, p. 12.
65 *South of My Days*, pp. 195–6.
66 Judith Wright papers NLA MS 5781, folders 748 and 749 ts, 'Chapter what: the fifties cont.' p. 2; permission to quote from transcriber Patricia Clarke.
67 Judith Wright papers NLA MS 5781, folders 748 and 749 ts, 'Chapter what: (of books and publishers)', p. 6; permission to quote from transcriber Patricia Clarke.
68 *Birds: Poems*, Angus & Robertson, Sydney, 1962.
69 *Kings of the Dingoes*, OUP, Melbourne, 1958; and *Range the Mountains High*, Lansdowne, Melbourne, 1962.
70 Wright, *Preoccupations in Australian Poetry*, OUP, Melbourne, 1965; *The Nature of Love*, Sun Books, Melbourne, 1966.
71 Quoted by Patricia Clarke, 'In love with a man and a mind: Judith Wright's relationship with Jack McKinney', *NLA News*, March 2001, xi(6), p. 4.

72 Fiona Capp, ‘In the garden: Judith Wright and Nugget Coombs’, *The Monthly*, 46, June 2009, pp. 42–9.

73 *Portrait of a Friendship*, p. 423.

74 *A Human Pattern*, p. 241.

CHAPTER TWO

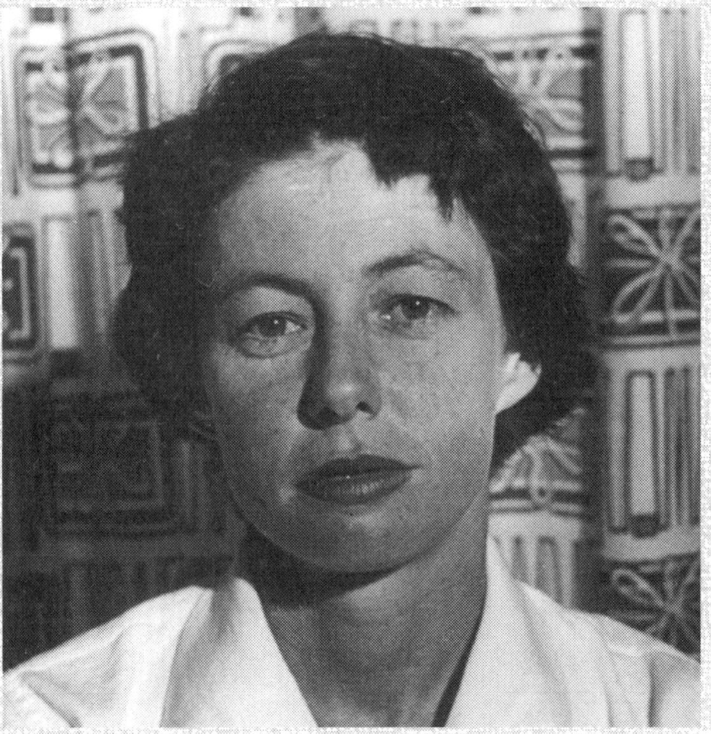

Thea Astley in the late 1950s

Thea Astley: Charting a new country

'I know the country I want to explore, but I don't seem able even to chart the coasts,' Thea Astley wrote to a friend in 1958 after the publication of her first novel, *Girl with a Monkey*.[1] She continued:

> It wasn't intended to be a novel in the strict sense – more a landscape with figures. It was a study in emotions. Technique interests me far more than characters or plot at the moment and until I find a style that I feel happy about I shall probably go on labouring with insignificant people performing routine tasks.

This is an early declaration of Astley's modernist ambition to write a new kind of novel. Its language resonated throughout her career – a landscape with figures, a study in emotions. What makes her fiction distinctive is the additional dimension of satire – her 'insignificant people performing routine tasks' inhabit Australian suburbs and small towns, where outsiders may become scapegoats for the doubts and fears of upright citizens. Not for her the flawed heroic figures in Patrick White or Randolph Stow.

Five years after *Girl with a Monkey* Thea Astley won the Miles Franklin prize for *The Well Dressed Explorer*, her third novel, and found a place on the literary map. She won the Miles Franklin again in 1965 with her next book, *The Slow Natives*, at which point in her career she took her place as the only woman among the leading modernist novelists of the postwar period, along with White, Stow and Hal Porter. Over the following thirty-five years she built consistently on this early success with a series of innovative fictions that pursued her central preoccupations: satirising Australian small-town life through portraits of its outsiders, and pursuing a love affair with the landscapes of the tropical north.

The literary country she chose to explore, the kind of fiction that was variously described at the time as 'poetic prose', 'metaphysical fiction', 'experimental modernism', was contested ground in 1960s Australia. An emerging cohort of academic critics, as well as adherents of the long-standing tradition of realist writing, were deeply sceptical of the value of postwar literary modernism. The various recipients of the Miles Franklin prize over the first decade of its existence illustrate this divided critical opinion. The first winner, for 1957, was *Voss* by Patrick White, whose previous book had been panned by the poet AD Hope as 'illiterate verbal sludge'.[2] The second winner was *To the Islands* by Randolph Stow, another experimental writer, whose work was often compared to White's.[3] The next two winners were realist writers Vance Palmer (*The Big Fellow*) and Elizabeth O'Conner (*The Irishman*). White won again in 1961 for *Riders in the Chariot*.[4] Astley shared the 1962 prize with George Turner, whose *The Cupboard Under the Stairs* is a straightforward psychological novel, while Astley's *The Well Dressed Explorer* undertakes a full-length ironic portrait of a man who believes himself to be a wit and a Don Juan. The shared prize reflected disagreement among the five judges: two had voted for Astley, two for Turner, and the fifth for a novel by Gavin Casey.[5]

Between this shared prize and Astley's next win, the Miles Franklin had been awarded to two realist novels, Sumner Locke Elliott's *Careful, He Might Hear You* and George Johnston's *My Brother Jack*. Astley's *The Slow Natives* set a new fictional agenda as well as a new style. Her subject matter was middle-class suburban family life; her themes were youthful rebellion and adult spiritual emptiness; her tone was ironic, sometimes satirical, sometimes lyrical. Here is the boy, Keith, taking his adolescent angst out into the surf:

> From the top of the sandhill he looked down the coast to Burleigh and the spot where, half a mile away, lollipop umbrellas had their colour sucked from them by the sun, spinning their windmills over a score of bathers who fried in the afternoon heat. Voices scrambled breathlessly upwards from the rear, so he stumbled into the dip on the seaward side and sprinted his confusion across the hard strip into the first gnawing line of surf. Dropping to his knees, he began to paddle his fibre-glass prayer mat out beyond the breaking water where purple currents moved along the sleeping coast, weeping purple, violet, cobalt rivers of salt salt tears. On the bosomy swell he knelt easily, holding the surf under him like a beating heart that moved him here and then there, that bucked a little when he shifted his weight, but, like blood, took his impulse for lost horizons farther and farther away from the beach and its puny people.[6]

'She has wit, and flashes of intelligence for a Brisbane girl turned schoolteacher,' wrote Patrick White with wonderful condescension soon after he had met Thea Astley in 1960.[7] Yet it was true that in the 1950s few 'Brisbane girls', and few 'schoolteachers', emerged as writers to be reckoned with. How did she do it?

Born in Brisbane in 1925, Thea Astley had ink running in her veins – her father was a journalist, and so too was her maternal grandfather. She considered joining the profession herself, but found that when she applied for a job, as a university graduate aged twenty-one, the Brisbane *Telegraph* considered her too old to take on as a trainee. Just as well, she later reflected – she would probably have been so driven by deadlines that there would not have been time for writing fiction. Her father Cecil sometimes reviewed books, and encouraged wide reading. As a girl Thea had loved Norman Lindsay's *The Magic Pudding* and *The Flyaway Highway* as well as the usual Australian girls' favourites, *Seven Little Australians* and the Billabong books, but she claimed that the book that impressed her most deeply as a child was *Les Misérables*.[8] Her father also loved music, and when Thea and her brother learned piano, they accompanied his singing. Thea often spoke of her love of music, especially *lieder* and jazz, but claimed she was not musical. Words were always her metier.[9]

She attended All Hallows' School, run by the Sisters of Mercy. It had a strong academic tradition, being the first secondary school for girls to open in Brisbane (1861) and the first convent school to present candidates for examination at the University of Sydney (the closest Australian university, where women students were admitted for the first time in 1881).[10] Although All Hallows' aimed to educate girls with 'deep faith and sound learning', Thea told an interviewer that in her day they were not encouraged to stay on for senior year and go to university.[11] Nevertheless, while she was training as a teacher at Brisbane Teachers College, she began studies for her Bachelor of Arts at the University of Queensland as an evening student. Her main subjects were Latin and French.[12]

She had started off, like many young writers, as a poet. While at university she published a few poems in the student paper, *Galmahra*, but a more important connection was with the group of Brisbane State High School students who had begun *Barjai*, a journal 'for youth'. Its founders were Barrett Reid and Laurence

Collinson, and others involved included Barbara Patterson (later Blackman), the painter Laurence Hope and Charles Osborne, who went on to become an eminent writer and arts administrator in London. Collinson, a painter as well as a poet, was the main link with the painters of the Miya studio, and *Barjai* number 20 represents impressive work by him, Hope, Pam Seeman and Joy Roggenkamp. The group cultivated ties with older Brisbane writers such as Judith Wright, art critic Gertrude Langer, James Devaney and JV Duhig (who gave financial support to *Barjai* as well as to *Meanjin*).[13] They published work by young people from all over Australia, including Brian Medlin in Adelaide, and Thelma Forshaw, Jill Hellyer and Grace Perry in Sydney. Women appear as often as men in the magazine, and Thea Astley published poetry there regularly from 1944 to 1946, serving as a member of the editorial committee for several issues.

Blackman describes Thea at Barjai meetings: 'good-looking in an angular way, [she] looked down from her height, and read pieces generally crackling and acrid.'[14] Here is the sestet of her 'Sonnet', which looks toward a future 'obliviscent' of present longings – her delight in obscure words and coinages was a feature of all her early writing:

> There where the doubtings of this comic hour
> Are swept into the dust-bin of forced laughter,
> I hope to banish you till years devour
> Your image, and love cuts its little whips,
> Yet who knows but I shall pause as you run after,
> To know the sudden terror of your lips.[15]

It was a lively group, which offered fresh perspectives to an eighteen-year-old convent girl whose education, she later maintained, had taught her not to question anything. After the war, according to William Hatherell, 'the Barjai-Miya group became the central force for progressive cultural practice in Brisbane,' and Collinson was contemptuous of the local cultural establishment's resistance to modernism.[16] There is evidence in the magazine that Freud and Henry Miller were read and discussed, as well as Eliot and Auden. Thea's poem 'Culture, 1945' mocks the attitude that 'of course there's no repression these days . . . We've Freud and Nietzsche at our fingertips . . .'[17] There was talk of communism, too: the editorial of issue 20 (1946) sees socialism as the way of the future, but only to solve humankind's material needs. Just as necessary is a new way of experiencing the world, with the emotions as well as the intellect: Judith Wright's recent talk to the Barjai group about emotional honesty was cited with approval here.

'My life changes,' Thea noted in a memoir of those days. 'I live through the week for those Sunday afternoon meetings at the Lyceum Club.' Some of the fathers worried that 'poetry readings might lead to communism. Most of our mothers worry. Poetry reading might lead to sex . . . They need not worry. Our politics are as romantic as our poetry, and *Barjai* meetings are desperately respectable.'[18] There is a lovingly re-created sense of community in this memoir. In an earlier interview, Thea had volunteered the comment that only the Barjai group got her out of her 'Catholic hangups about sex', 'impure thoughts' and so on: 'I became normal.' But, she added, she did not regret her Catholic upbringing, for it 'stimulated the metaphor glands'.[19]

In fact, Catholic writers constituted another strong group in Brisbane at the time, [20] and Thea had links to them as well. She knew the poets Paul Grano and Martin Haley, both a generation older. Grano was invited to talk to the Barjai group, and her notebook has a poem addressed to him.[21] A letter from her to Haley in 1944, inviting him to speak to a meeting of the Catholic Writers Movement in the Aquinas Library, suggests that Thea was already a member of that group when she joined Barjai.[22] Politically, the Barjai group might have been at odds with many of these writers, but Haley became a mentor to the young schoolteacher when she was sent out to country schools.[23]

Thea's first teaching post was in an infants' school at Mt Crosby, out of Brisbane. Then, after a year fulltime at university, when she'd fallen in love and spent time typing her boyfriend's thesis and so had failed history and economics, came the year in Townsville in far north Queensland. At the end of that year she had to re-sit the papers she'd failed the previous year,[24] and so her Bachelor of Arts was not conferred until April 1948. After that she taught at Mary Valley and other small towns out of Brisbane, where she again had to either board with a local family or live at the pub.[25]

This is the life described in her first two novels, of 'loneliness in country hotels', missing 'people & books & music & the interchange of ideas', as she wrote to Martin Haley in 1948. Writing from 'Rural School, Pomona,' she told him that this life had made her sick of introspection, and had overwhelmed the confidence she felt at nineteen. She wrote about her novel, what hard work writing was, 'the infinite erasings and scratchings needed to obtain a glimmer of style'; and told a funny story about the head teacher, who had 'an all-absorbing interest in himself' and who required her to make the school glue – to his recipe: '(Eheu Mrs Beeton)'.[26] This novel was presumably discarded, for she said later that she wrote *Girl with a Monkey* in 1955, some ten years after the experience of teaching in Townsville on which it is based.[27]

In August 1948 in Gympie she married Jack Gregson, an accountant who was ten years her senior and had been married before. Her parents disapproved of the match and the newlyweds moved to Sydney the following year, where they had little to do with either the Astleys or the Gregsons. Thea's brother Philip, who had become a Jesuit priest, kept in regular contact, sending birthday and Christmas cards.[28] After their only son Edmund was born in 1955, contact with Thea's parents was renewed.

Her father died in 1961 and her mother took over the letter-writing, at one point scolding Thea for writing about sex, using rough language and expressing anti-Catholic sentiments.[29] It seems unlikely that mother and daughter enjoyed a close relationship. Thea's comment that her father was a man who could never resist a wisecrack suggests that she would have had more affinity with him, but family relationships seem not to have been particularly warm and there had been a period during her childhood when her parents separated. By contrast, her long marriage to Jack appears to have been companionable and supportive of her writing. In an undated birthday card she thanks him 'for putting up with me'.[30]

From 1958 onwards Thea held fulltime jobs, first as a high school teacher, then as a tutor at Macquarie University (from 1968 to 1980). During these years the Gregsons lived in Epping, a suburb in the north-west of Sydney that was part of the great postwar suburban spread. Jack was employed in the NSW public service, and was for a long time in charge of music administration in the Education Department. To outward appearances they were an ordinary middle-class family – except that few women of Thea's generation and class worked fulltime. Postwar suburbia became a staple of her fiction, but her neighbours seemed blissfully unaware of this: even after she had published several novels, one of her neighbours expressed surprise to learn that Thea was a writer as well as a teacher.[31] Despite their literary and musical interests, the Gregsons did not mix much in those circles, although Thea got to meet other writers who were also loners (as she described herself). She invented an excuse to visit Patrick White at Castle Hill and introduce herself,[32] and they became friends. Joan Levick, who wrote under the name of Amy Witting, was a colleague at Cheltenham Girls High School in the early 1960s, and Thea encouraged her to send stories – successfully – to the *New Yorker.*

After the move to Sydney, Thea went on publishing poems in newspapers and journals. These later efforts are more assured and witty than the young girl's love poems in her notebooks and in *Barjai*. She once told the story of selling a poem to the *Sydney Morning Herald* under the name 'Philip Cressy' – and being paid as a man, five guineas instead of the usual three.[33]

By now her real commitment was to writing prose. In a statement that suggests how serious her ambition was, she told an interviewer that she had turned to prose when she 'discovered I'd probably never be any good at all as a poet of any stature'.[34]

Girl with a Monkey was highly commended in the *Sydney Morning Herald* novel competition, and as a consequence she received the following letter from Angus & Robertson's redoubtable commissioning editor, Beatrice Davis:

> We have read GIRL WITH A MONKEY with great pleasure, because of the quality of your writing. It is evocative and individual and you give an almost unbearably vivid picture of Elsie Ford's sensitivities and embarrassments – as well as of poor Harry's devotion.
>
> Would you care to come and talk about the MS? This piece is rather too slight, but I believe you could become a very good novelist indeed. May I hear from you?[35]

On the back of this letter are Thea's calculations of word length, apparently to counteract the 'too slight' comment. But the two women met, they got on well, and after this Davis always backed Astley.[36] The novelist paid tribute to the editor's influence in 'moulding and guiding' Australian literature, persuading Angus & Robertson to take on books like hers, which Davis knew to be important but did not expect to sell well.[37] According to her biographer, Davis influenced the Miles Franklin Committee on Thea's behalf.[38] Thea's tribute to Beatrice, on her retirement from Angus & Robertson in 1973, praised her 'capacity to advise without hurt, to correct without making the author feel ashamed or inadequate', a comment that speaks volumes about the novelist's sensitivity to criticism. 'Beatrice Davis has taught me more about writing than anyone else,' she went on.[39] Davis's acceptance of Astley's literary ambitions, unorthodox as they were at the time, and her promotion of the novels, proved to be a great advantage in the early part of the writer's career.

'I know the country I want to explore, but I don't seem able even to chart the coasts.'[40] Her phrase, 'a country I want to explore', suggests an affinity with White's 'country of the mind' (from the epigraph of *The Aunt's Story*, 1948). It was only after finishing her first novel that Astley discovered Patrick White, and when she read *The Tree of Man* she recognised at once that 'This is it. Someone can do it.'[41] Looking back later, she said that she felt affinity with White's metaphysical side, and also with Hal Porter's 'outrageously ornamented sickly imagistic style' which made White's style look spare by comparison.[42] She discovered Porter at around the same time, for she wrote a fan letter to him about his 1958 novel, *A Handful of Pennies*, praising him as not only an 'incredible handler of words' but also for 'a wistfulness in the poetry of your work'. She congratulated him on 'a contribution to world-class – not merely Australian – literature'.[43]

'Not merely Australian'. If her ambition was to be read by the world, not only by Australia, which writers did Astley admire? When in 1948 she wrote from Townsville to thank Haley for sending copies of *John O'London's Weekly* and the *Bulletin*, she offered the opinion that the *Bulletin* lacks the 'warm camaraderie of its earlier days', adding that she preferred that bit of 'magic' in the 'commonplace' to contemporary realists like Auden and Spender. This preference may refer to such regular contributors to *John O'London's* as Somerset Maugham and older writers such as Rebecca West and Max Beerbohm. It may have been here that she came across Graham Greene, whose influence critics have detected in her work, although she did not (to my knowledge) ever speak about this. That 'middlebrow' journal was an important conduit of literary education, though hardly an advocate of the modernist writing that Astley would soon look to for models.[44]

Later she was more openly scornful of the *Bulletin* tradition – 'bushwhackery', she called it – and was happy that a more cosmopolitan literature, interested in city and suburban life, had emerged. Her comment that Paterson and other 1890s writers 'were trying to flog [Australianness] and make it a saleable commodity' shows a clear rejection of such popular writing. After teaching a wider range of Australian literature at university, she came to regard *The Fortunes of Richard Mahony* as the great Australian novel. In the 1974 interview where she made these comments she expressed admiration for Thomas Keneally (by then a friend), but not for realist writers such as Kylie Tennant or Katharine Susannah Prichard.[45]

Like Judith Wright, her early literary heroes were all men. When interviewed in 1963 for an article in the *Bulletin*, she said that as well as White, other writers she admired were Durrell and Nabokov – she was clearly looking for contemporary models, beyond the local literary scene.[46] She looked as well to American writers – Hemingway and Sinclair Lewis among the older generation, Raymond Carver and John Cheever among her closer contemporaries. This was unusual among her generation of Australian writers, who generally took European and British modernists as models: it was not until the late 1960s and early 1970s that young poets and story writers like Frank Moorhouse turned to the United States for inspiration.

Astley later included female short story writers Carson McCullers and Mavis Gallant in her personal pantheon, and made impassioned statements about the cultural suppression of women and prejudice against women writers. But during her early years as a novelist Astley moved into the mode of writing from a male point of view which, she said later, she felt was the only way to be listened to. To be classified as a woman writer/women's writer would have been a fate worse than death. It was not until the early 1980s that she attempted to write from within the consciousness of a female protagonist.[47]

Her first two books were reviewed in the *Times Literary Supplement*, as well as locally, in both newspapers and little magazines: Beatrice Davis was getting her work widely noticed. *Girl with a Monkey* depicts a young teacher's final day in a remote north Queensland town as she prepares to break with her lover, a roadworker, and her consciousness flashes back to key moments of the past year. The novel won from Vance Palmer, a representative of the previous generation of realist novelists, the comment, 'definitely a promising writer'.[48] Sidney Baker in the *Sydney Morning Herald* placed her in a recent tradition, starting with Eve Langley's *The Pea Pickers*, and continuing with White's *Tree of Man* and *Voss*, of novels 'loaded with poetic imagery and symbolism'.[49] A place in such distinguished company perhaps nullified his objections to her use of flashbacks, and of words like 'gobemouche', 'sigillate', 'majuscule'. The *Bulletin*, despite calling it 'a highly promising first novel', was not impressed by the style ('influenced by James Joyce, [it] is pretentious: too much artifice, too much parade of erudition') and criticised Astley's handling of the subject: 'She allows her schoolteacher to evade for far too long the gratification of the roadworker's passion, so that the life is taken out of the story: these people are only pretending to be great lovers.'

Astley must have written to Douglas Stewart objecting to this review, as his reply amplifies the point about passion: 'I would say, so far as plot goes, beware of the girl who rejects passion – she has been Kylie Tennant's bane for years.'[50] These avuncular remarks about a novel that all agreed was 'promising' were offset by Astley's friend Laurie Collinson's review in *Overland*, which recognised the 'humorously ironic treatment of the girl and the detachment with which she, as narrator, observes her proletarian "lover" ' – who is not, for once, 'a sentimentalised projection of an author's political outlook'. Astley has 'an extraordinary facility with words', he wrote, and she is 'struggling towards a style which will be totally her own'.[51]

A Descant for Gossips (1960) fared better.[52] The novel moves between a pair of illicit lovers, who are schoolteachers in a county town and are hounded by its gossips, and a vulnerable young girl who is bullied by other students. Among the old guard of critics, Marjorie Barnard was fulsome in her praise, calling it 'great' and 'brilliant prose', and bringing out its compassion as well as its anger.[53] Sidney Baker returned to his 'prose poetry' theme and suggested that 'social satire' was a 'profitable direction' for this kind of writing which could use imagery to 'probe into the cobwebbed corners of behaviour'.[54] In this he anticipated the kind of writing that Astley would perfect over the course of her next few books. The *Times Literary Supplement* reviewer noted briefly that her tragedy was melodramatic but satire was her strength.[55] RG Geering was also firmly of the opinion that 'the main strength of the book is in its satire', and quoted this description, from chapter IV, of a party where sandwiches are handed around:

> Like communion breads, thought Moller, like tribal tokens of an infinite ill-will towards others outside the group. The crowd blessed themselves and ate the flesh of their victims with such overt smacking of scandalous lips it was really intolerable. Fragments of

> conversation, the clichés standing out skeletal, the frame on which the verbose platitudes fleshed themselves, reached Moller's ears . . .

He noted that her highly charged style can produce 'sharp visual effects' but also 'ponderous atrocities' and some strange coinages.[56]

A young male reviewer thought *A Descant for Gossips* sentimental but praised the use of speech – 'a three quarter written play lies embedded in the marquisite prose'.[57] This judgment is perspicacious about the contrast between Astley's convincing use of speech and her 'exquisite' descriptive prose that often glitters like marcasite rather than diamonds, but it indicates a problem that would dog readers' responses to Astley's novels. The predominantly ironic narrative often fails to deliver a clear moral stance, so that readers may respond to the same scene in diametrically opposed ways, seeing the narrator as either a pitiless critic or a sentimentalist indulging the character who is the object of irony.[58] There is also the recurrent reaction of, 'Who does she think she is, to criticise others so harshly?' The *Bulletin* opined: 'Though exclusive in her own attitudes, Miss Astley strikes at small-town snobbery without mercy and with an acidly clever pen.'[59] This is the kind of trouble that a satirist who is more of a moralist than a comedian is bound to get into.

The Well Dressed Explorer evoked just such opposing responses. 'Poor George,' wrote Kylie Tennant of the book's protagonist, whose life course is its subject.[60] He is an egotist of monstrous proportions, who believes himself to be a generous soul, albeit susceptible to love. Rosemary Wighton found him neither significant nor sympathetic.[61] Another reviewer, detecting a 'grey puritanism' beneath Astley's 'audacious' prose, asked why 'the authoress' identifies the man entirely with 'the squalor of his extra marital chasings', positioning herself 'in order to condemn'?[62] However, for Sidney Baker, while George is a 'forgettable' person, in Astley's hands he became a memorable character: 'he is psychologically valid'.[63]

For Nancy Keesing, too, 'The malice this time is in the narration,' as it depicts George throughout his life, a man who 'seeks his childhood idyll in the arms of every woman chance brings his way'. The following passage illustrates Astley's method, which to some is 'malice in the narration', and for other readers is 'position[ing] herself in order to condemn'. Either way, the issue is her mode of narration. A long-term girlfriend accuses George of being stingy, even as he expresses regret that he is not free to buy her presents like those he buys for his wife:

> His outraged face had swung a slow arc of disgust and prudishness upon her, the nasty little gold-digger. His finest sensibilities were outraged and he rewrapped his family gifts prissily with his mouth tucked in at the corners. When they parted finally he tried to tell himself she really had been rather grasping – but he knew it wasn't true. Still, he had given her a couple of books (two, said his accurate angel) and if they had been review copies, well, Marie had never known![64]

In Keesing's view, Astley succeeds best 'when she allows her malice full rein' and 'invents satirical aphorisms with some of the ease of Samuel Butler'. In fact, she thought the author was not hard enough on George; instead, she is hard on her women characters, cannot forgive their fondness for this absurd man.[65] This is another version of the sentimentality verdict – that Astley is too hard on some characters, too easy on others.

'Sentimentality' was an accusation targeted at any overt expression of feeling in much 1960s literary criticism, with its austere formalist standards and preference for irony and ambivalence. In the first extended commentary on Astley's three debut novels, academic John Burrows argued that her sympathetic portraits were sentimental and that her satire lacked the depth that charity toward her subjects would provide. At least in *Explorer* she had forsworn a schoolteacher's superior standpoint on her subjects, he wrote, but her attempt at 'the ambivalence of the true satirist' failed dismally: George remains 'an uneasy union of sentimentally observed virtues and scornfully observed follies and vices'. What's more, this critic detected the noxious influence of Patrick White in Astley's similarly 'vacuous, uncomprehending antipathy for suburbia'.[66] The expectation of ambivalence is a strange one, if we think of Jonathan Swift – or indeed White – as a 'true satirist'.

Astley would have been flattered by the comparison, despite the accompanying sneers at her attempt at a 'literary novel', and it was made by other reviewers who disliked her mannered style. She admired White greatly, and they were friends for several years, until a falling-out over her anxiety to find a paperback publisher for *Explorer*.[67] During that time he wrote her an extraordinary letter about a manuscript she had submitted to Angus & Robertson called 'The Little Lie'. Confessing that he had not liked the work, he went on to say that it was a falling off from *Descant*, and even there 'moral indignation was as far as you could go' without spiritual values. Lacking such values, she may have escaped from suburbia into 'a rackety career of novel writing', but that was not the way to go. His advice was:

> Read, think & listen to silence, & shell the peas . . . concentrating on the work in hand until you know what it is to be a pea – and drudge at the school, & sleep with your husband & bring up your child. That is what I mean when I say 'living', not going to parties and taking lovers (I don't suggest you have taken any!) Then, when you have become solid, you will write the kind of book you ought to write. You may even find that you have come to believe in God – in spite of the fact that you are a lapsed Catholic soul – which I personally believe to be the root of all matters.[68]

'Becoming solid' echoes his character Theodora Goodman in *The Aunt's Story*, and her desire to become a chair or a table. Did White's comment about her 'lapsed Catholic soul' point her in the direction of the themes of conversion in *Explorer*, and of faith and forgiveness in *The Slow Natives*? What might have happened to this manuscript that he disliked so much? Did she destroy it? Did it transmute into *Explorer*?[69]

The Slow Natives was greeted with superlatives by the majority of reviewers, before it went on to win the Miles Franklin and the Moomba Festival prizes. Neil Jillett praised it as 'almost brazenly stylish . . . limned with wit and pity', and its author as 'a novelist who is unquestionably in world class'. Like some reviewers of *Explorer*, he also distinguished between the tale and its mode of narration, noting that although the spirit is warm (he instances the convent scenes) 'the telling itself usually has a hep-cat crackle.'[70] 'A corner of Sarsaparilla' was the title of one review, reiterating the connection with Patrick White and admiring the sharper focus achieved by 'her dense, untidy and nervously rich style'.[71] In the *Sydney Morning Herald*, LV Kepert introduced his detailed account of the novel with the opinion that Astley's quality should be more widely recognised as a lively recorder of contemporary life, with sharp pen and 'detached cynicism', as JK Ewers had noted in his book *Creative Writing in Australia*.

Kepert added that 'her feminine insight and sympathy' proved 'disconcerting to a male reader when applied to stripping men characters of their outward poise and showing their ridiculous centres'.[72] Here, perhaps, is the nub of the problem for Astley's predominantly male reviewers: she is merciless in exposing the self-delusion and selfishness involved in the pursuit of sexual excitement. Yet they rarely notice, as Keesing did, that she is equally hard on her female characters, if not harder. Only children show up well under her piercing gaze in these early works.[73] Reviewers' nervousness about sex in fiction was commonplace in Australia at the time, although it is often unclear whether the subject itself was considered taboo, or they would prefer her to write about it in a more Lawrentian and lyrical way, as Douglas Stewart clearly did in his reviews of *Girl* and *Descant*.[74]

Reviews in the literary journals, appearing after *Natives* had won the Miles Franklin prize, were more restrained. *Overland* saw it rather contentiously as a 'realistic novel that tries just a little too hard to achieve symbolic significance', but thought the prize was justified because of the novel's 'awareness of contemporary urban life and its problems'.[75] *Southerly*'s critic praised the convent scenes but thought the sharp portrayal of Iris Leverson and the homosexual character Leo was undermined by lack of sympathy, and found the ending – where Keith is at first thought to have been killed in a car accident, and his father rediscovers his faith in life – both sentimental and melodramatic.[76] JM Couper, reviewing all of Astley's work for *Meanjin* in 1967, sought in vain some structure of values underpinning her irony. He read the four novels as successive attempts to find 'a form capable of keeping the recalcitrance of life within the definition and completeness of art' and found that *Natives* came closest to success, although he disagreed with its use of Catholicism, 'religious insistence where there is no belief to back it'.[77] Critics' attention to what they saw as faults of construction, and of excessive or inappropriate emotion, as well as their dislike of the treatment of sexuality in Astley's fiction, all suggest that they had no sympathy for her desire to create 'a landscape with figures' and 'a study in emotions' rather than a conventional novel.

And of course she was a woman, and a young woman at that, whose manner lacked the *gravitas* of a Judith Wright. The condescension to which she was subjected is chillingly shown in an exchange with Clem Christesen over Couper's article. Astley expressed herself disappointed: 'After reading Doctor Couper maybe I'll chuck the novel away.' Christesen replied that maybe he should have asked for a full article rather than a review article, but: 'Frankly, I didn't feel your work to date warranted an essay – it's not yet substantial enough.' This is after four novels, two of which won the Miles Franklin prize. He added '(Please don't be "affronted" by these remarks; perhaps you too might concede that you haven't yet written a really significant novel? But I'm quite confident you will do so.)'[78]

Nevertheless, Thea Astley had made her mark. She was now in a very different league from the unknown schoolteacher who started out twelve years before. Her books had won prizes, she was published by the prestigious Angus & Robertson. *Natives* was taken up by a New York publishing house, M Evans. It also appeared in paperback – the first of her novels to do so – in the Sun Books series recently established by Geoffrey Dutton and Max Harris, a welcome initiative for Australian writers in a market where the quality paperback was a recent innovation. Reviewers compared her with Christina Stead as well as Patrick White.[79] She had received grants to support the writing of both *Explorer* and *Natives*. Nevertheless, her books did not sell in large numbers, and she told an interviewer in 1966: 'You have to go outside Australia to make money as a writer. You never build a reputation here by winning prizes.'[80]

A few years after *Natives* she was appointed a fulltime tutor at Macquarie University, teaching Australian literature and creative writing.[81] In this role she joined the small band of women teaching in Australian universities during the 1960s and 1970s, even though for most of them an appointment as tutor was as far as they were permitted to climb the academic ladder. This appointment gave her more time for writing and a more prestigious position in the literary world than that accorded to schoolteachers. Further signs of recognition followed. Over the next few years she made two lecture tours in Queensland at the invitation of the Commonwealth Literary Fund.[82] She was also invited to edit the 1970 annual CLF-subsidised anthology of short fiction, *Coast to Coast*.[83]

This publication received negative reviews from the young men of the literary world, another indication, like the reviews of her novels, that her literary taste was not widely accepted – or not from a woman. One review began with the question, 'Who is this Thea Astley?'[84] No proponent of *Bulletin*-school realism, she was a modernist whose sensibility was equally alien to the new realism of the 1970s. Michael Wilding in *Meanjin* thought it disappointing that the anthology was not urban but 'suburban' in its themes, looking from a distance at the odd way other people live.[85] Unusually for *Coast to Coast*, the proportion of female to male writers was almost 50–50, and this may have influenced reviews. 'Sadly lacking in talent' was *Overland*'s judgment.[86]

The review that most upset Astley drew attention to her preference for self-conscious, and sometimes badly behaved, writing. The *Australian*'s reviewer faulted the stories as being too similar, having the 'common flaw' of intruding their telling rather than 'letting the story tell itself'. As a prime example of this flaw he accused Amy Witting's 'The Man with the Impediment' of adopting the Gothic 'in an inept attempt to entertain'. His criticisms add up to an indirect restatement of preference for realist writing, which does not draw attention to its fictitiousness and makes no explicit attempt to deal with 'moral and social issues'.[87] From this distance it is possible to see Astley's editorial choices as heralding the new postmodernist writing of the 1980s, but at the time the *Australian* critic's preferences carried the weight of authority: fiction should show, not tell; it should work obliquely; the writer should not intrude herself.

Astley was a forerunner of the postmodern fascination with

writing that draws attention to its own literariness. She belonged to the future rather than to the past of Australian fiction. Her approach to writing was certainly unfamiliar and challenging, and like Stead before her, she found that a female innovator meets even more resistance than a male one. Also like Stead, she was eager for an overseas readership, and looked outside Australian literature for her models. Beatrice Davis had described *The Well Dressed Explorer*'s protagonist as a character who 'may become as memorable in Australian writing as Sinclair Lewis's Mr Babbitt'.[88] This famous American satire on consumerism was also mentioned by an American reviewer of *The Slow Natives*, who referred to 'the author's feminine eye and ear for antipodean Babbittry'.[89]

The comparison with Sinclair Lewis reflects Astley's main literary innovations. She was essentially a satirist, and her stylistic affinities were with American writers rather than with British. Both qualities set her at loggerheads with the old guard of Australian literature, for many of whom social realism was the only true Australian writing, and with academic critics for whom literature must have a firm moral foundation, and should not draw attention to its workings.

Unlike Judith Wright's, Astley's early successes were not universally admired. Fiction was a more highly contested site than poetry at this time, and besides, she was satirising elements of the Australian way of life, including its patriarchal sexual mores, as well as experimenting with prose style and narrative structure. In 1970, at this turning point in her long and brilliant career, her future looked far from certain. Yet over the next three decades she continued to experiment with new subjects – post-colonial race relations, and women as protagonists – and a new technique of connected short stories forming a discontinuous narrative, which suited her 'figures in a landscape' better than linear narrative. Producing a new work every couple of years, she went from strength to strength, finding a wider readership and more appreciative critics. She won the Miles Franklin prize four times in all. On her death in 2004 Thea Astley AO was remembered as a 'creative force until the end' and 'a literary trailblazer'.[90]

Notes

1 Undated letter to Martin Haley, referring to his review of *Girl*, presumably in *Catholic Leader*: Haley papers, UQ Fryer Library 48, pp. 9–15.

2 Hope on *The Tree of Man*: 'The Bunyip Stages a Comeback', *Sydney Morning Herald*, 16 June 1956, repr. in *AD Hope: Selected poetry and prose*, ed. David Brooks, Halstead Press, Sydney, 2000, pp. 213–15.

3 HP Heseltine, *The Most Glittering Prize: The Miles Franklin Literary Award 1957–1998*, Australian Defence Force Academy, School of Literature and Communication and Permanent Press, Canberra, ACT, 2001, p. 26.

4 After White, Astley was the second writer to win it twice. She won four times in all: in 1972 with *The Acolyte* and in 1999 with *Drylands*, her final novel.

5 Heseltine, *The Most Glittering Prize*, pp. 13–16.

6 *The Slow Natives* [1965], Sun Books, Melbourne, 1966, p. 114.

7 David Marr, ed., *Patrick White: Letters*, Random House, Sydney, 1994, p. 229.

8 Geoffrey Dutton, 'What they read when they were young', *Bulletin*, December 23–30, 1980, p. 170.

9 Various interviews, including Jennifer Ellison, *Rooms of their Own*, Penguin, Ringwood, Vic, 1986, pp. 63–4; Candida Baker, *Yacker 3: Australian writers talk about their work*, Pan, Sydney, 1989; Ray Willbanks, repr. in *Thea Astley's Fictional Worlds*, eds. Susan Sheridan and Paul Genoni, Cambridge Scholars Press, Newcastle-upon-Tyne, 2006, pp. 21–35.

10 All Hallows' School website, <www.allhallows.qld.edu.au/>.

11 Interview with Suzanne Walker, National Library of Australia Transcript TRC275, 1974, pp.12–13.

12 Walker interview, pp. 11–13.

13 William Hatherell, *The Third Metropolis*, University of Queensland Press, St Lucia, 2007, p. 125.

14 'Brisbane in the Forties: My "Barjai" Days', *Meanjin*, 54(3), 1995, pp. 531–41.

15 Astley, 'Sonnet', *Barjai*, 17, 1944, p. 9.

16 Hatherell, pp. 123–4.

17 Not published till 1988; a copy of this poem exists in Astley's early 1940s' notebook, suggesting that was the date of composition.

18 Thea Astley and Vida Horn, 'Barjai Days: Hello Laurie, Hello Barrie', *Overland* 142, 1996, p. 36.

19 Walker interview, pp. 10–11.

20 Hatherell, pp. 79–85.

21 Astley papers, UQFL 97, folder 42, notebook. Later she attributed to his poetry her perception that 'the shabby areas of town and country . . . could be unashamedly declared as lyric argument' in 'Being a Queenslander', repr. *Thea Astley's Fictional Worlds*, p. 11.

22 Haley papers, UQFL 48, pp. 9–15.

23 The Brisbane Realist Writers Group was not formed until 1950, after Thea had left for Sydney. This group, which welcomed Aboriginal poet Kath Walker, was dominated by John Manifold in the 1950s and he is the object of Astley's satire in her story 'Journey to Olympus' (Hatherell, pp.166–7).

24 Walker interview, pp.15–16.

25 Willbanks interview, p. 24.

26 August 1948, Haley papers, UQFL 48, pp. 9–15.

27 Ellison interview, p. 58.

28 My thanks to Ed Gregson for this information about the family: interview, Sydney, February 2007.

29 Among the few letters from her parents preserved in the archive, this one is dated 5 November 1968, and refers to the novel *A Boat Load of Home Folk*.
30 Astley papers, UQFL 97, folder 152.
31 Ed Gregson, interview.
32 David Marr, *Patrick White: A life*, Vintage, Sydney, 1992, p. 356.
33 Letter from Sidney J Baker at the *Sydney Morning Herald*, 30 July 1956, in Astley papers, UQFL 97, Correspondence.
34 Interview with Hazel de Berg, 1964, National Library of Australia TRC 1/102.
35 Letter 4 March 1957, UQFL 97, box 21.
36 Walker interview, p. 18. She also told Walker that A&R knocked back two novellas – the one before *The Acolyte* was not good, 'I was very miserable at the time' (p. 31). Davis edited all Astley's books up to and including *The Acolyte*, after which she retired from A&R. Astley moved with her to Nelson.
37 Ellison p. 58.
38 Jacqueline Kent, *A Certain Style: Beatrice Davis*, Penguin, Ringwood, Vic, 2001, p. 157.
39 Kent, p. 157.
40 TA to Martin Haley, undated letter, Haley papers, UQFL 48, pp. 9–15.
41 Reported in 'Thea Astley in America', interview with Ray Willbanks, *Antipodes*, 2(2), 1988, pp. 107–8.
42 *Antipodes* interview, p. 108.
43 Undated letter, Mitchell Library, MSS7172, Ann and Roger Jennings papers.
44 See Jonathan Wild, '"Insects in Letters": *John O'London's Weekly* and the New Reading Public', *Literature and History*, 15(2), Autumn 2006, pp. 50–62.
45 Walker interview, pp. 3–4, 7 and later.
46 Patricia Rolfe, 'Novel Situation', *Bulletin*, 26 January 1963, pp. 14–15.

47 Ellison interview, pp. 56–7.
48 *Meanjin*, 17(4), 1958, p. 436.
49 'Australian Novels and Our Prose Poets', *Sydney Morning Herald*, 23 August 1958, p. 13; he also names Harrower's 'distinguished novel' *The Long Prospect*.
50 Letter 28 August 1958, Astley papers, UQFL 97, folder 141.
51 *Overland*, 15, 1959, p. 48.
52 Astley, *A Descant for Gossips*, Angus & Robertson, Sydney, 1960.
53 'Fiction Chronicle', *Meanjin*, 19(4), 1960, pp. 439–40.
54 'Social Satire', *Sydney Morning Herald*, 7 May 1960, p. 14.
55 *Times Literary Supplement*, 1 April 1960, p. 205.
56 'School for Scandal', *Southerly*, 21(2), 1961, pp. 53–4.
57 Alan Davies, 'A sentimental education', *Nation*, August 13 1960, p. 26.
58 Susan Sheridan, 'Violence, Irony and Reading Relations: Thea Astley's *Drylands*', *Thea Astley's Fictional Worlds*, pp. 164–75.
59 'Smalltown Gossip,' *Bulletin*, 22 June 1960, pp. 2, 58.
60 Brief notice, *Meanjin*, 21(4), 1962, p. 509.
61 *Australian Book Review*, February 1963, p. 71.
62 Bob Burns in *Prospect*, 7(1), 1964, pp. 28–9.
63 *Sydney Morning Herald*, 8 December 1962, p. 17.
64 *The Well Dressed Explorer* [1962], Penguin, Ringwood, Vic, 1988, p. 140.
65 Keesing, 'Back to the Plot', *Bulletin*, 15 December 1962, p. 40.
66 'Chalk and Cheese', *Southerly*, 23(4), 1963, pp. 276–80.
67 PW to Laurence Collinson, 27 November 1964, in David Marr, *Patrick White: Letters*, pp. 272–4.
68 PW to TA, 20 March1961, UQFL 97, folder 142.
69 He always thought *Explorer* 'a wretched book': PW to Laurence Collinson, 27 November 1964, *Patrick White: Letters*, p. 273.
70 'Australian Suburban Agony,' *Age*, 6 November 1965, p. 21.
71 Maurice Shadbolt, *Bulletin*, 27 November 27,1965, p. 55.

72 'Thea Astley's Lively Novel', *Sydney Morning Herald*, 16 October 1965, p. 18.

73 Susan Sheridan, 'Thea Astley: A woman among the satirists of post-war modernity', *Australian Feminist Studies*, 29(3), 2003, pp. 261–71.

74 See also Keesing's article, 'Australia's "Unlucky" Novelists,' where she hopes for more Australian writing about love affairs, not 'lust' affairs: *Southerly*, 22(2), 1962, pp. 84–9.

75 John McLaren, 'Recent Novels', *Overland*, 34, 1966, pp. 49–50.

76 Arthur Ashworth, Review, *Southerly*, 26(1), 1966, pp. 62–6.

77 JM Couper, 'The Novels of Thea Astley', *Meanjin*, 26(3), 1967, pp. 332–7.

78 TA to CC, 9 October 1967, CC to TA, 12 October 1967, *Meanjin* Archive, Melbourne University Library Special Collections, Astley file.

79 Mentioned by Keesing and also by anonymous US reviewer, 'Prodigal Parents', unidentified clipping, Astley papers, UQFL 97, folder 157.

80 Sascha Miles, 'Soul for Sale: Just for Jazz', *Woman's Day* with *Woman*, July 18 1966, Astley papers, UQFL 97, clippings file.

81 She had been doing some parttime tutoring there in 1967 while working fulltime at the Correspondence School: TA to CC, 9 October 1967, *Meanjin* Archive.

82 In 1969 and 1970: Walker, p. 21.

83 Astley, ed., *Coast to Coast.* Angus & Robertson, Sydney, 1970.

84 As reported by Janette Turner Hospital, 'A Writer Comes in from the Cold', *Sydney Morning Herald*, 14 October 1989, p. 80.

85 'Short story chronicle', *Meanjin*, 30(2), 1971, pp. 255–67.

86 Carl Harrison-Ford, 'Recent Fiction,' *Overland*, 48, 1971, pp. 59–60.

87 Brian Kiernan, 'A glut of sameness', *Australian*, 21 November 1970, p. 22. Astley said this was 'the only review that has ever really upset me', especially his attack on Witting, who had been published in the *New Yorker* (Walker, p. 32).

88 Unidentified clipping in Astley papers, UQFL 97, folder 157.

89 'Prodigal Parents' mentions Iris's taste for 'interior decoration and mild adultery'.

90 Rosemary Sorensen, 'Creative Force until the End', *Courier-Mail*, 18 August 2004, p. 3; Susan Wyndham, 'Journey of a Literary Trailblazer', *Sydney Morning Herald*, 21–22 August 2004, p. 79.

CHAPTER THREE

Dorothy Hewett with her three youngest children, Kate, Rose and Tom, about 1965

Dorothy Hewett's second run

> I was thirty-five yesterday. Last year I started seriously writing again, after years of giving it away to just live, bring up three little boys, and other things. So now I am making my second run, a very different person from the teenager who won first prize in a *Meanjin* Poetry competition with a highly precocious, embittered little poem called 'Dream of an Old Love'.

Thus Dorothy Hewett reintroduced herself in May 1958 to Clem Christesen, editor of *Meanjin*, after a silence of almost fifteen years. She went on to report that she was 'busy trying to write a novel' and had done 'a swag of short stories, but not much poetry until the last couple of months'.[1] The novel turned out to be *Bobbin Up*, the story of a group of women factory workers, published the following year by the Australasian Book Society, a left-wing press. It was highly commended for the Mary Gilmore Award (a competition sponsored by the trades union movement) and it launched her back into writing. Behind these brief words in her letter lies a complex tale of personal turmoil and political commitment that had caused her to 'give it away' for so long.

Photographs from the time of her literary success as a teenager and from the publicity tour she did for *Bobbin Up* certainly show 'a very different person'.[2] During the war years the young Dorothy had been glamorously unsmiling, with long blonde hair and dark lipstick. In 1959, with neat short hair and a shy smile, she appeared to fit the label of 'busy housewife' who 'finds time for writing'.[3]

Her writing, too, was very different. The prize-winning poem mentioned in her letter, originally published under the exotic pen-name of 'Jael Paris', begins:

> The sunlight hurts me like a diseased hand,
> I am the evil Chinese princess
> And you the diseased prince,
> Ricocheting in our turret of courtesans.
> The yellow hands of the sunlight hurt my heart.
> They pick at me like old men wanting my youth.

At the end of the poem both these golden lovers are aged and wizened, but it is the woman who suffers as she watches 'You with the young mouths of the courtesans'.[4] The poem is certainly both 'precocious' and 'embittered'. It also carries her trademark sexual directness, the only obvious link with her later prose work. The novel published seventeen years later begins:

> Shirl was nineteen years old, four months gone and just starting to show, bumping through Newtown on the back of a second-hand Norton.
>
> Through neon signs, traffic signals, lighted shop fronts, they slid on a long blurred streamer of speed down King Street. The summer wind, full of the smoke of bush fires from the Blue Mountains,

> whipped her skirt high above her knees. She was plastered against a leather-jacketed back with NEWTOWN ROCKETS exploded across it in crude white letters. A group of bodgies, holding up the front of a milkbar, bright as parakeets, whistled her shrilly down the wind.[5]

Here Hewett, communist writer, was describing proletarian life with a verve and sensuality far removed from the sober worker heroism that was the preferred mode of socialist realism. There is no sign of the earlier poem's exotic elements – which would certainly have earned disapprobation as 'decadent' from Leftist critics in the 1950s – but the prose has the rhythmic and imagistic power of poetry.

The writer now making her 'second run' had been silent for over ten years. The woman herself was now a 'very different person'. How did this happen, and why? Would this 'second run' be the end of the story of Hewett's becoming a writer?

In her autobiography, *Wild Card*, Hewett portrays herself as a flamboyant sexual and political rebel from the start. Born in 1923, she spent her childhood in the wheat-belt country east of Perth, at Wickepin, where she and her younger sister enjoyed the freedom of life on the farm and had correspondence lessons at home. When Dorothy was twelve, the family moved to the city and the girls attended Perth College, an academic private school for girls. Dorothy at first hated school, not knowing how to relate to other girls, until she decided that 'if I could be bohemian and outrageous . . . then I didn't have to fit in, I would make [the others] fit in with me'.[6] This, plus her difficult relationship with her mother, set her style of dealing with the world, as a wild rebel girl, defying all the rules of good womanhood.

She had early determined to be a writer and an actor. She read voraciously, encouraged by her father, who himself had little education. She and her sister had made up and acted out melodramatic plays derived from the plots of the movies they loved. Correspondence school had encouraged creative writing, and she wrote poetry that combined her knowledge of European and Aboriginal myths with bush settings.[7] At school she was introduced to modern English and American poets by the headmistress, an Oxford graduate. Starting an arts degree at the age of seventeen, Dorothy won a drama competition and this, her first play, was performed at the university. In the same year she won the *Meanjin* Poetry Prize. This, she said, was the 'beginning of it all, because I began to realise that I no longer had to just write in isolation'.[8]

Her mentors at this time included her university English lecturer, Alec King, *Meanjin*'s editor, Clem Christesen and the poet William Hart-Smith, whom she met when he spent some time in an army hospital in Perth. At university she edited and published in the student literary magazine *Black Swan*. At the age of twenty-one she won the ABC Poetry Prize for a long narrative poem called 'Testament', about lost loves – a boy, a girl, and the old farm of her childhood. She also wrote short stories and a number of other plays, and published poems in the Jindyworobak anthologies of 1941, 1942 and 1943, as well as in *Meanjin*, and in the Australian issue of the journal *Voices* edited by American serviceman Harry Roskolenko. She was, as she says, precocious.

Dorothy's busy writing, acting and political life at university, not to mention her many affairs of the heart, left little time or inclination to study. After failing French three times she left the university without taking a degree and worked at a succession of jobs, including court reporter. The account of this time in *Wild Card* abounds with remembered poses and roles, some in the theatre, most of them in life. Her emotional life was chaotic. When her first love left her to join the air force, she decided 'to be a whore', to pay him back. She joined the Communist Party. Still living at home, she had stormy rows with her parents. After another failed love affair she attempted suicide.

When she recovered she married her communist friend, Lloyd Davies, in 1945 and began work on the Communist Party paper, *The Workers' Star*, as a journalist. 'My salvation would be politics and marriage, in that order,' she wrote.[9] There was no room for writing poetry and plays in this salvation. Her preference for modernist literature was considered deeply suspect, and her lyrical and dramatic gifts were not suited to socialist realism.[10] Although she loved modernist poetry, and recalls that her prize-winning 'Dream of an Old Love' was influenced by Edith Sitwell and Ezra Pound's 'translations' from the Chinese, as a committed communist she did an about-face and wrote an article attacking the Angry Penguins as Pound's 'Australian godchildren', the inheritors of his arcane modernist poetics.[11] She read Wright's *The Moving Image* when it appeared and remembered this, almost thirty years later, as 'a tremendous experience' to see this relatively young woman with a sophisticated romantic sensibility 'taking charge of the Australian environment' and making of it a new kind of poetry.[12]

But Dorothy's own writing had stopped. The one poem from this period after her marriage, 'Clancy and Dooley and Don McLeod,' celebrated the heroes of the 1946 Aboriginal stockmen's strike in the Pilbara. It became famous in communist and socialist circles, and was in fact the first of a number of ballads she wrote, a form that she returned to in later years. But at the time it seemed to be an isolated phenomenon.

Communist politics and marriage to Lloyd Davies did not effect the desired salvation for Dorothy. She was sexually restless and hated being a fulltime mother to her son Clancy, born in 1947. Both her sexual and her political style offended Party officials and her affair with the Party leader in Perth ended with his threatening to put an end to her political career.[13] In 1949 she left lover, husband

and child and ran away to Sydney with Les Flood, a boilermaker and also a Party member. They lived together for nine years and she bore him three sons. They were poor, and she took a factory job, experience she used in *Bobbin Up*. She also took on the identity of Toddy Flood, distancing herself from Dorothy Hewett, the wild rebel girl who had defied the Party powerful in Perth.[14] She worked tirelessly for the Party, trying to be a perfect communist activist. And she committed herself wholeheartedly to Les and his working-class family and friends. She seems not to have had any contact with writers and Left-wing theatre in Sydney.

Tragedy struck when Clancy, the son she left in Perth, died of leukaemia. Dorothy's new relationship was difficult: Les Flood became more and more jealous and violent. In 1952 Dorothy and Les travelled with a delegation from the Union of Australian Women to a conference in Vienna, and then on to Moscow and China. On their return the relationship deteriorated: he beat her, they made up; the cycle was repeated. His employment became sporadic, and Dorothy's work for the Communist Party, and her jobs in the factory and in advertising, seem to have constituted the family's most reliable income.[15] Inheriting four thousand pounds from her grandmother, she was able to buy a house in Rockdale for the family to live in, but this became for her 'the house of madness'.[16] Les, diagnosed as a paranoid schizophrenic, accused her of trying to poison him and the children.

In 1956 'the miracle happens . . . I begin to write again after ten silent years'.[17] Frank Hardy, flush with the success of his notorious book, *Power Without Glory*, had moved from Melbourne to Sydney and set up a branch of the Realist Writers group. Dorothy joined and, encouraged by Frank, she produced several short stories and *Bobbin Up*. Hardy started her thinking in a different way about communism: he was sceptical of Party dogma on culture and aesthetics. He introduced her to other communist intellectuals, including David Martin, John Manifold and Stephen Murray-Smith, none of whom followed what she had considered the Party line. She came to see the Sydney communists she knew as philistines.[18]

Dorothy began to think that there might be more room for dissent within the Communist Party than she had believed, and that it was possible for her to be a writer and a loyal communist after all. There was a place for literature in the communist movement, and she could write about working-class people without making them into exemplars of all the revolutionary virtues, as required by Soviet-style socialist realism. She remained a Party member until 1968.

She stayed with Les Flood for a few more years. *Bobbin Up* was dedicated to him, yet he burned much of what she had written, once she started her 'second run'. He continued to be jealous and violent, and threatened to take the boys away from her. At the end of 1959 she left him and Sydney, and fled back to Perth in fear for her life, taking the children. There she made a new start, returning to university to finish her degree, with her parents' support. Soon she teamed up with Merv Lilley, a merchant seaman, a writer himself, and a sometime communist with anarchist tendencies. They had two daughters, and stayed together until Dorothy's death in 2002.

In the early 1960s she began publishing poetry and short stories, and writing plays again. In later years she wrote about the miracle of being able to write again as if it was solely the Communist Party that had silenced her. In a late poem, 'The Period of Silence', she wrote:

> Sometimes I could hardly breathe
> if your thoughts were ideologically incorrect
> if your words were inaccessible to the masses

better to be totally silent.
Once or twice I fell from grace
that was enough of guilt don't write
the doggerel of the Revolution.[19]

But there was another dimension to her silencing: the abuse she suffered in her life with Les Flood, which undermined her sense of self. In a somewhat apologetic preface to a new edition of *Bobbin Up* in 1985, she wrote that she had been 'silenced by political activism, the deep-seated anti-culturalism and socialist realist dogmas of the Australian Communist Party, plus the terrible struggle to survive'.[20] That 'the terrible struggle to survive' was psychological as well as material is clear from her autobiography, and such experiences would silence most women. When we look at what she wrote between *Bobbin Up* and the next major turning point in her career ten years later, when she left the Party and threw herself into writing for theatre and composing new, more confessional poetry, we discover a woman recovering her confidence in herself after a long period of self-hatred.

In fact her new outpouring of creativity in the 1960s coincided not with her repudiation of communism – that came later – but with her relationship with Merv Lilley and her return to university. She and Merv produced a jointly written book of poetry, *What About the People!*, published in 1962 by the National Council of Realist Writers, with an introduction by Frank Hardy. In 1968 Dorothy's first solo book of poetry, *Windmill Country*, appeared. At university she read extensively in English, American and Australian literature, began research for a Master of Arts degree, and successfully applied for a lecturing position in the English department, where she was employed for most of the next decade.

Undoubtedly the success of *Bobbin Up* restored her confidence in herself as a writer, but more than that, it gave her an entrée into the literary world of the Left, where she could be a writer and a communist as well. In the opening chapter of what was intended to be the second volume of her autobiography, Hewett recalls and pays tribute to 'all the old icons of the left who once came to celebrate the launch of a first novel by a young woman of thirty-five', including Stephen Murray-Smith, Ian Turner, Brian Fitzpatrick, David Martin, John Morrison, Alan Marshall and Aileen Palmer. Many of these were renegade communists who had left or been expelled from the Party over the events of 1956, Krushchev's 'secret speech' denouncing Stalin's crimes and the 'cult of personality', and the crushing of the Hungarian uprising. She met other writers as well, notably George Turner and Frank Dalby Davison, and wondered what her life would have been like in Melbourne rather than Perth and Sydney. 'I began to feel culturally deprived,' she wrote later. 'A whole period of Australia's literary life had come of age while I, enclosed in my proletarian gulag, had hardly been aware of it.'[21]

Frank Hardy and the Realist writers, and *Bobbin Up*, had started her off on the process of learning to write again (as she put it in *Wild Card*), but the kinds of writing she experimented with over the next decade owed nothing significant to the dogma of socialist realism. Rather, she drew for her poetry on folk traditions such as the ballad and for her rural-based stories on the Australian Lawsonian tradition. In both modes the implicit social critique was informed by her commitment to the political Left. The letter of congratulation on *Bobbin Up* she received from Katharine Susannah Prichard welcomed 'a comrade whose writing has such vital quality; & whose vision will be of great value to Australian literature – counterbalancing the "negative mysticism" of the White & Stow brigade [sic], & giving positive, stimulating incentives for the everyday struggles of life'.[22] This dismissal of the modernist fiction of Patrick White and Randolph Stow (it is not clear whose judgment Prichard is quoting here) invites Hewett to share Prichard's own position, as communist writers committed to writing 'as socialists and realists . . . using all our literary and psychological skill'.[23] And indeed Hewett's stories of the 1960s match this description of social and psychological realism, though it was not Hewett's style to aim for 'positive, stimulating incentives for the everyday struggles of life'.

In important ways, *Bobbin Up* was a once-off in Dorothy Hewett's writing career. It has more in common with her plays than with the realist short stories. Its style is impressionistic, laced with lines from popular songs and the sights, sounds and smells of urban life. It is structured as a series of portraits of the women who work at the Jumbuck spinning mill, seen at work and at home, on the bus and at the beach, with husbands, boyfriends, children, parents. These episodes dovetail into the drama of the strike in the final section. Nell, the communist, writes a pamphlet with her husband urging her fellow workers to protest against some of their number being laid off. Together the women stand up to the boss, and to the union representative, but every step along the way is fraught with doubt about whether they will continue to act in solidarity. The novel leaves them occupying the factory, singing 'He's got the whole world in his hands', a favourite protest song of the period. It is a small drama, with a less than triumphalist ending, but the women and their world are drawn with loving and vivid detail.

Dorothy Hewett in a later interview commented acutely that *Bobbin Up* wasn't really a novel at all but eighteen short stories loosely strung together. She said that she had not resolved this problem of structure because she lost interest in writing another long prose narrative and turned to plays.[24] However, the short stories she wrote around this time suggest a trajectory between the novel and the later plays, although it was not easy to see this because they appeared in various journals and were not collected until *A Baker's Dozen* appeared in 2001.[25] None of these collected stories revisits the scenes of Sydney proletarian life. Rather, most are set in the country where Hewett grew up, as were many of her poems of the 1960s. They are stories of ordinary people, their loves and griefs, not their politics, nor even their working lives.

The circumstances of their publication tell part of the tale of Hewett's comeback. She had obviously decided to send work wherever it might meet an appreciative audience. Several stories appeared in Left-wing anthologies, while *Australian Letters*, the glossy Adelaide-based journal edited by Max Harris and Geoffrey Dutton, published in 1962 the first of her stories to appear in a non-Left journal. *Westerly* published several more. *Overland* published both stories and poems, and its editor Stephen Murray-Smith became an important friend and adviser; despite this journal's break with *Realist Writer* and the Communist Party, Dorothy published in both. She did not publish a story in *Meanjin* until 1967, although in the meantime she had become friends with Clem Christesen when they shared a writers' tour in Russia in 1965, and they exchanged letters about this experience and its aftermath.

Dorothy acknowledged that Christesen did not have a high opinion of her poetry, but added, in defence of her expansive lyrical style: 'I am not convinced that I am wrong . . . re the "concentrated essence" school I mean.'[26] Murray-Smith sent poems back for revision: for instance, he commented on 'My love on whom the good sun shone' that the repetition of 'meaningless words' made some of her work read at times like 'a pastiche of your own style'.[27] These two judgments suggest that even editors who liked her work were uncomfortable with the expansive style and song-like refrains of her poetry. Yet fellow poet RD FitzGerald thought her 'Go down red roses' was 'the finest new poem that has come my way for several years'.[28]

Nevertheless it was *Overland*, together with Peter Leyden (a friend and former employer in Sydney), that published her book of poetry, *Windmill Country*, in 1968. This book reproduced thirteen of the thirty-two poems she had published in *What About the People!*, adding four from the 1940s, and sixteen new ones. Many of the new ones were originally published in *Westerly* and some in *Poetry Australia* and *Realist Writer*. There are a number of ballads, such as 'In Midland Where the Trains Go by', but the song-like qualities of the poetry extend further. As Nicole Moore puts it, 'other poems, like the lament "Go Down Red Roses", use traditional form and imagery from ballads and working-class writing but extend the forms through disrupting the rhyme scheme or over-extending it.'[29] 'Red Roses' introduces its refrain part-way through:

> When the footsteps die at the end of the empty street,
> When the faces die in the neon sign and the pub closes,
> The door shuts, the ship pulls out of the dock, this is the end –
> And go down all my red roses.
> I weep for you, my love, who will not be loved,
> You wandering men with a swag of dust on your shoulders,
> Carting a holey blanket to the world's end,
> . . .
> And the Southern Cross has a wan and a wandering light,
> And the neon sign's blood-red, blood-red as a rose
> Oh! tears and mud and regret where the Yarra flows,
> And the seagull screams on the ship and the wild wind blows
> Go down red roses . . . [30]

Several of her poems also exist as songs, such as 'Where I Grew to Be a Man', better known as the song 'Weevils in the Flour'; and 'My Love on Whom the Good Sun Shone', which became a song in her play *The Chapel Perilous*.[31] Other poems of her 'second run' include 'Country Idyll', which uses this new facility with song to revisit the theme from her 1940s poetry of women destroyed, but heroically so:

A glittering girl went out one day
On a dappled horse through the meadow hay . . .

O she rode down to the gliding river
And the water covered her face forever, . . . [32]

Poems in *Windmill Country* which point the way to her later, more directly autobiographical, work include 'My Fortieth Year', 'Unanswered Love Letter' and 'Legend of the Green Country', a narrative poem in nine parts. This won Hewett the ABC poetry competition in 1965, twenty years after her earlier success with 'Testament'. In 'Legend' the poet demythologises her family history, denouncing her grandfather's greed as 'his flocks and acres/ Drowned under salt'. On this farm now the 'dead orchard' only produces green and bitter apples. She casts herself as 'Eve, spitting the pips in the eye of the myth-makers.' Yet in the same poem she creates a myth of her father, heroic despite the fact that his vision of regenerating the land is laughed at:

Only the man with the cornet, who rode with Remarque
Across his saddle bows, only he loved the soil,
Running it through his fingers, he sensed its dying,
Its blowing away on the winds of time and cut timber
He saw the salt of its death rising.
. . .
You tried to give us
A vision of greenness and water, who were bred out of desert and
  scrub

And sheep crying and crow . . . our father whispered 'Trees' and he blew 'Tipperary'.[33]

'The Hidden Journey' is another long poem in *Windmill Country* that explores a crucial experience for Hewett: her visits to Russia, and her disillusionment, which gradually led to her leaving the Communist Party in 1968. On her first visit in 1952 she was a joyous believer:

But sometimes in the river of sleep
A doubt surfaced, bumping like a stone, and would not be pushed under
And I would see the prison train pulled into Moscow Station.[34]

Her subsequent visit in 1965 had deepened the disillusionment. She wrote to Clem Christesen, who had been on the same trip, about conformity in Soviet literature, and the difficulty of writing the truth about this 'when one feels that there are unscrupulous people who will make Cold War capital out of it'. But, she continued, it is important to speak the truth for the sake of the Russian writers who are 'fighting this good fight in USSR, in other socialist countries and in Western culture'. She acknowledged his reasons for distrusting the Communist Party but 'I still believe in the idea, and my Party membership, although often bitter and difficult, is important to me.'[35]

Many of those Russian writers are named in 'The Hidden Journey' with its nightmare vision of all the writers who have died or been exiled for their attempts to speak the truth about their lives:

Sinyavsky carried Pasternak's coffin shoulder high up the grassy meadow,
Mayakovsky floats like a cloud in trousers over this city,

Blessed, with a powder burn on his forehead, Yesenin's shadow swings
Back and forth on the stairs, Eisenstein's voice screams confessions
Endlessly into the amplifiers, where is Meyerholt's grave and Babel groping
Short-sightedly, shabby and plump, bespectacled, tender as blue lilacs
Shambling down Gorky Street? . . . I will speak with the tongue,
The iron tongue, the tongue of the bell, the gift of the dumb.[36]

The year this poem was first published saw the Russian invasion of Czechoslovakia. This event, following vain efforts to intercede on behalf of the imprisoned writers Andrei Sinyavsky and Yuli Daniel, apparently triggered Dorothy Hewett's decision to leave the Communist Party.

However inevitable Hewett's break with the Party may seem in retrospect, her decision had traumatic consequences. For one thing, it cost Dorothy her friendship with Katharine Susannah Prichard. The women had become friends when Dorothy returned to Perth, and she named her first daughter 'Katharine Susannah'. Now Hewett sent Prichard a petition to sign, asking for the release of Sinyavsky and Daniel, and Prichard wrote a formal letter of objection. She accused the authors of the petition of playing into the hands of the CIA, and expressed her anger at 'this fatuous sympathy for the criminals without indignation at the outrageous crime they have committed to destroy the memory of Lenin and the whole history of the Soviet Union in its stand for world peace'.[37] In 1969, Hewett quoted from this letter in her obituary for Prichard, adding: 'The postscript was typical: "Sorry for this difference of opinion, dear Dorothy." We never met again.'[38]

Dorothy's obituary was severely critical of Prichard, but her critique reveals as much about Hewett herself: 'In the clash between the artist's pagan and poetic sensibility . . . and the moralising Marxist religieuse, it is the latter who finally wins the battle.' This was the conflict that Hewett had also suffered for over twenty years, and she was not about to sympathise with a writer – perhaps especially one who was a mother figure to her – who resolved it differently. She implicitly accused Prichard of a failure of leadership when she wrote: 'With her basically unassailable reputation, her wide circle of readers . . . she could have been a great force for "socialism with a human face".'[39] Aleksander Dubcek's slogan of the Prague Spring in 1968 partly described Hewett's post-communist politics, although the anarchism of her 'pagan and poetic sensibility' was equally strong in the work she did during the next thirty years of her writing life.[40]

If Hewett's 'second run' began with the novel *Bobbin Up* in 1958 and continued with the short stories and poetry she published over the next decade, her 'third run', as a major dramatist and poet, can be said to have started around 1968. A new kind of confessional poetry with its 'politics of the senses' emerged, as John McLaren pointed out, in 'Alice in a German Garden', published in *Overland* the same year as *Windmill Country*.[41] Hewett's next collection, *Rapunzel in Suburbia* (1975), announced her new and powerful mixture of the mythic and legendary and the personal and everyday. The final poem, 'Grave Fairytale', took up the Rapunzel theme:

> I sat in my tower, the seasons whirled,
> the sky changed, the river grew,
> and dwindled to a pool.
> The black Witch, light as an eel,
> laddered up my hair
> to straddle the window sill.[42]

Throughout this third run in her career Hewett continued to publish poetry with *Overland* and *Westerly* and occasionally with *Meanjin*. As the 1970s moved into the 1980s and the number of literary magazines increased, she often published in the new ones edited by younger people: Carole Ferrier's feminist *Hecate*, as well as *Helix*, *Scripsi*, *Outrider*, *Heat* and others. She was very much at home with the developments in poetry, influenced by such American writers as Robert Lowell, which happened in the 1970s. Her poetic milieu was radical with political overtones, rarely establishment outlets like the newspapers. Nevertheless she began to be recognised as an important voice in Australian poetry, and published several more volumes of poems.

Becoming a playwright was a breakthrough of a different order. Theatre reaches out to a larger audience than poetry. It requires the cooperation of many people to produce, and it must make an immediate impact on its audiences. Theatre can be the most political of genres, in that it dramatises ideas, makes statements. Hewett described it as 'a peculiarly aggressive art form with a brutal, unprotected contact with the audience', one thing that made theatre a difficult field for women to enter.[43] She certainly met more than her fair share of outrage for the sexual and linguistic explicitness of her plays, at a time of heightened conflict over censorship.[44] The question is, how did she, a woman in her forties, living in Perth, manage to crack the deeply masculinist theatre scene in the eastern states?

She had long been fascinated by the problems of writing plays. Both *Bobbin Up* and the longer narrative poems had pointed in that direction, and she had begun a play set in Redfern that Les Flood committed to the flames. When she returned to Perth, Philip Parsons, an old friend from university drama days and now a lecturer in drama at the University of Western Australia, asked her what had happened to all the plays she had wanted to write as a girl. This encouraged her to return to that idea of the Redfern play and, she said, '[I] never wrote my MA, just got more and more involved in this blasted play, which got longer and longer.'[45]

It was Parsons, by then in Sydney, who organised a production of that 'blasted play', *This Old Man Came Rolling Home*, at the Old Tote Theatre in 1968. It was noticed, but 'low life in Redfern' was considered old-fashioned nostalgia.[46] Even Katharine Brisbane (her friend, married to Parsons) noted in her review its 'old-fashioned quality' but blamed the naturalistic production for 'pushing the poetry out in the cold' – adding that Hewett was 'primarily a poet'.[47] It was really only with her next plays, *Mrs Porter and the Angel* and *The Chapel Perilous*, that Hewett began to create her trademark non-naturalist theatre. This style, she wrote, maintained the link with older forms of popular entertainment such as 'melodrama, farce, burlesque and panto', reaching towards 'the metaphysical dimensions of the individual'.[48]

Philip Parsons helped Hewett establish herself as a playwright to be reckoned with. He gave feedback on her drafts and promoted her plays in the eastern states, arranging rehearsed readings and full-scale productions. He and Katharine Brisbane set up Currency Press as a publication outlet for Australian plays. *The Chapel Perilous* was one of the first texts to appear, in 1972, just a year after its stage debut. Aarne Neeme, another of Parsons' protégés, directed some of the most satisfying productions of Hewett's plays, including the premiere of *The Chapel Perilous* at the New Fortune Theatre in Perth in January 1971. The play rapidly achieved productions in Melbourne, Brisbane and Sydney as well. It was a huge success, and made a lasting impact on Australian theatre. Its heroine, Sally Banner, became a household name, signifying the bold new women of the women's liberation movement.

Dorothy Hewett and her family moved to Sydney to live in

1973, when she received her first Literature Board grant. Over the next twenty years and almost as many theatrical productions, she established herself as Australia's most accomplished woman playwright. As Nicole Moore has written: 'Her writing for the theatre encompasses social realism, musicals, sprawling melodrama, experimentation with time and visual space, defamiliarisation and audience involvement, a lyrical poetics and a love of an "Old Australian" vernacular that still marks her as a playwright of the early 1970s.'[49]

Sociable, politically engaged, yet with a romantic degree of faith in her individual calling, Dorothy Hewett built up a large cast of friends and colleagues around her. She was the great multi-talented woman writer of her generation. In both her plays and her poetry she was a brilliant self-mythologiser, although the self she created was many-faceted rather than a unified image. This capacity for self-invention stood her in good stead when she needed to stage not one but two returns to the literary field during the early part of her career, as we have seen here. The 'second run' that started with *Bobbin Up* established her as a communist writer (though not always an ideologically sound one), adept at both fiction and poetry. The 'third run' left her Communist Party affiliation behind and established her as a major lyric poet and a leading dramatist in the non-naturalist mode that marked her out from other contemporary playwrights.

Notes

1 The letter, dated 22 May 1958, is signed, 'Dorothy Hewett (Mrs Dorothy Flood)': Hewett File, *Meanjin* Archive, Melbourne University Library Special Collections. Although she refers here to having sent some poems, in fact *Meanjin* did not publish any of her work until 1967.

2 Both reproduced in Dorothy Hewett, *Wild Card: An Autobiography 1923-1958*, McPhee Gribble, Melbourne, 1990.

3 The *Age*, reported in Hewett, 'Excerpt from "The Empty Room", an autobiography in progress' *Overland*, 160, 2000, pp. 4–10, 8.

4 *Dorothy Hewett: Collected Poems 1940–1995*, ed. William de Grono, Fremantle Arts Centre Press, Perth, 1995, pp.19–20.

5 *Bobbin Up*, Seven Seas, Berlin, 1961, p. 9.

6 Interview with Hazel De Berg, 1973, National Library of Australia, Oral History Collection 658, 2/26.

7 See the collection of poems and a play she wrote between the ages of eight and eleven: *The Gipsy Dancer & Early Poems*, ed. Christine Alexander, with others, Juvenilia Press, Sydney, 2009.

8 De Berg interview, 1/5.

9 *Wild Card*, p. 111.

10 *Wild Card*, pp. 112–13, 122.

11 *Wild Card*, pp. 90, 113.

12 De Berg interview, 1/7.

13 *Wild Card*, p. 143.

14 *Wild Card*, p. 174.

15 *Wild Card*, pp. 213–27.

16 *Wild Card*, p.192.

17 *Wild Card*, p. 246.

18 *Wild Card*, p. 248.

19 *Overland* 153, 1998, p. 49.

20 Dorothy Hewett, *Bobbin Up*, Preface, Virago, London, 1985.

21 'Excerpt from "The Empty Room", an autobiography in progress,' *Overland*, 160, 2000, 4–10.

22 KSP to DH, 8 September 1959, Dorothy Hewett papers NLA MS 6184 box 7, folder 48.

23 Typescript statement signed KSP in Hewett papers, NLA MS 6184 Box 7, folder 48.

24 De Berg interview, 2/17.

25 As Nicole Moore has pointed out in 'Dorothy Hewett' in *Companion to Australian Literature*, eds Nicholas Birns and Rebecca McNeer, Boydell and Brewer/University of Rochester Press, New York, 2007, pp. 321–34.

26 DH to CC, 16 April 1963, *Meanjin* Archive.

27 SM-S to DH, 3 November 1961, Hewett papers, NLA MS 6184, Folder 3. Stephen Murray-Smith criticised the matter of some poems later in the 1960s: he could not publish 'Green Country' because of its length, but even so, 'I am slightly unsympathetic to the romantic-realist bush epic and/or family chronicle,' the 'heroism' in the poem 'jars with me'. He pointed out obscurities in 'Last Summer' and 'Two Faces'. He finished by asking her for 'some more outward-looking, less lacerating verse for a change – ironic or humorous – comment on e.g. university life, your children? . . .', concluding, 'Please don't be cross. This is what I'm here for. Even if I don't know what I'm talking about': SM-S to DH, 30 October 1966, Hewett papers, NLA MS 6184, box 1, folder 10.

28 RGF to SM-S, 30 June 1962, requesting permission to read this poem at his CLF lecture in Townsville, Hewett papers, NLA MS 6184, folder 3.

29 Moore.

30 *Collected Poems*, p. 51.

31 *Collected Poems*, p. 413.

32 *Collected Poems*, p 67–8.

33 *Collected Poems*, p. 77.

34 *Collected Poems*, p. 91.

35 DH to CC, 1 September 1965, Hewett file, *Meanjin* Archive.

36 *Collected Poems*, p. 94.

37 KSP, 18 April 1967, Hewett papers, NLA MS 6184, box 1, folder 2.

38 'Excess of Love: The irreconcilable in Katharine Susannah Prichard', *Overland*, 43, 1969, pp. 27–31.

39 'Excess of Love', pp. 29–30.

40 For a fuller discussion of Hewett's political and artistic transition over the 1960s period, see Susan Sheridan, 'Dorothy Hewett's Paths to *The Chapel Perilous*', *Westerly*, 54, July 2009, pp. 170–88.

41 *Writing in Hope and Fear*, Cambridge University Press, Melbourne, 1995, p. 71.

42 *Collected Poems* p. 152.

43 'Creating Heroines in Australian Plays', *Hecate*, 5(2), 1979, pp. 73–9.

44 Theatre and censorship: According to Barbara Blackman, *Hair* was a huge hit in Sydney in 1969, and Harry Miller was a hero: 'I think it overcame the censor by sheer momentum. And it will be a great breakthrough for the theatre . . . it will run for years and people will at last have found out what going to the theatre is, and . . . they will flock to see HAMLET in the same way': *Portrait of a Friendship: The Letters of Judith Wright and Barbara Blackman 1950–2000*, ed. Bryony Cosgrove, The Miegunyah Press, Melbourne, 2007, p. 238.

45 De Berg interview, 2/18.

46 *Bulletin* review, 30 March 1968.

47 Review, 29 March 1968 (newspaper not named), Hewett papers, NLA MS 6184, box 32, clippings file.

48 Hewett, 'Shirts, Prams and Tomato Sauce: The all-Australian theatre', *Contemporary Australian Drama*, ed. Peter Holloway, Currency Press, Sydney, 1981, pp. 77–87.

49 Moore, 2007, p. 330.

CHAPTER FOUR

Rosemary Dobson with her youngest child, Ian, in 1962

Rosemary Dobson: A clear vocation

Rosemary Dobson always had a clear 'sense of what was due to the poetry'.[1] As a young woman she was fortunate in having the support and encouragement of her family, school and colleagues to follow her vocation.

She was also lucky in her time, being able to find a niche in Sydney's lively literary and artistic scene of the early 1940s. This was a period of cultural growth as well as turmoil, with new painters and poets beginning to make their mark. She later described it as a time which 'initiated much that has enriched our literature since', despite the constraints of cultural cringe, censorship, attacks on modernism and isolation from the arts in other places. In a lecture she gave in 1973, she observed that at this time isolation was especially restricting for painters although poets were readily influenced by the other arts.[2]

It is characteristic of Dobson that she took both painting and poetry and their interactions as her subjects in this lecture. She had an active interest in both art forms, and many of her early poems take paintings – sometimes actual, sometimes imagined – as their subjects. One of her best-loved poems, 'The Bystander', begins:

> I am the one who looks the other way
> In any painting you may see me stand
> Rapt at the sky, a bird, an angel's wing,
> While others kneel, present the myrrh, receive
> The benediction from the radiant hand.[3]

Evoking the world of Renaissance painting she evokes at the same time, with deft understatement, some of the great themes of Christian art. These few lines also show the qualities that, as she said many years later, she stood by: 'Simplicity, clarity, austerity', 'wit, the high-spirited as well as the spiritual, and a certain waywardness or originality – a stepping outside of the expected'.[4]

In her early twenties, she began to publish poetry in the *Bulletin*'s literary page, then edited by Douglas Stewart. This meant that, when she was introduced to Beatrice Davis of Angus & Robertson, that ambitious and discerning editor recognised her as an already impressive poet. Davis arranged for Rosemary to begin work at the publishing company, first as a proofreader, then graduating to the editorial section.[5] This was to provide her with interesting work and a decent income for the next decade. It also brought about her meeting with Nan McDonald, a fellow poet of her own age, who became a firm friend. They in turn made friends with Francis Webb, and Rosemary also met older poets whose work she 'knew and revered' – Kenneth Slessor, RD FitzGerald, Kenneth Mackenzie and Hugh McCrae.[6] It was at Angus & Robertson, too, that she met her future husband, Alec Bolton. The Sydney literary world welcomed her, and she never looked back. Despite some gaps, which at the time seemed to her to threaten failure, each time she returned to her vocation with a new maturity and renewed insight. Her output has been continuous and her publishing career marked by consistent recognition as a distinctive and important voice in Australian poetry.

Born in Sydney in 1920, Rosemary Dobson lost her father when she was only five and her sister Ruth was seven. Arthur Dobson was the son of the English poet and essayist Austin Dobson. He was a good deal older than his Australian wife Marjorie, whom he met at the Dickens Society after he had come to Australia to work as a civil engineer. Left a widow with few resources and two small daughters, Marjorie Dobson endured straitened circumstances. Such an early experience of material insecurity left its mark on the small family, but Marjorie Dobson was a resourceful and courageous woman. She corresponded regularly with members of the family in England and in late 1928 one of the several Dobson aunts, Lissant, travelled to Australia to visit them. Like a fairy godmother, she arranged for her sister-in-law to meet Susannah Williams, the head of the Women's College at Sydney University, who in turn introduced her to Winifred West, the headmistress of Frensham, a progressive non-denominational girls' boarding school in Mittagong south of Sydney.[7]

These two were exemplars of their generation of educated women. Susannah Williams, an Australian who had taken a degree in classics at Newnham College, Cambridge, was the head of Women's College from 1919 to 1935.[8] The connection with her might have been made through Lissant's two sisters, who were educators. A report of Lissant Dobson's visit in the Melbourne *Argus* noted that there were five daughters and five sons in Austin Dobson's family, and that all the girls save Lissant, the one who stayed at home to care for ageing parents, had followed professions. Besides the two who were teachers in England, one was a doctor, and another worked in the Women's University Settlement in Bombay.[9] Winifred West, who was born in Frensham, Surrey, in

1881, read medieval and modern languages at Newnham College, Cambridge, from 1900 to 1903. After teaching at Guernsey Ladies' College for a few years she came to Sydney, where she formed a lifelong friendship with Phyllis Clubbe. The two women founded Frensham in 1913, a school which prided itself on emphasising the arts as well as academic and sporting excellence, while eschewing competitions, marks and prizes.[10]

As a result of their meeting, Miss West offered Mrs Dobson a position as housemistress, and a scholarship for one of her daughters. When Mrs Dobson replied that she could not leave the other daughter behind, Miss West invited her to bring them both. Rosemary and Ruth received an excellent education at Frensham, and Rosemary dedicated her book, *Cock Crow* (1965), to Winifred West, whom she named as one of several influential women in her life.[11]

At Frensham Rosemary thrived. In the library she used to read the *London Mercury*, where she learned to admire the 1930s modernists Auden, Spender and Day-Lewis, as well as the established English poets. She was passionately interested in the visual arts, and after finishing her school studies spent some three years at Frensham as an apprentice art teacher. In 1937, during her final year as a student, a volume of her poems, with her own linocut decorating the cover, was published at the school, where West had employed Joan Phipson (later an acclaimed writer for children) to set up a printing press modelled on the Hogarth Press of Leonard and Virginia Woolf. Dobson was always interested in book design, later working with her husband Alec Bolton to set up the small specialist Brindabella Press in Canberra. Of the relationship between the sister arts, she has said that it was through her study of painting, design and drawing that she acquired the discipline and concentration that transferred to the craftsmanship of her poetry.[12]

As a child Rosemary had written poetry, not in emulation of

her grandfather (whose poetry she learned about only later) but simply because she wanted to.[13] Going on to detail the material circumstances of her childhood and education, she added: 'I think that this insecurity, so foreign and incomprehensible to most of my contemporaries at school, gave me an eagerness to pursue my aims and to hold tenaciously to what I regarded as precious. Poetry and painting were already of the greatest importance.' 'To hold tenaciously to what I regarded as precious' captures her sense of poetry as a vocation, and her continuing preoccupation throughout her work with capturing moments of intense apprehension, whether in poetry or painting or in nature. She described this as 'a search for something only fugitively glimpsed; a state of grace which one once knew, or imagined, or from which one was turned away'.[14]

At the age of twenty Rosemary Dobson took herself off to Sydney, having inherited a small amount of money from her grandfather's estate. For two years she attended classes at Sydney University as a non-matriculated student without taking a degree, as Judith Wright had done. She took as many classes in English as she could, sitting for the examinations and writing essays: 'that under-the-counter education was marvellous,' she later recalled, adding, 'it's a pity that students can't do it now'.[15] At the same time she attended art classes with Thea Proctor in the evenings, meeting a very different group of people.

Later through Angus & Robertson she met another crowd of contemporary and older poets such as Nan McDonald and Francis Webb. Working at Angus & Robertson was an excellent way of acquiring a literary education. The publishing department was housed above the bookshop in Castlereagh Street, right in the heart of the city, and writers would climb the stairs to visit Davis and other members of the editorial staff. Alec Bolton, an editor there for many years, observed that there was a feeling of family belonging about the place. He recalled the massive volume of manuscripts received during the 1950s, when the company published titles on every subject and took on large projects including a ten-volume encyclopedia of Australia, the initial volumes of the *Dictionary of Australian Biography*, and Miller and Macartney's pioneering literary history of Australia.

Beatrice Davis, who commissioned mainly fiction, was influenced in her literary choices by Douglas Stewart and the *Bulletin.*[16] She determined that Angus & Robertson would 'bring the best in Australian literature and the best of the writers within our sphere' for 'good writers bring the best publicity and prestige'.[17] These poetry and serious fiction titles were often supported by the Commonwealth Literary Fund.

Stewart was an important and long-standing mentor to the young Dobson. She had visited him in his office at the *Bulletin*, after sending to the Red Page her poem, 'Australian Holiday, 1940', 'a reflection upon the isolation of Australians in the early years of the Second World War', which she regarded as 'my first worthwhile adult poem'. She described waiting nervously to see Stewart, beset by 'shakes and trembles' and 'a fearful inability to shape my words', but to her relief she observed that the great man's hands were also shaking.[18] She subsequently formed a friendship with him and his artist wife, Margaret Coen. It was through this couple that she met Norman Lindsay, with whom they shared a studio in Bridge Street.

Norman Lindsay painted her portrait, as Thea Proctor had done. She later told Graeme Kinross Smith:

> I violently disagreed with a number of his ideas, and I suppose I preferred Thea Proctor's reserve to Norman's overwhelming personality. But I liked him so very much. He had great generosity, great enthusiasms, and affections and it was wonderful to know him.[19]

Although Dobson published occasionally in *Meanjin Papers*, *Hermes* and *Poetry*, the *Bulletin* was the favoured destination for her early poetry. Most of the poems collected in her first book, *In a Convex Mirror*, had initially appeared there.[20] This book was published in 1944 by Dymock's, the booksellers, with Douglas Stewart's encouragement and help.

It was favourably reviewed in the places that mattered: *Southerly*, *Bulletin*, *Meanjin* and *Poetry*. However, AD Hope's criticism in *Poetry* that her 'graceful, decorative' poems were 'reflective, but her reflection gives rise to no original thought'[21] was a minority one – and he later regretted it.[22] Other reviewers were in no doubt that 'Miss Dobson's poetry is distinguished by intellectual and technical power of a high order'[23] and she already has 'a distinctive poetic personality' and a style 'both concise and precise'.[24] Dobson's epigrammatic force and grace were commented upon, with one reviewer quoting the final stanza of 'Young Girl at a Window':

> Over the gently-turning hills
> Travel a journey with your eyes
> In forward footsteps, chance assault –
> This way the map of living lies.
> And this the journey you must go
> Through grass and sheaves and, lastly, snow.[25]

Both the reviews just quoted grouped Dobson's book with those of two older women poets, much to her advantage.[26] One can see why such a gendered grouping might have displeased the poet herself; but this situation did not last long. Judith Wright, already well known for individual poems such as 'South of My Days', published her first book, *The Moving Image*, in 1946. Dobson reviewed it, recognising and acknowledging a poet with ambitions similar to her own. She began with a quietly confident statement that

Australia's recent ballet and film productions, as well as fine poetry, should show 'those on the other side of the world that it is not the antipodean Terra Incognita it once was held to be'. Wright's poems, she wrote, are 'essentially Australian, and they are sure and beautiful', indicating their range from the long title poem through some 'exquisitely-told narratives in brief' and landscape poetry that 'results from a harmonious fusion of mind and eye'.[27]

Both Dobson and Wright struck their early reviewers as already mature, and were readily included in the ranks of Australian poets who mattered in the immediate postwar years. Stewart, for example, writing to Rosemary in London in 1948, expressed impatience with little magazines as 'minority affairs', adding: 'what needs doing is for Faber to publish you, me, Judith Wright, FitzGerald, Slessor and Webb.'[28] In his eyes, at least, she was already one of the leading Australian poets, worthy of recognition in London as well as at home.

Dobson's second book, *The Ship of Ice*, was published by Angus & Robertson as part of its bid to 'bring the best of the writers within our sphere'. The long title poem had won the *Herald* poetry competition in 1946, and the book contained a sequence, 'The Devil and the Angel', as well as poems reflecting on paintings, stories and other artefacts. It was reviewed less widely than her first, but by the time it was released, Rosemary was in London. Expanding on his review of this book, Stewart wrote to her there: 'You'll have more to say yet, but as far as you've gone you've travelled first class.'[29]

In late 1947 Rosemary travelled with her mother to England. Ruth Dobson, engaged in the long and difficult process of establishing herself as a diplomat in the days when the doors to such a career were firmly closed to women, had been working in the Australian High Commission in London since June 1946 (she was advisor to the Australian delegates at the Paris Peace Conference that year, and at many sessions of the United Nations in Geneva).[30]

During the eighteen months she spent in London, Rosemary worked as an editor at Harrap's publishing house[31] and travelled in Europe. She visited Florence, where she was able to see many of the pictures that inspired her poems: 'The group of painting poems, like "Child with a Cockatoo", belong to the period when I returned from overseas' she later told an interviewer.[32] Many poems in *Child with a Cockatoo* (1955) imagine the painter's (or the writer's, or the printer's) relationship to their work; but the title poem is inspired by the detail of a particular portrait, the presence of a sulphur-crested cockatoo with 'its cynic eyes half closed', which, like 'a disregarded prologue to an age', presages 'Terra Australis, unimagined land'.[33]

She wrote to Norman Lindsay that she had met his sons, Jack and Philip, in London. Philip Lindsay later wrote about her in his series of essays on 'Poetry in Australasia' in the London *Poetry Review* in 1949–50. The article began by noting that Rosemary was Austin Dobson's granddaughter but, by comparison with him, her sense of humour saved her 'daintiness' from resembling his archness. Detecting the influence of Stewart and maybe Slessor, he concluded that she was an original with 'a delicate and graceful vision'.[34] In the same issue her poem 'The Missal' appeared:

> The lovely, lost, italic curve
> Enrapt his soul. All day he stared
> At A for Apple. Dimly heard
> The beating of the holy wings
> In D for Dove; but shut his ears
> To sound's delight, instead preferred
> The E of Eden, marked how stood
> The mainstroke like a flaming sword.
> The F for Fall. How brief the flight
> With dark descender, black as night! . . . [35]

This and other poems first published in *Poetry Review* in 1949 and 1950 – 'The Midnight Reader' and 'Painter of Umbria' – were all reprinted in *Child with a Cockatoo.*

The Australian English Association's journal *Southerly* published Dobson's report from London describing an eager interest in Australian literature.[36] She mentioned having attended several poetry readings, including one where she herself read, and where she met someone from the Council of the Poetry Society, which published *Poetry Review*. Much later Rosemary recalled having met the 'vital and volatile' Muriel Spark,[37] who edited the journal for a brief period during 1947–48, and whose attempts to modernise the journal roused the wrathful opposition of older, established Society members.[38]

Through Douglas Stewart, Rosemary met the Left-wing novelist Sylvia Townsend Warner and her lover Valentine Ackland.[39] Both women were poets, although Warner was better known for her fiction, beginning with *Lolly Willowes* (1926). Although both were still, in the late 1940s, members of the Communist Party and wrote for the magazine *Our Time*, they were far from programmatic or polemical in their writing. Both in their different ways favoured the classical quality of the writer 'vanishing off the page', in order to render the immediacy of the thing or experience observed[40] – a quality that Dobson had already made her own. Both women sent positive comments on the younger poet's work, although Warner warned against the note of 'jauntiness' in the poem, 'The Devil and the Angel'.[41] For Dobson's third book, *Child with a Cockatoo*, however, Warner's praise was unstinting.[42]

Back in Sydney after her London sojourn, Rosemary Dobson rejoined Angus & Robertson. In 1950 she met her future husband Alec Bolton coming out of Beatrice Davis's office after a job interview. 'He'll do,' said Davis, and he joined the firm.[43] A book editor and designer, he shared Dobson's fascination with the visual arts and always supported her work. He, too, had lost his father as a young child, and he and his brother had spent their early years in Sydney where Alec's education at Sydney Grammar School had been enabled by a half scholarship. He had attended the University of Sydney after serving in the Royal Australian Navy during the war. He and Rosemary married and moved to live in Neutral Bay. Their experience of parenthood began in anguish when their first child died soon after birth. 'The Birth (2)', in Dobson's *Child with a Cockatoo*, explores this loss:

> Unknown, never to be known, lost
> Beyond darkness, beyond the reach of time,
> Brought forth from darkness as a wave
> That breaks upon the edge of day
> And knows but for a moment shore,
> Landfall, the earth. So there was light
> And human hands, before the tide
> Returned you to the oblivious night.[44]

Child with a Cockatoo, Dobson's third volume of poetry, appeared in 1955 and was extensively reviewed. AD Hope, reviewing it together with a reprint of *The Moving Image*, wrote that both Dobson and Wright had mastered their craft in their first books. Wright's position in Australian poetry was already assured, 'But Rosemary Dobson is emerging as the most perfect of our poets. Her range is smaller than Judith Wright's but she commands everything within her range with a surer touch.'[45] A major review in the *Bulletin* by Douglas Stewart declared that in this volume she had 'clarified and made manifest her personal vision of life' in poetry that was 'gay, graceful, witty, deep and humane'.[46] David Campbell's review explored the theme of time in her work: he no longer found it strange, he wrote, that she should write so much about painters and paintings, for in these 'she has discovered a territory in which she is completely at home, where her wit may play with conceits on Time . . . ; where she may move from canvas to canvas, from century to century . . .'. Turning to the final poems, he observed that 'this trend of thought is like a tragic background' to their passionate immersion in the present moment.[47] Other readers, too, noticed a new level of intensity in this volume. Sylvia Townsend Warner wrote to Dobson from London, referring to her lost daughter and the 'emotional crux' that had her writing as she never had before: 'your whole technique has taken wings and soared.'[48]

Like Judith Wright, Dobson was fully established as a poet by the age of thirty-five. First Wright and then Dobson was invited to edit the annual Angus & Robertson anthology *Australian Poetry*. Earlier volumes in this prestigious series had been edited by poets FitzGerald, Slessor and Stewart and academics HM Green and RG Howarth. The young women editors set a precedent for the appointment of other women – Nan McDonald and later Nancy Keesing, Leonie Kramer and Dorothy Auchterlonie (Green) – before the series ceased publication in 1970.

Wright remembered being criticised for including so many poems by women in her 1949 volume – twenty of the forty-seven. In fact the *Bulletin* review (presumably by Douglas Stewart) accused her of 'bad tactics' by including so many female poets and so many experimental works. He wrote plaintively: 'One does not expect Ern Malley . . . Nor, being male, does one expect to be knocked flat on opening the anthology by an Amazonian phalanx of nine successive poems by women.' This confrontation, he wrote, made him think of 'beer and boots and other things uncompromisingly masculine'.[49] Dobson's *Australian Poetry* published the following year had the same proportion of women, fifteen out of thirty-six, but no reviewer gave her a hard time for this. In fact, the

Bulletin review singled out for praise poems by McDonald, Wright, Elizabeth Riddell and Nancy Keesing. If the reviewer was Douglas Stewart again, he was now being conspicuously pro-woman. He did not criticise the strong representation of women in Dobson's anthology, but praised her selection of good 'anthology-pieces, standing detached from the authors' and the 'unusual sense of form' evident in their arrangement.[50] No doubt the difference was that he knew and liked Dobson, and her choice of poems was more to his taste.

In 1955, the year that *Child with a Cockatoo* was published, Rosemary gave birth to her first child, her daughter Lissant. Two sons, Robert and Ian, followed, and with the joy of these children also came the heavy demands on Rosemary's time and energies that three small children inevitably require. The years of intensive child-rearing took their toll on her literary productivity, and there was a ten-year gap before Dobson's next volume of poetry, *Cock Crow*, appeared in 1965.

Cock Crow opens with a section of poems concerning pregnancy, birth and motherhood. The title poem, often quoted, addresses the dilemma which, Dobson felt, affected any creative person when life's responsibilities had to take precedence over creative work. The poet walks away from the house into the darkness while:

> My mother and my daughter slept,
> One life behind and one before,
> And I that stood between denied
> Their needs in shutting-to the door.[51]

But her illusion of being 'separate and alone', 'cut off' from both the pain and the love of human bonds, is shattered when, like Peter denying Christ, she hears the cock crow thrice, and re-enters the house. The poems in the second and longer section of the book turn most often to legendary tales and, like 'The Rape of Europa', create modern Australian settings and variations on classical myths. There are also character sketch poems like 'Amy Caroline' and 'Captain Svenson'.

This book won the Myer Award for Australian Poetry in 1966. RD FitzGerald praised it as a 'splendid book of poems', expanding Dobson's range and showing that although she 'may have slowed down her pace', she had not stood still. In a long and thoughtful review he recognised as central 'the motif of the self-imposed limitations on scope, adventure and liberty involved in a fealty to love and an acceptance of duty', pointing out that this motif generated poems in the second section of the book, as well as the motherhood poems.[52] This calm formulation of the 'self-imposed limitations' on the poet who is also committed to love and duty was close to Dobson's own, and did not specify – as a later reading might do – that the roles expected of mother and wife are hardly the same as those of father and husband. A younger poet, Andrew Taylor, found the book overall to lack 'virtuosity and ironic bite', although he mentioned that 'such subjects as the bearing of children . . . are explored with tact and sensitivity'.[53]

The times were changing rapidly, and by the mid 1960s the current taste for vitality and irony caused some critics to place Dobson's 'poignant and tender visions of the commonplace'[54] or poems 'on the homely experiences of a woman'[55] in the category of minor poetry. Her reticent style was misread as 'delicate and bland', offering 'an optimistic celebration of physical life' which is 'the precise opposite of an Anne Sexton or a Sylvia Plath', according to Charles Higham's account of Australian poetry for an American audience in 1966.[56] To be considered an insufficiently fierce and confessional woman poet must have been deeply disappointing for Dobson, who had consciously striven for qualities of 'clarity and an edge of wit', which women were not expected to manifest.[57] Nevertheless, she must have been pleased to see her first book in ten years in print, to have her 'wit and irony as well as an overall womanly sensitivity' recognised,[58] and to receive the praise of FitzGerald, a poet whom she especially admired.

'Yes of course you will write again . . . But of course you feel guilt, too. So do I,' wrote Judith Wright to Rosemary Dobson in 1958. 'We're bound on two wheels going different ways: it's hard to learn how to yield to either without being torn apart.'[59] Many years later Judith Wright, in another letter, recalled their early days:

> visiting you and Nan upstairs in Castlereagh Street, putting as much of both of you into that 1948? Anthology as I dared (remember, poetry wasn't supposed to be for women?) getting called down for it; seeing you again when I came to Sydney and stayed with Beatrice and she gave that party, after we'd both had babies, and discussing how poetry and babies came from the same place . . . [60]

Here in a nutshell lay their dilemma – 'poetry wasn't supposed to be for women,' especially when they became mothers, yet in their experience, 'poetry and babies came from the same place.' Both Wright and Dobson wrote memorable and path-breaking poems on this subject. 'Annunciations' from *Cock Crow* turns on the conceit of poems and babies, of the word made flesh:

> Lulled by the drumming of my blood,
> The distant thunder of my heart,
> You slept upon the moving tide
> Of darkness, sealed in mortal flesh.
> Once more immortal wings were stilled,
> I heard the word that bade you come.[61]

Despite frustrations during this period, Rosemary Dobson kept up her connections with writers and writing. She and Nan McDonald sustained their friendship with Francis Webb through the turbulent years when he was often hospitalised for his mental illness. The letters collected in her archives testify to friendships with David Campbell, Patrick White, Tom Shapcott and others continuing through the 1950s and early 1960s.

She avoided getting caught up in Cold War literary politics, however. In 1956 James McAuley invited her and her husband to his home, and soon afterwards wrote urging her to join the editorial board of his new magazine, *Quadrant*. In response to her 'misgivings' about becoming 'part of the Right', for 'one must write as an individual',[62] McAuley assured her that such a commitment was necessary to oppose totalitarianism, for 'the Left in this sense is outside the realm of morally permissible politics.' In her quiet way Dobson resisted his dogmatism, agreeing merely to offer poems to *Quadrant*.[63] She did in fact publish a poem in its initial issue, as did Judith Wright (the only women to do so), but did not become a frequent contributor.

Her friend Nan McDonald wrote in response to Rosemary's dilemma over this invitation, 'leave it to people with more time or less to do with it.' She said that McAuley had only one job, probably with short hours, but, she added sceptically, 'I may be wrong of course, he might do a lot for his wife at home.'[64] This exchange suggests a further dimension of the woman writer's dilemma – with her own writing and her family responsibilities, she had not the time (even if she had the inclination) to become a public intellectual, joining editorial boards and publishing opinion pieces.

In the same letter as his invitation to join *Quadrant*, McAuley invited Dobson to join 'the new Poetry Society' in 1956 (with Campbell, Hope and Harold Stewart). This was probably the Poetry Society of Australia, which had been established in

1954 by Imogen Whyse. It published *Prism*, then *Poetry Magazine* (1961–70) then *New Poetry* (1971–82). Dobson appears not to have taken up this invitation, as she continued to favour the *Bulletin*, where she published poems throughout the 1950s and early 1960s. She also appeared regularly in the annual anthology, *Australian Poetry*, and was one of the featured poets in the *Australian Letters* poets and artists series, where she and Judith Wright were the only women poets to be represented.[65] The painter with whom her work was teamed in this series, Ray Crooke, designed the dust jacket for her 1965 book, *Cock Crow*. She in turn wrote a monograph about his work, published by UQP in 1971.[66] Dobson and Wright were again the only women whose work appeared among the living poets in the Angus & Robertson *Australian Poets* series, along with FitzGerald, Hope, McAuley and Douglas Stewart.[67]

A further period of silence from Rosemary Dobson marked the family's five-year stay in London from 1966 to 1971, when Alec Bolton was appointed to manage Angus & Robertson's London office. Although they travelled and visited many galleries, museums and historical sites, Dobson felt unable to write poetry during these years. Looking back, she thought this was because she was taking so much in at the time, and could only write about it later, back in Australia.[68] Her friend Nan McDonald, having offered detailed comments on several of Rosemary's poems, referred to her 'thinking you are Australia's forgotten poet' and advised her to be content and keep writing, for literary recognition is 'a fearfully hit-or-miss thing'.[69] She did, however, complete the monograph on Ray Crooke and, after a visit to her sister in Athens, began a series of poems based on the writings of the ancient Greek travel writer Pausanias.[70]

Back in Australia, the family moved to Canberra, where Alec Bolton had been appointed the National Library's first publishing director. Rosemary Dobson renewed her vocation as a poet. Revived friendships with poets David Campbell and Alec Hope, and the establishment of Brindabella Press (where Alec produced fine hand-printed books of poetry and stories) fed her creativity. Over the next few years she produced several volumes of new poetry as well as translations from the Russian of Anna Akhmatova and Osip Mandelstam, and edited an anthology of poetry and prose for ANU Press.

The literary critic Marie-Louise Ayres placed Rosemary Dobson among her contemporaries in this way:

> Unlike the work of her female contemporaries, such as Judith Wright and Dorothy Hewett, hers has never been overtly political, has invited no controversy, and has eschewed the confessional . . . Her commitment to classical forms might align her more closely with her male contemporaries, such as Hope, McAuley, Campbell and Brissenden.[71]

Yet Dobson always acknowledged the crucial role played in her life by women – her mother, her grandmother, her teachers, Beatrice Davis, Nan McDonald. For her, this female identification did not take on a political dimension, although she conceded that as a young woman, 'the feeling that one's ambitions should be curtailed simply because of one's sex did not enter my mind. If I had been more socially aware perhaps I would have realised how fortunate I was.'[72]

In the late 1970s Dobson became involved with Sisters Poets, a feminist publishing enterprise. For them she edited a selection of new poets, *Sisters Poets 1* (1979) and was represented with Wright, Harwood and Hewett in *Journeys*, edited by Fay Zwicky (1982). This seems at first glance an unexpected commitment, for Dobson (like her contemporaries) had resisted classification as a woman poet, even when feminists of the 1970s began to transform the term into a badge of honour. She remained sceptical, although involved. After her experience of editing *Sisters Poets 1* which, in the publishers' words, 'should reflect the concerns of women and offer a feminist perspective', she offered the opinion that:

> The difference that being a woman made to my writing is that, being aware that women historically are thought to be more emotional and gentler as writers than men, I determined quite consciously to work with clarity and an edge of wit – or as near as I could come to it. But these are qualities I admire and would aspire to anyway.[73]

A late poem, 'Divining Colander', applies that 'clarity and an edge of wit' to experiences of loss and old age. It is dedicated to Alec Bolton who died in 1996:

> The kitchen vessels that sustained
> Your printed books, my poems, our life,
> Are fallen away. The words remain –
> Not all – but those of style and worth.
>
> And here, in Age, I feel the need
> Of some Divining Colander
> To hold the best of all since done
> And let the rest slip through.[74]

Notes

1 Rosemary Dobson, private communication, February 2010.

2 Dobson, *A World of Difference: Australian poetry and painting in the 1940s*, 3rd Blaiklock Lecture, Wentworth Press, Sydney, 1973.

3 Rosemary Dobson, *Selected Poems*, Angus & Robertson, Sydney, 1973, pp. 43–4. Subsequent quotations from the poetry are from this edition.
4 David McCooey, 'A conversation with Rosemary Dobson', *Antipodes*, 10(2), 1996, pp. 107–10, p. 110.
5 The biographical information in this chapter is drawn from a number of sources, but is most consistently dependent upon Joy Hooton, 'Rosemary Dobson: A life of making poetry', Hooton, ed., *Rosemary Dobson: A celebration*, National Library of Australia, Canberra, 2000.
6 McCooey, 'A conversation with Rosemary Dobson', p. 108.
7 'Rosemary Dobson in conversation with John Tranter', 2004, pp. 1–2. Accessed from AustLit database, 5 January 2006.
8 Patricia Horner, 'Williams, Susannah Jane (1875–1942)', *Australian Dictionary of Biography*, vol. 12, Melbourne University Press, Melbourne, 1990, p. 506.
9 *Argus*, 19 January 1929, p. 8.
10 Priscilla Kennedy, 'West, Winifred Mary (1881–1971)', *Australian Dictionary of Biography*, vol. 17, Melbourne University Press, Melbourne, 1990, pp. 447–8.
11 'Statements: Rosemary Dobson', *Poetry and Gender*, eds David Brooks and Brenda Walker, UQP, St Lucia, 1989, p. 32.
12 'Rosemary Dobson', in Barbara Williams, *In Other Words: Interviews with Australian poets*, Rodopi, Amsterdam, 1998, p. 5.
13 Dobson, 'Australian Poets in Profile: 2. Rosemary Dobson', *Southerly*, 40(1), 1980, pp. 3–10.
14 *Poetry and Gender*, 1989, p. 33.
15 Kinross-Smith, 'The intricate, devised, hearing of sight: A profile of Rosemary Dobson', *Westerly*, 3, September 1974, pp. 55–63, p. 57.
16 Bolton, 'Angus & Robertson in the 1950s: Publishing in an age of innocence', *Publishing Studies*, 1 Spring 1995, pp. 12–20.
17 Quoted in Neil James and Elizabeth Webby, 'Canon around the hub:

Angus & Robertson and the post-war literary canon', *Southerly*, 57(3), 1997, pp. 51–66, p. 51.

18 Dobson, 'Starting out', *Australian Book Review*, 161, June 1994, pp. 55–6.

19 Kinross-Smith, p. 59.

20 'Australian Holiday' (*Bulletin*, 7 May 1941) was the first, followed by 'Cherry Picking' (10 June 1942), 'Foreshore' (4 November 1942) and 'In a Convex Mirror' (18 November 1942). In *Meanjin Papers*: 'The Idlers' in 1(10) Spring 1942, 'Cockerel Sun' in 1(11) Summer 1942, and one each in *Hermes* 47(1), 1941, the Sydney University Arts magazine, and *Poetry* 6, 1943, the quarterly edited by Flexmore Hudson.

21 Review of *In a Convex Mirror*, *Poetry*, 17, 1945, pp. 24–26.

22 Years later he began a reassessment of her work with 'a full confession and repentance' that he was wrong to criticise her for basing her poems often on other works of art: 'Rosemary Dobson: Portrait in a Mirror', *Quadrant*, 16(4), 1972, pp. 10–14.

23 Elizabeth Hamill, *Meanjin Papers*, 5(2), 1946, pp. 170–1.

24 Thelma Herring, 'Writer and Reader: Women Poets', *Southerly*, 5(4), 1944, pp. 57–60.

25 *Selected Poems* (1973), p. 4.

26 Norma Davis and Janet Beaton.

27 Dobson, 'New Poetry', *Australian Book News and Library Journal*, December 1946, pp. 255–6.

28 DS to RD, 21 January 1948, Dobson papers, National Library of Australia, MS 4955, folder 15.

29 DS to RD, n.d. 1948, Dobson papers, NLA, MS4955, folder 14.

30 Sylvia Marchant, 'Dobson, Ruth Violet Lissant (1918–1989)', *Australian Dictionary of Biography*, vol. 17, Melbourne University Press, 1990, pp. 321–2.

31 See her 'From London' in *Southerly* 9(2), 1948.

32 John Thompson, 'Poetry in Australia: Rosemary Dobson', *Southerly*, 28(3), 1968, p. 204.

33 *Selected Poems* (1973), pp. 57–8.

34 Lindsay, 'Rosemary Dobson', *Poetry Review*, 41(3), 1950, pp. 144–8, p. 148.

35 *Selected Poems* (1973), pp. 60–61.

36 'From London,' *Southerly*, 9(2), 1948, pp. 130–31.

37 Rosemary Dobson, private communication, February 2010.

38 Susan Sheridan, 'In the Driver's Seat: Muriel Spark's Editorship of the *Poetry Review*', *Journal of Modern Literature*, 32(2), Winter 2009, pp. 133–42.

39 Warner asks after him in a letter inviting Rosemary to visit: STW to RD, 15 April 1948, Dobson papers, NLA, MS4955, folder 15.

40 Wendy Mulford, *This Narrow Place: Sylvia Townsend Warner and Valentine Ackland: Life, letters and politics 1930–1951*, Pandora Press, London, 1988, p. 190.

41 VA to RD, 5 May 1948, Dobson papers, NLA, MS4955, folder 15; STW to RD, undated [1948], Dobson papers, NLA, MS4955, folder 16.

42 STW to RD, 15 September 1955 and 29 February 1956, Dobson papers, NLA, MS4955, folder 15.

43 Dobson, private communication, February 2010.

44 *Selected Poems* (1973), p. 73.

45 Untitled review, AD Hope, *Meanjin*, 14(4), 1955, p. 573.

46 *Bulletin*, 1 June 1955, p. 2.

47 David Campbell, 'Time and the Mirror', *Southerly*, 17(1), 1956, pp. 42–4.

48 STW to RD, 15 September 1955 and 29 February 1956, Dobson papers, NLA, MS4955, folder 15.

49 Anon., 'Review of *Australian Poetry 1948*, edited by Judith Wright', *Bulletin*, 6 July 1949, p. 2.

50 Anon., 'The Year's Verse', *Bulletin*, 18 October 1950, p. 2.

51 *Selected Poems* (1973), pp. 83–4.

52 *Southerly*, 26(2), 1966, pp. 132–7.

53 *Overland*, 35, Summer 1966–67, pp. 55–6.

54 Brian Elliott, *Australian Book Review*, October 1965, p. 232.

55 Anon., *Times Literary Supplement*, 16 September 1965, p. 799.

56 'Letter from Sydney', *Hudson Review*, 19(4), Winter 1966–67, pp. 645–52.

57 Dobson, 'Australian Poets in Profile: 2. Rosemary Dobson', *Southerly*, 40(1), 1980, pp. 3–10, p. 10.

58 Thomas Shapcott, untitled review, *Australian Book Review*, 3(7), 1964, p. 132.

59 JW to RD, 15 August 1958, Dobson papers, NLA, MS4955, folder 14.

60 JW to RD, 2 September 1991, in Wright, *With Love and Fury*, eds Clarke and McKinney, National Library of Australia, Canberra, 2006, p. 477.

61 *Selected Poems* (1973), p. 79.

62 RD to JMcA (draft), 23 February 1956, Dobson papers, NLA, MS4955, folder 16.

63 JMcA to RD, 26 February 1956, Dobson papers, NLA, MS4955, folder 15.

64 NM to RD, undated note, Dobson papers, NLA, MS4955, folder 23.

65 Susan Sheridan, '*Australian Letters* and Postwar Modernity', *Australian Literary Studies*, 23(3), 2008, pp. 264–78.

66 Dobson, *Focus on Ray Crooke*, UQP, St Lucia, 1971.

67 Mary Gilmore was the only other woman in this series, along with Shaw Neilson, Kendall et al.

68 Tranter interview, 2004, p. 6. Accessed from AustLit database, 5 January 2006.

69 NM to RD, 17 November 1970, Dobson papers, NLA, MS4955, folder 21. The collection includes extensive letters detailing this friendship, which lasted until McDonald's untimely death in 1974, after a long illness.

70 Kinross-Smith, p. 62.

71 Ayres, 'Rosemary Dobson', *Australian Writers 1915–1950*, ed. Selina Samuels, *Dictionary of Literary Biography*, vol. 260, 2002, pp. 99–105, p. 105.

72 Statement, *Poetry and Gender*, p. 32.

73 'Rosemary Dobson', *Southerly* 40(1), 1980, pp. 3–10, p. 10.

74 *Australian Book Review*, 282, June–July 2006, p. 54.

CHAPTER FIVE

Dorothy Auchterlonie Green as co-principal of the Presbyterian Girls' College, Warwick, about 1958

Dorothy Auchterlonie Green: Woman of letters

Late in her life, Dorothy Green made some acerbic remarks about the problems women face in becoming writers. 'The woes of writers are at bottom self-inflicted. No-one is compelled to be a writer,' she wrote, and quoted Rilke's 'Advice to a Young Poet' on the need to examine one's motives in joining the company of writers.[1] Her concluding recommendations for gender equality reiterated her distaste for any separate consideration of women. Women's wrongs could best be righted, she believed, when 'women make common cause with men against the forces of privilege which hold both sexes equally in subjection'.[2] I want to consider the triumphs and frustrations of her career as a woman of letters in the light of her gender, while noting that this is not an approach with which she would consistently have agreed.

Dorothy Auchterlonie Green was an important member of her cohort of Australian women writers, and the only one of this group of nine who seriously pursued an academic career in preference to a vocation in creative writing. As Dorothy Auchterlonie she published three books of poetry, and as Dorothy Green a monumental study of Henry Handel Richardson, a complete revision of the two-volume *History of Australian Literature* originally written by her husband, HM Green, and many essays and reviews. In her youth she worked as a journalist and wrote for newspapers and women's magazines, though the principal trajectory of her professional life was as a teacher. She taught in schools during her years as a university student and in the 1950s while her children were young. She was appointed to her first academic post, at the newly established Monash University, in 1961, and later taught at the Australian National University and at the Australian Defence Force Academy in Canberra. Her scholarly work and teaching formed the core of her professional life whereas, by contrast, Thea Astley's university post enhanced but did not take over from her principal commitment to writing fiction.

Green's biographer Willa McDonald has argued that Green saw her real calling in life not solely as a writer nor as a teacher, but as a social critic, encompassing both roles.[3] Her model for this vocation was the famous freethinker John Anderson, her philosophy teacher at Sydney University, who believed that criticism and opposition to social institutions were vital to democracy. McDonald's perspective, though it gave due weight to the strong critical vein in Green's poetry and prose, considered Green's writing an adjunct to her social critique and her spiritual searching. To categorise her poetry and literary essays in that way, I think, gives them too instrumental a place in her life. Certainly some of Green's strongest poetry is satirical, and her essays are always animated by an oppositional stance but, for her, poetry had intrinsic value as a way to 'make sense out of chaotic experience and live with it'.[4] Beyond its subjective value for her, she felt that literature had broader and deeper significance. It is, she wrote, 'humanity thinking aloud, communicating its experience of all that is, holding a great continuous discussion throughout the ages and across the world'.[5]

She valued the role of reader as in a sense co-creator with the artist. She distinguished between the roles of reader and critic, and often told correspondents that she 'hated' literary criticism, despite the fact that she practised and taught that craft. Her essay 'The Critic' identifies the analytical kinds of literary criticism she so disliked, but she offers the following account of the relationship between writer, reader and critic, which retains a vital role for the critic as a teacher, one that she herself played with outstanding verve and skill:

> [T]here can be no real response to literature unless the reader shares to some extent the artist's capacity for 'negative capability', his capacity to become: a tree, a dog, a lake, a human being of the opposite sex. This capacity, if fully exercised in the real world, is implicit in the operations of justice, and a lively teacher of literature, a vital literary criticism, would enable students to make the connection for themselves. Literature is the most effective means of enlarging this capacity for active empathy, because it is not subject to the limitations of time and space: a book carried in the pocket can put a girdle round the earth in a few seconds and abolish millennia.[6]

This recognition that the 'capacity for active empathy' required by literature must be exercised in the real world in pursuit of justice was what linked her critical essays and her poetry.

While this late essay appears to reconcile the poet Dorothy Auchterlonie and the critic Dorothy Green, her dismissive comments about criticism suggest that she experienced her two writing selves as opposed to each other. Although several of Green's male colleagues were productive and respected poets as well as academic critics and teachers, she seemed to experience this combination of activities as a source of conflict in her life. She complained at times that she never did what she really wanted to do, but what other people wanted her to do. Beneath the complaint one might discern a classic feminine conflict between individual freedom and commitment to the welfare of others, in her case intensified by the need to earn a living for herself and her children.

As a girl, Dorothy Auchterlonie was lively and talented. She loved music and poetry, and was academically gifted. Although her parents were poor immigrants from the north of England, she remained at North Sydney Girls' High School throughout the Depression years and matriculated in 1932. As a pupil teacher at a small private girls' school, she attended Sydney University in the evenings, encouraged by the school's headmistress Florence Cortis. She took a Bachelor of Arts degree in English, philosophy and French, and a Master's with honours in English literature. Her Master's thesis topic was the work of Thomas Lovell Beddoes, a strange figure of the nineteenth-century Romantic movement, who published poetry while he was still a student at Oxford but never completed any of his later dramatic and poetic works before he died by his own hand at the age of forty-six. Today he is celebrated as a Gothic writer, but his work was little known in the 1930s. It would be interesting to know how Dorothy came across his work and why she decided to write her thesis about him.

She was at the University of Sydney at the same time as Judith Wright and Amy Witting, but as an evening student she might not have met them, although she and Wright became friends later in life. Like Witting, Dorothy was close to the young James McAuley, with whom she shared a passion for music as well as poetry. They combined her talent as a singer with his for jazz piano when they gave concerts to old soldiers' homes and the like. She was actively involved in university life, attending Freethought Society meetings led by the charismatic John Anderson, writing poetry and contributing to university magazines.[7]

In 1938 she co-edited the three issues of the journal *Hermes* with RW Rutledge, a science student, who was active in the Freethought Society and had worked on *Honi Soit*, the student paper.[8] They produced a fine-looking magazine with a striking woodcut of the god Hermes in silhouette on the cover, and Dorothy wrote the editorials. She later told an interviewer she was pleased with the 'revolutionary discussion of issues' they published.[9] During the second half of the year their collaboration was done by correspondence as Rutledge was employed in northern New South Wales. His letter congratulating her on the Trinity term issue included praise for her poem 'l'eau verte de Lethe' and 'the one about the pool' which reminded him of Housman.[10] In the same letter he apologised for writing as if he thought she had nothing to do but *Hermes*, and made sensible suggestions as to how she could control her workload. Indeed, he sounded almost possessively solicitous of her welfare when, referring to her insomnia, he told her to be careful of her health: 'I want to return to find you quite well.'[11]

Not so her other steady correspondent, James McAuley. He was living in exile from Sydney in Bungendore, out of Canberra, and he sent her poems for critical comment. He too congratulated her on *Hermes*, although he was amusingly critical of some contributions, including his own 'Four Poems from a Series' and his story 'Two till Six'.[12] At the end of this same letter he mentioned her 'address' about Beddoes which was published in the *Union Recorder*: 'I'm positive that you could produce a full-dress study that would be really good, and which you could publish,' he added encouragingly. She apparently sent him a few of her own poems, but he did not comment extensively in return, although he praised her 'poem about the Magdalene', which she later published as 'Question for Thomas'. It begins:

> Would there have been a bitter tree,
> Or vinegar on Calvary,
> Or lesser miracle have been,
> if Christ had kissed the Magdalene?[13]

The opening lines were 'inspired', McAuley wrote, and: 'The form you chose has the same kinship to popular poetry, to "rhymes" and "ballads" that delights me in Blake.' He was less positive about her contributions to *Arena*, the Arts faculty magazine: 'Your story has a dramatic core to it, but I feel that it is insufficiently thought into and realized. The poem, too, suffers in this way.' He added insult to injury by continuing: 'Perhaps it is merely my male prejudice that makes me think that your thought is still lost in your sex, trammeled by its subtle implications. Or does that seem nonsensical to you?'[14] Dorothy's response is lost to posterity, but she would surely have scoffed at the Freudian idea that a woman's mind is confined by her body.

Thanking her for her detailed attention to his poems, McAuley wrote in this same letter: 'I need someone to lay a finger on lines whose weakness I may dimly sense but not have the initiative to tackle . . . But actually I suspect my debt to you is deeper than that: it has been a great heartening of my own self-distrust to know that someone else expects a great deal from me.' Signing off, as usual, 'Yours, Jim,' he then added a postscript: 'Could you find me the meaning of the French word "chlorose", please?'

Clearly, McAuley regarded Green as a handmaiden, albeit a respected one, to his genius. In these letters he was sometimes deferential, sometimes patronising; he did not flirt. He offered ideas about books and music as well as his poetry. He was keen on

Wagner, and said he wanted to hear her sing something from the 'Frauenliebe' cycle – a reference to her beautiful singing voice.[15]

This exchange, and the appearance of Green's long poem *Kaleidoscope* in the 'Prelude' series published by her university colleague Bessie Mitchell in 1940, show her as a young woman who was serious about her poetry, and about literature and ideas.[16] The poem was a satire on modern life, a mode of writing that remained a favourite with her. In 1967 she published *The Second Coming*, which mocked official Australian responses to the visit of US President Lyndon Baines Johnson ('All the way with LBJ!') during the Vietnam war. *Kaleidoscope* traced the progress of a modern pilgrim up from Wynyard underground railway station into the streets of Sydney to participate in the delights of modernity – paying his insurance premium, making a withdrawal from the bank, visiting the 'proletarian park', crossing the Harbour Bridge ('like a coat-hanger in the sky') to Luna Park and other mind-dulling mass entertainments and the waste they generate: 'For men, of gods the prototype,/Would take a star to light a pipe.' The neat rhyming couplets were accompanied by small witty marginal 'ornaments' drawn by Bessie Mitchell.[17]

After graduating Dorothy was keen to leave teaching for journalism. She took a cadetship with the *Daily Telegraph*, then moved to the Australian Broadcasting Commission (ABC), where she was the first woman journalist appointed as a news reporter. These were the war years, with unprecedented opportunities for women. But she did not escape the tragedy of the war when her only brother, a merchant seaman, was reported missing in action in 1942. She had lost her mother to cancer some eight years earlier, and her father had died when she was a child. Now she was alone in the world.

At her request for an appointment out of Sydney, the ABC put her in charge of the national news service in Brisbane, at that time the hub of the Pacific war effort.[18] In Brisbane she met Clem and

Nina Christesen, who would become her lifelong friends. She had sent material to *Meanjin Papers*, as Judith Wright had done, with a note congratulating the editor on the plentiful creative work, and emphasis on historical criticism, that made his journal unique in Australia.[19] Now she was in Brisbane they invited her to visit, and she published several reviews in the journal, as well as four poems, including 'Question for Thomas' (quoted above) and 'Morning and Evening':

> Morning breaks and I must go
> Where my true love waits for me;
> The sun-lit hours are long and slow
> And the red road winds so endlessly.
>
> Evening falls, and I must go
> Far from my love, far from delight;
> How swift the sunlit hours grow
> To clouds that hide him from my sight![20]

Love found and lost again was a theme close to her heart. By May 1944 she had returned to Sydney, and there she married Henry McKenzie Green, the university librarian and an eminent man of letters – poet, critic and literary historian. He had divorced his first wife, the mother of his two adult daughters, to marry Dorothy, who was thirty-five years younger than he. Divorce and remarriage were no light matters in those days, and the decision must have taken enormous courage on both their parts. Mrs Eleanor Green was a literary figure in her own right, an expert on Henry James.[21] Harry (as he was known) retired from his university post, and continued to support his first wife on his small pension.[22]

Like her contemporary Judith Wright, who also fell in love

with a much older man who had a first wife to support, Dorothy thus became the main breadwinner of the family. Her first child, a daughter, was born in 1945 and her second, a son, in 1952. The family lived in Glenbrook, in the Blue Mountains outside Sydney, and Dorothy would commute by train to the ABC offices in the city where she had casual employment, relieving when the newsroom was short-staffed. As a married woman, she was no longer considered for fulltime employment, even if she had been in a position to take it. She also earned money reviewing books on ABC radio, and writing articles for magazines such as *Walkabout* (where she published pieces on Judith Wright and Kylie Tennant) and women's magazines. For *Woman's Day* she wrote a controversial series on kindergartens, and for the *Australian Women's Weekly* a series on 'Poets in Private'.[23] She also contributed to its series on famous women (the 'Famous Trollops series' as she called it dismissively)[24] and published a story about a woman artist's tapestries, depicting Sturt's journey along the Murray, made for the 1951 Jubilee of Federation.[25] Like most of the educated women who were her contemporaries Green was dismissive of the women's magazines of the time, yet the *Australian Women's Weekly*, for one, incorporated a substantial news component and sections on literature, film and the performing arts.[26]

Harry was working fulltime on his monumental *History of Australian Literature*, which took him until 1960 to finish – it was known in the family as 'the Bloody Book'.[27] Dorothy helped him with this work, as well as being 'cook, bottle-washer, washerwoman & sempstress too'.[28] Her letters to Clem Christesen offer a vivid glimpse of her frustrations. A sign of things to come, when she would often reach the end of her tether with weariness, appeared in 1950 when Clem invited her to contribute to *Meanjin*'s 'Writers on Grub Street' series: 'I want you to be waspish in your inimitable way, and turn out a sizzling article.'[29] She answered crossly that she couldn't afford to spend time doing this kind of writing when the women's magazines paid her grocery bills. Besides, she fumed, 'I don't want to make things easier for artists. There are too many phony ones' (naming two well-known men, a publisher and an academic).[30]

As for writing poems for *Meanjin*, she insisted that 'I don't regard myself as at all "fit" yet to be a writer . . . I regard it, you see, as a sacred vocation'.[31] There was some contradiction here, as she also wrote that she was 'more concerned with the future of mankind than that of literature' – a lofty distinction that recurred in later letters. But all in all, she protested too much: she did care deeply about her own writing, and expressed herself despondent about neglecting it, and sick of writing about other people's.[32]

The only poems she published during these years at Glenbrook appeared in the *Bulletin*. They were 'The Tree', the first of her trilogy of poems about Christian mythology[33] and 'After-Dinner Speech', which was occasioned by JD Pringle (then editor of the *Sydney Morning Herald*) calling for 'a Dryden or a Swift' for Australian poetry. What would happen, she asked, if such satirical poems appeared on the editor's desk in this self-censoring country?[34] Green took satirical writing seriously, and it was also a creative outlet for her anger, but Kylie Tennant advised her not to waste time on such diversions: 'You are a woman with an original mind but you are still groping about looking for the thing you can do best. Now I believe you are a really creative person and you shouldn't bother with journalism at all . . .'[35]

Despite the fact that Tennant signed off this letter with a cynical reference to having a book review to finish, Dorothy would have been flattered by this account of her talents. The view that journalism and creativity were incompatible was a common one at that time, and one that Dorothy herself sometimes expressed. For this and other reasons – her husband, now in his seventies, was sometimes ill, and Dorothy could no doubt foresee the time when she would have to be the family's sole breadwinner – she began to look for a way out of casual journalism. In 1954 she wrote to the poet Alec Hope, a friend from her Sydney University days, to ask his advice about applying for an advertised job in English at the University of New England at Armidale – could he write a reference for her, and could she ask Ian Maxwell to do the same?[36] She needed to look for a job before too long, 'for obvious reasons', and she was sure she would fail to get the ABC job, for 'I know ABC politics too well.' The only other position on the horizon was as an English teacher at the Presbyterian Girls' College at Warwick, out of Brisbane.[37]

This was the job she secured, and in early 1955 the Green family moved to Queensland. But Dorothy did not look forward to teaching again, anticipating all her writing ideas 'gradually leaching away'. As she wrote (somewhat tactlessly) to Alec Hope: 'Once one begins teaching Eng Lit it's pretty well the end.'[38]

As it turned out, 'teaching Eng Lit' was the least that PGC asked of her, and soon Dorothy was sharing the position of school principal with her friend Betty Crombie, a job that, she said, was barely manageable by working sixteen hours a day, seven days a week. Much as her achievements at the school over the next six years were admired, both as a teacher and an administrator who tried to improve girls' education (these are detailed in Willa McDonald's book), Dorothy complained to her friends that it was a punitive regime. 'I cannot survive the Presbyterian Way of Life,' she wrote to Hope.[39] 'Behind Bars' was the address on another of her [undated] letters to him, where she wrote that 'when I read the latest articles in *Meanjin*, *TLS* and the *Listener*, I feel how illiterate I have become and realize that in my present incarnation I have namoore to seye' [sic]. She went on, 'I am now rising 42 and looking back on my life, I find I have spent the greater proportion of it doing things I didn't want to do at all.' A later margin note in her hand added: '! now 70 & nothing has changed.'[40]

Nevertheless, she did write poetry at this time, exchanging poems with Hope and publishing several herself: 'Magpies at Night',[41] 'Nativity',[42] '*Anser Barbara*'[43] and 'The Second Tree'.[44] One of her most powerful works, 'The Second Tree' begins with Christ's journey to Calvary:

> They watch him as he walks towards the Tree:
> Black, like an upraised finger on the hill,
> No scarlet fruit, no leaf's green broidery,
> Disturb the fierce direction of its will.

Midway through the poem the focus shifts from the human witnesses to Christ himself:

> He watched them, as he walked towards the Tree,
> Heavy with love, with pity and despair:
> All these I have created endlessly,
> To doubt and dread, to dream, exult and dare—
>
> Only to know me from a vast abyss,
> To apprehend me from the end of space
> To touch me, blindfold, in a moment's bliss,
> And to deny me if they see my face . . . [45]

Perversely perhaps – for he was constantly asking her for contributions – she sent 'The Second Tree' to *Meanjin* when Clem Christesen was on leave. Geoffrey Serle, the acting editor, returned the poem to her with a string of queries, which she refuted one by one, ending haughtily: 'I hope you will refuse to publish it if you are in the least doubtful about it; I am not anxious for an encouraging pat on the head.'[46] Serle instantly replied that it had never been refused. Some six months later Dorothy wrote to Christesen that her poem had not appeared, so might she have it returned? It 'may be' her last poem.[47] A huffy exchange followed, but the poem eventually appeared in the 1958 Spring issue of *Meanjin*.

A year later, when she must have been close to breaking point, Dorothy wrote an angry letter to both the Christesens, accusing them of neglecting her and her family, when 'I have practically obliterated my essential self, my creative impulse, all I wanted to do in scholarship, and my physical strength, to keep things going' in a job she hated. She accused Clem of 'cant' and of treating Harry 'truculently and patronisingly'.[48] Clem's reply was that of a sensitive friend, careful to address what he perceived to be her major anxiety, about the welfare of the children if anything should happen to her and Harry. He assured her that he and Nina would stand by their promise to care for them, and reminded her of his encouragement over the years, his conviction that 'You were the brightest of the whole damn bunch.' He was not above touting for sympathy himself, telling her what long hours he and Nina both worked.[49] Her reply to this letter was warm and loving, saying that she felt 'lonely and dehumanised' in her job at the school, and that 'all my life I have never really been able to believe that anyone could be interested in me – a basic insecurity.'[50]

The friendship was repaired, but Dorothy's desperate state was unrelieved. In a letter to Alec Hope decorated with a hammer and sickle and star she reported that 'It is impossible for a poem to be too violent – for me at the moment anyway. I am in a constant bad temper . . .' She was looking for a way out of teaching and into academe, and had asked him about an advertised job in his department. She continued defensively, 'the hortus siccus [literally 'dry garden'] of Eng Lit is not the summit of my ambition: I have none, except to find a corner to work in which will enable me to have part of my mind to myself' – as well as allowing her to fit in with children's holidays. 'But I don't know that I can escape from [her present job] by writing to Ian [Maxwell] or anyone else I know in English departments. It wasn't very easy for me to write to you . . . not easy at all, in fact. I still have a lump where I swallowed.'[51]

The letter was full of contradictions. The problem was, of course, that although she disclaimed 'ambition', she had the highest regard for her own abilities, envied people who seemed to have jobs fall into their (male) laps, and hated to ask for favours. Like many of her contemporaries she sneered at 'teaching Eng Lit', yet she wanted to be offered a job that was worthy of her. The university seemed to offer an environment that would nurture both her 'essential self', her 'creative impulse' and 'all [she] wanted to do in scholarship', and pay a decent salary besides. She knew male academics like Alec Hope and James McAuley who wrote poetry and undertook teaching and scholarly work as well. Yet she could see clearly, she wrote to Clem Christesen, that 'it seems easier for a camel to go through the eye of a needle than for a reasonably competent female to get an academic job without pulling strings.'[52] In the end, her appeal to Christesen for help bore more fruit than her appeals to Hope. He advised that there was a better chance for her in English at the new Monash University rather than at Melbourne where, it was rumoured, Maxwell felt 'troubled' by the number of women on his staff.[53] Her Monash application was successful and she was offered a lectureship starting in 1961.

'When I get used to the idea that I am supposed to read, that it is not considered a sinful waste of time, I think I shall feel better. It is quite extraordinary not having to think of two hundred different things at once,'[54] wrote Dorothy to Alec Hope in early 1961, after taking up her Monash appointment. This looked like the turning point in her professional life, the point where she had found a way to write as well as to earn a good living by teaching. She was then forty-five years old.

The transition, at a mature age, from journalism and school teaching to the university was not unusual at the time among her male colleagues. What was very unusual was to find a woman being appointed to a tenurable academic position at all. There were even fewer women career academics – in literature or in any other field – than there were women writers. Dorothy Green was one of the few. She was at least as well qualified as her male peers, with a Master of Arts with Honours from Sydney University, and she had published a number of poems, stories and reviews in serious magazines.

She had high expectations that this new appointment would bring her a satisfying career as well as a secure income. Yet the happiness which seemed so close was not to be. Within eighteen months of this move, the event she had anticipated with such anguish happened. Her husband died, leaving her a widow with two children, aged seventeen and ten. The poem, 'In Absentia', alludes to her loss:

> Here is the empty cup you drank from; here
> The pillow holds the pressure of your head,
> Your shadow stands behind me in the glass,
> And when I stretch my arms along the bed
> They trace the enchanted circle of our fear.[55]

Her grief was searing and her anxiety about the future was acute. In this vulnerable state she had a brief affair with a colleague, which ended badly. These events drove her over the edge, and she suffered a nervous breakdown.[56] She recovered gradually, helped by the prospect of another academic post but in a different place, where she already had one friend. In early 1964 she left

Melbourne to take up a temporary lectureship at the Australian National University, where the English department was headed by Alec Hope.

Again, this situation promised well. In addition to teaching English literature and drama, she joined Tom Inglis Moore in teaching the Australian literature course that he had pioneered. Over the next few years she gained tenure, was promoted to senior lecturer, took study leave overseas (in 1968) and held a research fellowship at the History of Ideas Unit at ANU (in 1969). Her creative as well as her critical work flourished. The ANU Press published a volume of her poetry, *The Dolphin* (1967), and she was invited to edit the prestigious Angus & Robertson annual anthology of poetry the following year.[57] She also undertook a massive project of literary scholarship on Henry Handel Richardson and her fiction, published as *Ulysses Bound* in 1973.[58]

The Dolphin marked the return of Dorothy Auchterlonie, poet. A number of satires on contemporary events link this book with her earliest publication, yet the overall impression of the book is one of estrangement and loss. The poems, composed over the years since the 1940s, show a continuing preoccupation with themes of love and death, explored in formally exact verse. Auchterlonie's poetry is far removed from the certainties of her prose.[59] Reviewing the book, poet Bruce Beaver perceived a tension between 'the joyous aspect of the creative principle' signified by the dolphin and the 'harsh shore and harsher inland of the human condition'.[60] He quoted from the poem 'Chess by the Sea':

> The tide is rising with the wind,
> Wave answers wind in the black pines,
> The dolphin dies upon the beach –
> Behind your head, the darkness shines.

Cold, cold upon the widowed sand,
Death opens up his ancient game;
His hooded face is white and wise,
He moves a pawn and names my name.[61]

The title and the imagery of this poem recall Ingmar Bergman's film *The Seventh Seal* (1957) about confronting death in the absence of God, which Auchterlonie almost certainly would have seen.

Ulysses Bound, Dorothy Green's study of Henry Handel Richardson, was widely reviewed and acknowledged as breaking new critical ground. Her analysis of the springs of the novelist's creativity in the complexities of her psyche is acutely perceptive and grounded in a thorough knowledge of the philosophical and social contexts of the work. What struck contemporaries most forcibly was Green's forthright insistence that postwar Australian critics did not take religious ideas in Richardson's work seriously, nor her work's place in relation to European literary and philosophical traditions.[62]

By any standards, these years were marked by a series of professional successes. Yet Green resigned from the Australian National University in 1972 declaring that it had been the worst experience of her working life. Certainly, she experienced two major disappointments there – her perception that the English department had downgraded Australian literature when, on Inglis Moore's retirement, she was asked to take on his job without promotion to his position of associate professor; and her unsuccessful application for the chair in Australian literature at the University of Sydney, passed over for her old rival Leonie Kramer (with whom she had long-standing disagreements about the work of Richardson and more generally about approaches to literary criticism).[63]

Considering the times and from this distance, neither decision seems unjustified. Promotion opportunities were few in those days, and senior lecturer was the position most academics were expected to aspire to. Inglis Moore had taken a lifetime to become associate professor, and Kramer was already at that level, whereas Green was a lecturer with only a few years' experience of university teaching and relatively few publications. Yet her decision to resign from her teaching position turned out well. It opened up new possibilities for her, which brought new commitments and different forms of recognition, including the Order of Australia in 1988.

Dorothy Green emerged as an influential freelance critic in the 1970s and 1980s. From 1972 until 1976 a Commonwealth Literature Fund grant enabled her to resign from teaching and devote herself fulltime to scholarly and critical writing. After that she was employed first as a tutor and then as a lecturer in literature at the Royal Military College Duntroon.[64] There she enjoyed warm collegiality of a kind that she had not experienced before. As well as completing the massive task of revising her husband's path-breaking *History of Australian Literature*, she published critical essays on such writers as Christina Stead and Patrick White, and numerous reviews. She went on writing poetry and in 1983 published *Something to Someone: Poems*, with Brindabella Press. Living in Canberra she made friends with other women writers of her generation who had moved there – Rosemary Dobson and Judith Wright – and with Christina Stead, after the latter returned to Australia to live.

Refurbishing her old skills as a journalist, Green published reviews and opinion pieces as well as scholarly articles. Her name appeared regularly in quality newspapers and weeklies including the *National Times*, bringing her a wider readership than most literary academics enjoyed. She was admired by a generation of younger intellectuals such as Humphrey McQueen and Drusilla Modjeska for her continuing 'critical engagement between literature and modern social thought'.[65] She contributed to feminist enterprises such as Shirley Walker's essay collection *Who Is She?*[66] and to the ABC women's program *The Coming Out Show*.

The pressure on her intellectual creativity was relieved when she turned away from the academic world to some extent and directed her rage outwards, to governments and politicians. She used her skill with language and reasoning to make eloquent attacks on militarism in all its forms, and abuses of science and education. It was only when Green became the 'warrior for peace' of Willa McDonald's study, active in political movements against war and conscription, uranium mining and nuclear arms, that she was able to reconcile her various professional selves as poet, critic, teacher and now social critic and public intellectual.

This new phase in her professional life, as a mature woman with grown children, in turn fed into her literary work, where her 'capacity for active empathy' could now be given full rein. Her reputation as a literary scholar grew: she was invited to deliver the prestigious Colin Roderick lectures at the James Cook University of north Queensland (published as *The Writer, the Reader and the Critic in a Monoculture* in 1986), and was made an honorary member of the newly formed Association for the Study of Australian Literature, which after her death instituted an annual lecture in her honour. A conference about her work was held in 1990, with papers published in a special issue of the journal *Southerly*. When she died in 1991 she left unfinished two major literary projects, on the novelist Martin Boyd, and on the biologist and writer Grant Watson.

Unlike her female contemporaries who saw themselves primarily as writers and sought recognition among publishers, editors, critics and readers, Dorothy Green saw herself, for much of her life, primarily as a scholar and looked for recognition to the university, a strongly patriarchal institution which she nevertheless respected deeply. Consequently she experienced much of her professional career as a series of bitter disappointments.

She had great talent, drive and belief in her own judgment, an excellent education and good contacts in the literary and the academic world. Yet she constantly felt overworked and under-recognised, trapped by the circumstances of her life and unsure of her capacity as a poet. As her friend Clem Christesen wrote in exasperation, she complained about not being recognised, yet when invited to contribute to symposia and journals she usually refused, pleading pressure of other work.[67]

Even though, in others' eyes, she always had talent and huge potential, she seems never to have been truly comfortable in her own skin. Neither her Anglican faith nor her family and friends could reassure her sufficiently of her value. Her material circumstances were never easy but, in addition, because of her perfectionism she could never undertake a job at less than 150 per cent commitment and was often physically and emotionally exhausted. For instance, when revising the *History* she set herself the task of re-reading every book that Henry had written about.[68] This profile suggests a peculiarly feminine form of perfectionism and 'victimism,' of never-ending toil, impossibly high standards set for herself and others and acute sensitivity to slights. Fortunately, no one else was as hard on her as she was on herself, and the contempt she sometimes expressed for 'teaching Eng Lit' and for journalism was not shared by others. She won widespread admiration for her poetry, her literary scholarship, her reviews and social criticism, and for her inspirational teaching.

Notes

1 Green, 'Men and Women Writers', *Writer, Reader, Critic*, Primavera Press, Sydney, 1990, p. 156.

2 Green, 'Men and Women Writers', p. 174.

3 Willa McDonald, *Warrior for Peace: Dorothy Auchterlonie Green*, Australian Scholarly Publishing, Melbourne, 2009, p. 44. This chapter is deeply indebted to McDonald's research on Green's life.

4 Maurice Dunlevy, 'Dorothy Green the Woman', *Canberra Times*, 30 December 1967.

5 Green, 'The Place of Literature', *The Music of Love: Critical essays on literature and life*, Penguin, Ringwood, Vic, 1984, p. 155.

6 Green, 'The Critic', in *Writer, Reader, Critic*, p. 147.

7 McDonald, *Warrior for Peace*, p. 7.

8 Alan Barcan, *Radical Students: the Old Left at Sydney University*, Melbourne University Press, Melbourne, 2002, p. 77.

9 Richard Campbell, 'Dorothy Green, 1915–1991', *LiNQ*, 18(2), 1991, pp. 110–11.

10 RR to DA, 19 August 1938, Australian Defence Force Academy Archives, Green papers, MS20, box 6, folder 36.

11 RR to DA, 14 July 1938, ADFA Archives.

12 JM to DA, undated [1938], Dorothy Green papers, NLA, MS5678, box 85, folder 146. 'Glaucon' was the pseudonym McAuley used for his prose pieces.

13 Dorothy Auchterlonie, *The Dolphin*, ANU Press, Canberra, 1967, p. 10.

14 JM to DA, 'circa 7 Nov' [1938], Dorothy Green papers, NLA, MS 5678.

15 She originally wanted to pursue a career as a mezzo-soprano but this proved impossible for financial reasons; she claimed late in life that 'everything else has been, in a way, a substitute' for that lost career (McDonald, *Warrior for Peace*, p. 3).

16 Dorothy Auchterlonie, *Kaleidoscope*, Viking Press, Sydney, 1940.

17 The other 'Preludes' volumes ornamented and published by Bessie Mitchell were by Elizabeth Riddell, Elisabeth Lambert and Harley Matthews; all were reviewed by Thelma Herring in *Southerly*, 2(2), 1941, pp. 30–32.

18 McDonald, *Warrior for Peace*, pp. 12–16.

19 DA to CC, 4 August 1943, from ABC News, Sydney, offering a short story for publication. *Meanjin* Archive, Melbourne University Library Special Collections, Dorothy Green file.

20 *Meanjin*, 3(1), Autumn 1944, p. 38; repr. in *The Dolphin*, p. 13.

21 *Biographical Register*, Sydney University Women's College, vol 1, 1892–1939, 2006, p. 42.

22 The *Biographical Register* lists Eleanor Green as principal of Day Nurseries and Nursery Schools College in the 1940s.

23 Dunlevy, 'Dorothy Green the Woman'.

24 DG to CC and NC, undated letter [mid 1950s], *Meanjin* Archive.

25 Susan Sheridan, 'Cold War, Home Front: Australian women writers and artists in the 1950s', *Australian Literary Studies*, 20(3), 2002, pp. 155–66. There may be other *Women's Weekly* articles as yet unidentified.

26 Susan Sheridan, with Barbara Baird, Kate Borrett and Lyndall Ryan, *Who Was That Woman? The* Australian Women's Weekly *in the postwar years*, UNSW Press, Sydney, 2001, pp. 3–4.

27 For instance, in HMG's note to AD Hope [n.d. 1954], copy in Dorothy Green papers, NLA, MS 5678, series 1, folder 1. In this note he tells Hope he has suggested to Beatrice Davis that A&R might be interested in publishing a volume of Hope's poetry.

28 DG to CC, 16 June 1946, *Meanjin* Archive.

29 CC to DG, 21 July 1950, *Meanjin* Archive.

30 DG to CC, 3 August 1950, *Meanjin* Archive.

31 DG to CC, 1 November 1950, *Meanjin* Archive.

32 DG to CC, undated [1950], *Meanjin* Archive.

33 *Bulletin*, 20 June 1954, p. 24; repr. *The Dolphin*, pp. 3–4.

34 *Bulletin* 21 July 1954, p. 2; repr. *The Dolphin*, pp. 39–40.

35 KT to DG, 2 July 1954, Dorothy Green Papers, NLA, MS5678, series 1.4, box 85, folders 150–52.

36 Hope was at this time Professor of English at Canberra University

College, and Maxwell, who had taught Dorothy at Sydney University, was Chair of English at Melbourne University.

37 DG to ADH, no date [1954], copy in Dorothy Green papers, NLA, MS5678, series 1, folder 1.

38 DG to ADH, 1 December 1954, copy in Dorothy Green papers, NLA, MS5678, series 1, folder 1.

39 DG to ADH, 1 July, no year, copy in Dorothy Green papers, NLA, MS5678, series 1, folder 1.

40 DG to ADH, undated [1957], copy in Dorothy Green papers, NLA, MS5678, series 1, folder 1.

41 *Bulletin*, 20 June 1956, p. 24.

42 *Sydney Morning Herald*, 11 August 1956, p. 11.

43 *Bulletin*, 19 March 1958, p. 56; repr. *The Dolphin*, p. 17.

44 *Meanjin*,17(3), Spring 1958, pp. 251–53; repr. *The Dolphin*, pp. 5–7.

45 *The Dolphin*, pp. 5 and 6.

46 DG to GS, 22 October 1957, *Meanjin* Archive.

47 DG to CC, 19 May 1958, *Meanjin* Archive.

48 DG to CC and NC, 4 November 1959, *Meanjin* Archive.

49 CC to DG, 27 November 1959, Dorothy Green papers, NLA, MS5678, series 1, box 2, folder 10.

50 DG to CC, undated [late 1959], *Meanjin* Archive.

51 DG to ADH, undated [late 1959, early 1960 – she is reading McAuley's *End of Modernity* (1959)], copy in Dorothy Green papers, NLA, MS5678, series 1, folder 1.

52 DG to CC, 20 February 1960, *Meanjin* Archive.

53 CC to DG, 15 June 1960. NLA Green Papers MS5678, series 1, box 2, folder 11.

54 DG to ADH, 1 February 1961, copy in Dorothy Green papers, NLA, MS5678, series 1, folder 1.

55 *The Dolphin*, p. 31.

56 McDonald, *Warrior for Peace*, p. 43.

57 ADFA Archives, Green papers, MS20, series 1: Douglas Stewart to

DG 16 August 1967; Vivian Smith to DG 11 March 1967 invited her to contribute poems to *Quadrant*, an invitation she apparently did not take up.

58 Green, *Ulysses Bound: Henry Handel Richardson and her fiction*, ANU Press, Canberra, 1973.

59 This disjunction is demonstrated convincingly by Marie-Louise Ayres, 'The Mainland of Grief: Dorothy Auchterlonie', in '"Me" is not a stable reality: Negotiations of identity in the poetry of Dorothy Auchterlonie, Rosemary Dobson, Dorothy Hewett and JS Harry', unpublished PhD thesis, ANU, Canberra, 1994, pp. 41–50.

60 Beaver, 'Poetry of Joy, Protest,' *Sydney Morning Herald*, 8 February 1968.

61 *The Dolphin*, p. 23.

62 For instance, Bernard Hickey, 'Richard Mahony's Success', *Journal of Commonwealth Literature*, 10(3), 1976, pp 81–4.

63 McDonald, *Warrior for Peace*, pp. 62–4.

64 A campus of the University of New South Wales.

65 Drusilla Modjeska, 'Introduction', Dorothy Green, *The Music of Love: Critical essays on literature and life*, Penguin, Ringwood, Vic, 1984, p. 1.

66 Green, 'Power-Games in the Novels of Henry Handel Richardson', in Walker, ed., *Who Is She? Images of Women in Australian Fiction*, UQP, St Lucia, 1983.

67 CC to DG, 26 June [1967], Dorothy Green papers, NLA, MS5678, series 1, box 2, folder 11.

68 McDonald, *Warrior for Peace*, pp. 65–6.

CHAPTER SIX

Gwen Harwood, 1967

Gwen Harwood takes on the poetry pundits

In her memoir, 'Words and Music', Gwen Harwood described her childhood experience of poetry, like music, as something that was 'in the world waiting to be listened to'.[1] Often the ease and brilliance of her poetry gives this impression, that the poetry was already there, immanent in the world, ready to be conveyed into words. Yet the child's experience of a world replete with music and poetry changed into a more active conception of creative work, as she suggests in one of her earliest published poems, 'Alter Ego':

> Who stands beside me still,
> nameless, indifferent
> to any lost or ill
> motion of mind or will,
> whose pulse is mine, who goes
> sleepless and is not spent?

This other self 'knows what I was, will be,/and all I am' – another image of immanence, something that is 'in the world waiting to be listened to'. It transcends time, just as:

> Mozart said he could hear
> a symphony complete,
> its changing harmonies clear
> plain in his inward ear
> in time without extent. . . .

The alter ego is a presence that she 'cannot name or see, save as light's sidelong shift', yet which she apprehended:

> that morning when I came
> from childhood's steady air
> to love, like a blown flame . . .

She conjures that presence to:

> Wait, then, beside my chair
>
> as time and music flow
> nightward again. I trace
> their questioning voices, know
> little, but learn, and go
> on paths of love and pain
> to meet you, face to face.[2]

If it was in the transition from childhood to womanhood that Gwen Harwood realised that poetry was her vocation, it was nevertheless not until she was in her thirties, with her four children at school, that she began to write for publication. She later insisted that she was 'a late publisher' rather than a poet who discovered her vocation late.[3] The poise and depth of the poems that she began to publish in the mid 1950s, such as 'Alter Ego', support this self-characterisation. As her friend the poet and academic Vincent Buckley put it, she 'became an important presence in Australian poetry, in the course of a few weeks it seemed, late in the 1950s. A few poems in *Meanjin* and other places, and it was clear that here was a poet of unusual power and kind'.[4]

At the time Gwen Harwood did not see her arrival on the literary scene in such triumphal terms. In those early years she experienced frustration with magazine editors, not only when they rejected her poems, but when they failed to acknowledge her submissions, accepted poems but delayed publication, or published poems without payment. At the same time as she was recounting these adventures in letters to friends, she was inventing a series of pseudonyms and sending to those same editors poems by 'Walter Lehmann', 'Francis Geyer' and 'Miriam Stone'. Many of these fared better than the work of Mrs Gwen Harwood of Hobart, Tasmania. In some anthologies, more than one of these poets appeared.[5] It was only with the publication of her first book in 1963 that Gwen Harwood openly acknowledged her responsibility for Walter Lehmann; she acknowledged that she was Geyer and Stone in her second volume (1968).[6]

These inventions complicate the story of her early publishing career, as well as later evaluations of her achievement. What is most striking about her early publishing career, however, is the volume and versatility of poetry she produced in the decade between 1956 and 1967, represented in her first two volumes of *Poems* and also in the thirty-odd additional poems from this period, which appear in her *Collected Poems*.

Gwen Foster (as she was born in 1920) later claimed that as a young woman she was without ambition, and was certainly not interested in going to university. She characterised herself, in memoirs and youthful letters, as a mischievous, mocking girl, and if her cartoon-style verbal portraits of her parents are any guide, she took after her father in her capacity for play and performance – with words, music, and scene-setting. From her mother, who had been a schoolteacher and was a busy committee woman, she perhaps took a negative example of the sort of woman she did not want to be.[7] Family life in suburban Brisbane was happy and satisfying, and Gwen lived at home, like most girls at this time, until she married at the age of twenty-five. The household included her maternal grandmother, who spent a lot of time with Gwen and recited to her the first poems that she remembered hearing. As a child her favourite poets were Byron and Tennyson, and later Donne, Wyatt and Hopkins.[8]

A musical family, the Fosters held evening parties where guests played and sang, and Gwen and her younger brother both proved to be gifted musicians. Her father had a radio shop, and the family owned a large collection of records as well as a good library. Her mother hoped Gwen would be a concert pianist, but the girl 'knew' she was not good enough ('once she played for Rubinstein, who yawned,' as she recorded in the poem 'Suburban Sonnet'). Nevertheless, she gained the highest certificate in music while still a pupil at Brisbane Girls' Grammar School, and afterwards her music teacher's diploma. She went on to learn composition from Dr Robert Dalley-Scarlett, a Handel scholar and organist at All Saints Anglican Church.

This association led Gwen to become his assistant organist, a member of the Handel Society choir, and to 'take to High Anglicanism with fervour'. As she wrote in 'Words and Music':

> My years at All Saints' were spent in a loving circle of friends. We were drawn together not by religion but by affinities of temperament. After Benediction we would go down to Basil's coffee shop . . . [or to her home] to listen to the late quartets, make

> ourselves toast, argue endlessly about the nature of the world, plan an ideal society for that time when we would have children of our own whom we would keep from sorrow. We discovered the great Russians . . .

Gwen and her friends read the Thomist philosophers Maritain and Gilson, as well as Kant. At the centre of this group was Peter Bennie, a curate and graduate of Melbourne University with 'a dazzling academic reputation and a way of making each of us seem gifted and special'. He introduced them to modern literature – *The Waste Land*, *Ulysses*. 'He had written poetry and looked at my first derivative efforts.' He was her first great love, the 'most unsuitable love affair' that drove Gwen, when it ended, to join – for a brief six months in 1941 – a community of Anglican nuns.[9]

Combining as it did music, poetry, philosophy and theology, young Gwen Harwood's post-school education was extensive, though informal. It included, too, an appreciation of painting that had begun with her school art teacher Vera Cottew. Through her subsequent friendship with Vera she met some Austrian refugees, who introduced her to such European expressionist artists as Munch, Redon, Heckel, Kirchner and Ensor. She described the impact of these works in a tone of high drama:

> [T]he haunting prints from Redon's dreams took hold of my imagination and led me towards intense and radical new feelings. I lost my old certainties. It was good to find that my inner life was more complex than any experience: the paintings and lithographs said: *you are known*.[10]

Art that asserted the truth of dreams, and revealed an inner life 'more complex than any experience' left her 'shaken to bits'. Yet it also offered confirmation of her sense that it was not external events – 'experience' – but the inner life that fed the poetic imagination. This, it seems to me, is an important key to understanding the paradox of such powerful and diverse poetry coming out of the apparently quiet contented suburban life that Gwen Harwood led, both as girl and as woman.

Such a loss of 'old certainties', after her earlier enthusiasm for Anglo-Catholicism, also suggests that a quiet secure religious faith was not to be hers. This impression is reinforced by an anecdote she related in 'Time Beyond Reason', another memoir of the war years. She writes of being 'unconverted' in a blinding flash, on reading Cyril Connolly's *The Unquiet Grave*. This wartime journal of reflections and quotations, fragments shored against the uncertainties of the times, sustained her in a new faith. She realised that 'for me the new and the old Jerusalem would always be the Queensland of my childhood, the natural world with its creatures, the people, some of them long dead, who had brought me to this moment.'[11] Her friend Alison Hoddinott described this as 'her final conversion from a religion that required redemption from this world to a religion of the natural world and human love and friendship'.[12]

As for 'experience', for the remainder of the war period, when Brisbane was buzzing with troops and rumours of invasion, 'I ended my dilettante life by going to work in the War Damage Commission.' It seems that she took a job only because it was expected for the war effort, not because her family expected her to earn her living. In letters during this period (later collected as *Blessed City*), she relates hilarious stories of how she relieved the boredom of public service life by teasing her superiors and playing havoc with the switchboard.[13]

The recipient of these letters was Thomas (Tony) Riddell, a Melbourne friend of Peter Bennie, whom she met when he was posted to Brisbane and then to Darwin in the Royal Australian

Navy Volunteer Reserve. Bennie and Riddell encouraged her to send out her poems and stories for publication, but she resisted their suggestions; nor was she connected with Brisbane's Barjai group of young writers and artists, of which Thea Astley was a member, and Judith Wright an admired mentor.[14] It seems that during the years before marriage Gwen was too preoccupied with sorting out her values and her relationships to attend seriously to the question of a vocation in writing. She later wrote that she looked on this period as a 'stormy long-delayed adolescence',[15] and told Tony Riddell that Peter Bennie 'understands me as no one else does, and changed me, many years ago, from a neurotic child into a "reasonable woman"'.[16]

It was through Riddell that Gwen met her future husband Bill Harwood, a fellow member of the RAN Volunteer Reserve, in late 1943. At the end of the war they married and moved to Tasmania, where he had a lectureship in language studies in the English Department at the university. Though she described this move as a form of exile from her 'blessed city' of Brisbane, it also occasioned another key turning point, when the young Gwen Harwood – creative but 'not ambitious' – read her husband's copy of Wittgenstein's *Tractatus* on lonely winter afternoons in Hobart: 'When I came to the end I felt like someone who'd come upon a new religion . . . when I read in Wittgenstein "Not how the world is, is the mystical [sic], but that it is" I took my first step towards being a poet.'[17] Other intellectual influences at this time included the German Romantic and modernist poets Goethe, Hölderlin, Heine, Rilke and Trakl,[18] and during the 1960s she read widely among younger contemporary American poets such as Berryman, Dickey, Nemerov and Swenson.[19]

She published a handful of poems in 1949, one each in the *Bulletin*, *Meanjin* and *Southerly*, but did not start sending out a steady stream of work until the mid 1950s. She had little time for writing: in the first seven years of their marriage she bore five children, the second a still-born daughter. With the birth of twins in 1952, the family was complete, and by the time all four children were at school, Harwood had begun the decade of intense artistic creativity that would result in her first two volumes of poetry, in 1963 and 1968. Her *Poems Volume II* received high praise, and in the same year, 1968, Dorothy Green included in *Australian Poetry* two of her poems as well as two each by Hope and McAuley.

During this first decade Harwood wrote quickly, published widely, and met early success when three of her poems were accepted by Hal Porter for *Australian Poetry 1957*, and two by Vincent Buckley for *Australian Poetry 1958*. She won the *Meanjin* Poetry Prize in 1959 for 'Caro Autem Infirma' ('But the flesh is weak'), and again in 1960 for 'I Am the Captain of My Soul'.

These two poems illustrate some of the distinctive qualities of her poetry. The first, with its title from the biblical quotation in Latin, works on oppositions between spirit and flesh, dream and waking, darkness and light, to dramatise a struggle (imagined in terms from Gerard Manley Hopkins) with 'the protean inscape of self'. The title of the second, by contrast with these learned allusions, recalls a popular Victorian poem, only to contradict its confidence in the power of the self in the opening words: 'But the Captain is drunk . . .' and the epigraph from Wittgenstein: 'The human body is the best picture of the human soul.'

The group of eight 'Professor Eisenbart' poems from this period deploy her characteristic combination of satire and lyric, and include some of her most-loved and frequently discussed works. The professor and his mistress mock ordinary lives around them and in turn are mocked by the poet, yet they transcend the satiric mode in such lines as:

She cradled his Darwinian head.
Its intricate landscape of fine lines and scars,
ridges and hollows, veins' meanderings'
grew desolate in sleep. Above them spread
a leaf-divided tissue of space and stars.[20]

Despite her successes, in her letters to friends over this period Harwood, in the words of Gregory Kratzmann, 'chronicled her exasperation with what she saw as the amateurism, unprofessionalism, tardiness and cronyism of editors'.[21] In those early years Douglas Stewart, Geoffrey Dutton and Max Harris, and Kenneth Slessor (then editor of *Southerly*) were the objects of her scorn, as was Clem Christesen, whom she always referred to by initials only, 'CBC'. About these and other editors Harwood recounted to her correspondents a succession of lively and sometimes scandalous stories – for, as well as being an accomplished poet, she was an unparalleled letter writer. She never let a good story go unadorned and recounted her victimisation with relish – 'operatic as ever', as she described herself in 'Words and Music'. But it is also clear that her wit was fuelled by rage. For example, although she had published two poems in the new journal, *Australian Letters*, in 1958 and 1960, she complained to Tony Riddell that: '*Australian Letters* promised to print an Eisenbart in No. 5 and another in No. 7; neither has appeared. They have left two letters unanswered. You see what they do print – that pixie poem [which she had quoted to him].'[22] This was the burden of her complaint – editors published rubbishy verse, which showed they had no discrimination, and undermined the value of getting published in their magazine; furthermore their unbusinesslike correspondence amounted to insult.

Her main publication outlet in the first decade was Clem Christesen's *Meanjin*, followed by the *Bulletin*, then James McAuley's *Quadrant* and *Prospect*, the Melbourne Catholic magazine of which Vin Buckley was co-editor from 1959 to 1961. Her relations with Christesen were especially fractious. She sent Riddell the following acrostic sonnet (with its echo of Milton's 'When I consider how my light is spent . . .'), expressing her resolve to take revenge. The title refers to a poem actually published in *Meanjin*, and the acrostic reads 'Wreck that train':

'On a second reading of "Goods Train"'

When I consider how I used to write
Rhythmical verse, and keep my meaning wed
Ever to form; and see the rubbish spread
Carelessly through *Meanjin*: all the spite

Knavishness, nastiness, readiness to fight
That mar my lovely nature, make their bed
Here. I resign poetic maidenhead.
A-whoring I shall go, this very night.

There'll be no peace for Editors who take
Things like 'Goods Train'. I'll prostitute my art.
(Reserved exclusively for CBC
Are several 'translations', each a fake.)
I'll tout myself all round, a lyric tart.
No-one will know who is or isn't
G[23]

It was the *Bulletin*, not *Meanjin*, which bore the brunt of her most notorious poetic hoax. The story is well known: on 5 July 1961 the *Bulletin* published a pair of sonnets by Walter Lehmann, named for the famous medieval lovers, Eloisa and Abelard. When it was noticed that their first lines read acrostically 'So long Bulletin' and

'Fuck all editors' there was an uproar, not least because this use of the f-word was traced to Gwen Harwood, the 'Tas. Housewife' behind the Lehmann mask. She was besieged by journalists and feared that Donald Horne, then editor of the *Bulletin*, would instigate obscenity proceedings. Her relations with close friends Vivian Smith (who disapproved of the hoax) and Vincent Buckley (whom she suspected of having revealed her identity) were disrupted for some time. Yet she bounced back and kept successfully sending Francis Geyer and Miriam Stone poems to the *Bulletin*. Indeed, that journal published more than half of the poems she saw in print in 1961, an extraordinarily prolific year for Harwood. It also the year when the *Bulletin* changed hands and lost its long-time literary editor, Douglas Stewart.

Yet it was Clem Christesen and *Meanjin* that were the objects of her ongoing rage. In a letter to Alec Hope months after the *Bulletin* acrostic scandal, she summarised her complaints:

> CBC has treated me shamefully for years; he never pays me for the poems (I know he pays some others); he accepted one poem saying it was 'strikingly original' and returned it later with a rejection slip; when I wrote about this again he returned the poem again, without any letter, but with a nasty comment from some editorial assistant who spelt the possessive adjective as 'it's'. I don't care for his literary manoeuvring and will certainly do him over if I feel like it with acrostics up down and diagonally.[24]

The *Meanjin* correspondence files fill out the details of this conflict over the poem, 'Memento Homo' ['Remember, man [that thou art dust']]. Christesen accepted it, with two others, writing that it was 'the most strikingly original and the least personal', and added, 'I'm becoming more and more interested. Could you let me have a biographical note one of these days?'[25] Yet a year later he returned this highly praised but still unpublished poem without comment. Harwood expressed her disgust, and two months later, sent him another handwritten broadside: 'Dear CBC, I am SICK of the way you treat me – I have just heard from a friend in Melbourne that some of my ms poems were being shown round in Melbourne . . .' She added, 'You have not bothered to reply to my letter about the rejection of Memento Homo,' and concluded, 'you are not running a Parish Gazette. I really am very angry. I suppose you'll show this letter round too for people to giggle at.'[26]

In response to this she was sent an apology by David Moody, *Meanjin*'s poetry editor, with an explanation of how it might have happened that a joke on her envelope (intended for Christesen) became known to others in the Melbourne University English Department common room over tea.[27] But she heard nothing, apparently, from Christesen. It's no wonder she was angry, if sending Christesen a joke was a way of establishing some epistolary intimacy with him, despite her frustration at his incompetence. She clearly did not expect her letter to be passed on, unread, to a third party, the poetry editor.

In February 1960 Harwood wrote again to Christesen, responding to the news that she had won the annual *Meanjin* Poetry Prize with a cross query about why the prize money had been reduced from 10 guineas to 10 pounds. Yet to this note, she added in handwriting, 'with kind regards to you personally'. But he seems to have been immune to her charm – and perhaps intimidated by her – because from this time onwards there are no copies of Christesen's letters to Harwood in her *Meanjin* file, only his instructions to his secretary about how to reply to hers.

The 'Wreck that train' acrostic sonnet quoted above suggests that these frustrations with Christesen and other editors led Harwood to experiment with fakes – acrostics, pseudo translations and pseudonymous poems. Other sources suggest additional motivations – finding places for the profusion of poems she was producing at this time and experimenting to see how carefully editors read submitted work, or whether they would accept male poets more readily than female ones.[28] Whatever her intentions, it was clear that these pseudonymous publications revealed yet another failing on the part of editors – their clear preference for interesting European male poets over married female ones called Miriam Stone or Gwen Harwood. Geyer and Lehmann were regularly invited to meet editors for lunch next time they were in Sydney or Melbourne,[29] and Geyer was invited to read at the Adelaide Festival, though he declined.[30] The *Meanjin* archive shows that Geyer was treated with great respect by Christesen.[31]

Yet Harwood's experiments produced additional poetic personae, not just *noms de plume*. Geyer, Lehmann and Stone all had distinct poetic concerns, even voices. As many critics have observed, Lehmann allowed Harwood to articulate strongly passionate feelings and sometimes misogynist ideas, while Geyer was more sharply defined as a migrant writer and failed musician, whose poetry frequently expressed alienation and loneliness. Miriam Stone was invented as a stereotypical 'lady poet' who nevertheless allowed Harwood to contribute forcefully to the poetry of female complaint.[32] Harwood in later comments often stressed her life-long delight in masks and disguises, and recent criticism has fruitfully explored the creative potential of her pseudonymous writing.[33]

She also delighted in parody, which can be detected in traces of other poets in her own works and is brilliantly illustrated in her 'Variations on a Theme', where variations on the nursery rhyme, 'Here We Go round the Mulberry Bush', parody the work of Buckley, Dobson, Smith, McAuley, Hope, Geyer and Harwood. The series was originally planned as a hoax, to mock Leonie Kramer's editing the 1961 *Australian Poetry*. When Kratzmann reprinted it in *Collected Poems* he included the fake Editor's Note, which had been omitted from earlier publications: 'Australian poets in the past have shown such poverty of imagination that I myself have set the theme for this year's poetry.'[34]

Despite all these difficulties and diversions – perhaps because of them – Harwood was certainly not silenced. During the single year 1961 she published an astonishing twenty-seven poems in journals, under her three current names, as well as selecting more than fifty for the volume she sent to Angus & Robertson. After that volume had been published and enthusiastically received in 1963–64, she had no further problems having her work accepted and recognised in her own right.[35]

In her early years of publishing Harwood was sustained and encouraged by a number of important friendships, in addition to her lifelong friendship with Tony Riddell. At first her literary friends in Hobart were confined to Vivian Smith and his wife Sybille, and occasional meetings with Hal Porter through his friendship with Ann and Roger Jennings; her friendship with the painter Edwin Tanner also dates from this period.[36] Then, from 1959 onwards, she met Alec Hope, James McAuley and Vincent Buckley when they came as visitors to the English Department. In the early 1960s the musicians Rex Hobcroft and Larry Sitsky inspired her to work on her poetic language along more musical principles, and to take on a new dimension of writing, as a librettist.[37] But it was 'the professors' – McAuley, Hope and Buckley – who played a crucial rolc in encouraging Harwood to publish and to take on a public profile as a poet. She was initially critical of all these men, but they became good friends.

James McAuley moved to Hobart in 1961 to take up the chair of English at the University of Tasmania. As Jennifer Strauss points out, their shared passion for music formed the basis of the friendship between Harwood and McAuley, 'although she had little affinity with his political views and had been critical of his aesthetic judgment as poetry editor of *Quadrant*'.[38] He introduced her to visiting writers (although she did not always feel properly acknowledged as a writer rather than a faculty wife)[39] and encouraged her to take part in poetry readings and radio and television appearances, as a result of which she gradually became known beyond the readers of literary magazines. But she refused his invitations to review for *Quadrant*, and Buckley's to review for *Prospect* or the *Bulletin*, saying she did not want to write prose.[40]

When she first met Alec Hope she professed herself to be bitterly disappointed in him as a critic, though 'I adore the poet who wrote "Imperial Adam", "The Return of Persephone", "The Lamp and the Jar".' She described making him jump through a succession of hoops: his knowledge of contemporary American poets, of her own work, of Vivian Smith's. She wrote scornfully of his lecture on the poetry of Vin Buckley: 'a former student of Hope's, they take in each other's washing.' Yet at the end of the same letter, she reports how she told him 'in ravishing tones' how she loved his poetry and he asked her to lend him one of the American poets of whom he had professed himself ignorant.[41]

Over the next two years as they corresponded, Harwood joked to friends about her infatuation with him: in a letter to Alison and Bill Hoddinott she invented a *jeu d'esprit* of estimating how high a building you would throw yourself off for the sake of which men, putting Hope on the highest, along with their mutual friend Edwin Tanner.[42] Her public tribute to him, the poem 'To AD Hope' is both serious and gaily admiring of him as '*Glücklicher Dichter*! Poet as smiling man.' It begins with a witty anecdote, which sets up the themes of spirit and flesh that will move through the Eden myth to become a debate about the nature of poetry.[43] The poem may be read as making a public claim to Hope as both a mentor and a friend. Although Hope did not, as she had wanted, review either of her first books, he did publish an article, 'Gwen Harwood and the Professors', where he claimed to go in fear of her mockery; when, years later, he responded in kind to her poem 'To ADH', he called her a 'remarkable and rather terrifying poet'.[44]

Both Hope and McAuley encouraged Vincent Buckley to write to her, and these two met in 1961.[45] Harwood's first note to him promised wryly that 'I have 4 school age children and am quite used to listening; it will be a pleasure to listen to you for a change,' but she was soon writing of him to Tony Riddell that 'he was, contrary to expectations, not a scapular-bedecked knowall; he combined firmness and sharpness and arrogance with merriment and humility; it works quite nicely with Irish charm. I rather loved him in spite of my prejudices.' To the Hoddinotts she reported that 'Vincent & I spent the evening drinking endless pots of tea and tearing the literary field to rags,' and he 'uttered the lovely sentiment that I was now second only to AD Hope'.[46]

Such a combination of tearing down the opposition and building up her reputation was irresistible. Gwen's letters to Buckley suggest that she was more comfortable with this younger man's belligerent charisma than with the much-admired Hope's charm. They were soon deep in conspiracies to hoax and parody; indeed, Buckley's parody of Harwood's style, 'The Sentry', was published under the Harwood name, and reprinted in successive volumes of hers, and he published a poem as Francis Geyer in *Meanjin*.[47]

These new friends – all male, all academics – played no small role in the period of intense creativity that brought an end to Gwen Harwood's isolation in Hobart, launched her publishing career and culminated in the publication of her first book in 1963. Hope had suggested that she should think about publishing a volume[48] and wrote of her in his pamphlet, *Australian Poets 1950–1962*:

> One of the most interesting poets to emerge in this decade is Gwen Harwood, who has not yet published a volume of verse. She ranges from poems of great concentration and purity of feeling to a series of sardonic poems which together make up a comic apocalypse of characters, centring on the fabulous Professor Eisenbart. An incorrigible leg-puller, she writes under a number of different names.[49]

In 1961 she was the only woman among the ten poets discussed by Chris Wallace-Crabbe in 'The Habit of Irony: Australian poets of the fifties'.[50] Vincent Buckley also wrote about her in the company of other major writers (McAuley, Webb, Wright and White) in 'The Search for an Australian Identity'.[51] Buckley played a role in helping her to select and edit a volume of her poems, which she sent to Angus & Robertson in September 1961.[52] She heard nothing for months and asked McAuley to follow up when he visited Sydney. His enquiry was soon followed by an offer of publication,[53] but the book did not appear until early 1964.[54] Harwood's relationships with 'the professors' proved to be the best possible defence against 'the editors' on whom she had declared war.

The first review of *Poems 1963* appeared in *Meanjin*, the scene of some of her best and worst publishing experiences. This was a good one. David Moody, the poetry editor, welcomed 'the genuine originality of the sensibility' expressed by the poems, praising their 'clarity and concentration, their 'harmonising of complex image and rhythm', which 'bespeak a discipline of more than words'. His lengthy review considered the relationship between her satires (which he liked less well) and the savagery underlying her best lyrics, and whether the conflict between revulsion and acceptance they enacted might be a function of her 'wholly feminine' sensibility. Harwood told Tony Riddell that she detected 'the usual superior attitude'[55] but she would surely have been pleased that this review concluded by placing the book on a par with Hope's *The Wandering Islands* and as a contender internationally.[56]

Other reviews were equally enthusiastic: she was described as 'almost the best poet writing in Australia nowadays . . . combining, as nobody else does, the feeling of Mary Gilmore and Judith Wright with the craftsmanship of McAuley and Hope';[57] having written a first volume for which 'achievement' rather than 'promise' is the appropriate word;[58] displaying 'astonishing versatility';[59] and demonstrating 'an austere and mature intellectual poetry' with impressive scope.[60]

This last reviewer, Flexmore Hudson, commented that 'some of her work has a sinewy toughness and a power that are rare in women's poetry', but also noted, as if in compensation, that 'under the mask of Walter Lehmann, the reticent Gwen Harwood tells the truth of her tenderness and compassion'. The examples of Judith Wright and Rosemary Dobson had apparently failed to prepare male critics for these dimensions of Harwood's art. Most reviewers commented on her femaleness, and expressed some disquiet about the satires, as if the two were incompatible. JM Couper in *Poetry Magazine* praised her satirical comments on literary criticism, quoting the lines that compare Indians in the Amazonian forests feeding on the 'half-digested fruits' taken from the stomachs of apes and parrots with the way 'towering spirits caught/by your prick-eared wit are opened/ and an after-image of rapture, a fragment of passion/ savoured and sucked'. But he added hastily that it would be wrong to 'confine these poems within a literary context' for so many of them are 'sensitive, deeply won from a woman's experience'.[61]

The notional opposition between the literary and the womanly could not have been more vividly expressed. Similar assumptions about femininity being incompatible with cultural sophistication and art had greeted both Dobson's poems about paintings and Wright's philosophical themes. The only really negative review of Harwood's *Poems 1963* appeared in *Prospect*, the Melbourne liberal Catholic journal where Harwood had published poems (as had Francis Geyer) when it was edited by Vincent Buckley. There Evan Jones (a colleague of Buckley's whom Harwood had met and liked) recorded that he no longer believed 'Mrs Harwood' to be 'a genuine bluestocking': 'she did not really understand Ryle', and stood accused of anti-intellectualism (and 'sheer vulgarity') because of the lines in 'Critic's Nightwatch' about critics being 'solitary masturbators'. Apparently rattled by finding her poems hard to interpret, he wrote that her poetry only 'startles because it walks on such a fine edge between banality and nonsense'.[62]

Gwen Harwood's letters from this period make few references to these reviews, although she later referred to the 'praise lavished' on her first book. If the published letters are any guide, she was more readily hurt by the carelessness of editors than the opinions of critics – her criticisms of Angus & Robertson (like other poets, she made up variations on the name such as 'Arthritic and Rheumatic' or 'Anguish and Robbery') for delays, bad cover design and so on, were numerous by comparison.

Her second book, *Poems Volume II*, appeared in 1968 and by this time 'there was no doubt that she was recognised as a major writer'.[63] The reviews included some longer critical essays on her work by Chris Wallace-Crabbe and Dennis Douglas.[64] During the 1970s further critical essays appeared, and the publication of her *Selected Poems* in 1975 ensured that her work was read in universities and schools. She began to accept invitations to literary festivals, although she was always ambivalent about public life, fearing to become 'a performer instead of a poet'.[65] Her reputation went from strength to strength until her death in 1995. Her work has been the subject of several book-length critical studies, and her biographer Gregory Kratzmann has edited an invaluable collection of letters, as well as the *Collected Poems* (with Alison Hoddinott, the editor of her letters in *Blessed City*, and author of one of the critical studies).

The story of Gwen Harwood's emergence as a poet has several distinctive features when compared with that of her women contemporaries. She is the only poet in this group who did not attend university, though her reading of poetry and philosophy was probably wider than anyone else's in the group, and enriched her poetry. Unlike Judith Wright or Dorothy Hewett, she did not need to earn an income for her family, and could afford to focus on writing poetry. She was thus able to combine wholehearted wife-and-motherhood with an emerging literary career. Despite occasional expressions of self-doubt, she seemed to sustain her confidence and energy through the drama of her campaigns against incompetent editors. Yet she was even better at cultivating allies than she was at excoriating enemies: despite feeling isolated and even exiled in Tasmania during the early years of her marriage, she made lasting and inspiring friendships during that marvellous decade when she began to publish. She made a distinctive place for herself in the very male-dominated world of literary academe, revelling in its gossip. Much as she loved and admired the male poet professors, she freely competed with them, whereas Dorothy Green, who sought to make her career in the academy, felt unwelcome.

It was as a mature woman, supported by her husband and friends, that Gwen Harwood first published her work. She encountered some barriers but dealt with them productively by inventing those disguises that are key to her versatile and witty poetry. Like Rosemary Dobson, she exhibits 'wit, the high-spirited as well as the spiritual', that springs from a ground of belief.[66] Erudite and passionate, visionary and savage, the intellectual range of her poetry is matched by its emotional range. She and Dorothy Hewett, different as they were temperamentally, recognised their extraordinary position as poets – weavers of enchantment, partaking of the divine, but still earth-bound human women. Each wrote poems dedicated to the other. In 'Dorothy, reading in Hobart', Gwen Harwood exhorts her sister poet to:

> Charm with your haunting vox humana
> Merlin from his malign enchantment.
> Melt the black frost, mysterious angel.
> Heaven's long emptied of its gods.
> Fill the void with a woman's voice.[67]

This is exactly what she did herself.

Notes

1 'Words and Music', *Southerly*, 46(4), 1986, pp. 367–76, p. 369.

2 *Gwen Harwood: Collected Poems*, UQP, St Lucia, 2003, p. 3.

3 *A Steady Storm of Correspondence: Selected letters of Gwen Harwood, 1943–1995*, ed. Gregory Kratzmann, UQP, St Lucia, 2001, p. 40.

4 *Cutting Green Hay*, Penguin, Ringwood, Vic, 1983, p. 167.

5 One each by Harwood, Geyer and Lehmann in *Australian Poetry* 1961, and one each by Harwood, Stone and Geyer in *Australian Poetry* 1964: Jennifer Strauss, *Boundary Conditions: The poetry of Gwen Harwood*, UQP, St Lucia, 1992, pp. 22–3.

6 Having established the habit of inventing alternative poetic personae, Harwood added others later in her career, Timothy Kline and Alan Carvosso.

7 These portraits inhabit the letters she wrote to her friend Thomas Riddell during 1943, published in *Blessed City*, ed. Alison Hoddinott, Angus & Robertson, Sydney, 1990.

8 Harwood, 'Lamplit Presences', *Southerly*, 40(3), 1980, pp. 247–54, p. 249, and 'The Evanescent Things', in Jenny Digby, *A Woman's Voice: Conversations with Australian poets*, UQP, St Lucia, 1996, pp. 44–66, p. 49.
9 'Words and Music', pp. 372–4.
10 'Words and Music', p. 375.
11 'Time Beyond Reason', in *Gwen Harwood*, ed. Robert Sellick, CRNLE, Adelaide, 1987, pp. 13–21, 19–20.
12 Hoddinott, *Gwen Harwood: The real and the imagined world*, Angus & Robertson, Sydney, 1991, p. 26.
13 'Time Beyond Reason', p. 18; *Blessed City, passim.*
14 She did publish one poem, 'The Rite of Spring', in *Meanjin*, 3(3), 1944, p. 77.
15 Letter to AD Hope, 14 March 1961, *A Steady Storm*, p. 120.
16 Letter to Riddell, 4 September 1953, *A Steady Storm*, p. 46.
17 Quoted in Strauss, *Boundary Conditions*, p. 13.
18 Jennifer Strauss, 'Gwen Harwood', *Australian Writers 1950–1975*, ed. Selina Samuels, *Dictionary of Literary Biography*, vol. 289, Gale Research, 2004, pp. 107–113, p. 110.
19 GH to TR, 9 May 1962, *A Steady Storm*, p. 159.
20 'Panther and Peacock', *Collected Poems*, p. 54.
21 Kratzmann, *A Steady Storm*, 40.
22 GH to TR, 7 April 1960, *A Steady Storm*, p. 95.
23 GH to TR, 20 July 1960, *A Steady Storm*, pp. 102–3.
24 GH to ADH, 18 September 1961, *A Steady Storm*, p. 141.
25 CBC to GH, 11 December 1958, Harwood file, *Meanjin* Archive, Melbourne University Library Special Collections. Her response to this request is quoted and discussed in Sheridan, 'Suburban Sonnets: "Mrs Harwood", Miriam Stone and domestic modernity', *Australian Literary Studies*, 23(2), 2007, pp. 140–52, p. 141.
26 GH to CBC, 9 December 1959, Harwood file, *Meanjin* Archive. 'Memento Homo' did not appear until 1961, in *Quadrant*, 5(4), Spring 1961, p. 72.

27 DM to GH, 18 November 1959, Harwood file, *Meanjin* Archive.

28 See discussion of the varying motivations claimed by Harwood, or attributed to her, in Strauss, *Boundary Conditions*, pp. 21–4.

29 Harwood, quoted in Hoddinott, *The Real and the Imagined World*, p. 90.

30 Kratzmann, *A Steady Storm*, p. 41.

31 See Sheridan, 'Suburban Sonnets', p. 142.

32 A point noted by Stephanie Trigg, *Gwen Harwood*, Oxford Australian Writers, Oxford University Press, Melbourne, 1994, pp. 37–9 and further discussed in Sheridan 'Suburban Sonnets', pp. 148–50.

33 Cassandra Atherton, *Flashing Eyes and Floating Hair: A reading of Gwen Harwood's pseudonymous poetry*, Australian Scholarly Publishing, Melbourne, 2006.

34 *Collected Poems*, pp. 587–8.

35 Strauss, 'Gwen Harwood', *Australian Writers 1950–1975*, p. 111.

36 Kratzmann, *A Steady Storm*, pp. 39–40.

37 See, for example, Harwood, 'Lamplit Presences', *Southerly*, 40(3), 1980, pp. 247–54.

38 Strauss, 'Gwen Harwood', *Australian Writers 1950–1975*, p. 112.

39 Kratzmann, *A Steady Storm*, p.154; she told Riddell that 'Jim did not mention my poetry when introducing me' to John Betjeman, GH to TR, 30 November 1961, *A Steady Storm*, p. 146.

40 Letter to Alison and Bill Hoddinott, *A Steady Storm*, p. 140, is one of several such references in the letters of this period.

41 GH to Tony Riddell, 11 July 1959, *A Steady Storm*, pp. 75–6.

42 GH to A. and B. Hoddinott, 6 November 1961, 'Letters from Gwen Harwood', Fryer Library, UQFL332, folder 1.

43 *Collected Poems*, pp. 195–6. It was first published in *Meanjin*, 26(4), 1967.

44 Article published in *Australian Literary Studies*, 5, 1972, pp. 227–32; 'To Gwen Harwood', poem first published in AD Hope, *A Book of Answers*, Angus & Robertson, Sydney, 1978.

45 Kratzmann, *A Steady Storm*, p. 41.

46 *A Steady Storm*, pp. 121, 122, 127.
47 GH to TR, 5 December 1961, *A Steady Storm* p. 157.
48 Letter to GH quoted in GH to Tony Riddell, 18 September 1959, *A Steady Storm*, p. 80.
49 Hope, *Australian Poets 1950–1962*, Melbourne University Press, Parkville, Vic, 1963, p. 7.
50 *Meanjin*, 20(2), 1961, pp. 164–74.
51 *Hemisphere*, 8(1), 1964, pp. 14–17.
52 Kratzmann, *A Steady Storm*, p. 41.
53 Reported in letters November 1961, *A Steady Storm*, pp. 143, 144.
54 Reported in letter to Riddell, 9 December 1963, *A Steady Storm*, p. 185. The publication date is 1963 but it was not released until early 1964.
55 GH to TR, 18 December 1963, *A Steady Storm*, p. 187.
56 'The Poems of Gwen Harwood', *Meanjin*, 22(4) 1963, pp. 418–21.
57 TH Jones, 'Able to be romantic', *Quadrant*, 8(2), 1964, pp. 73–6, p. 76.
58 HP Heseltine, *Bulletin*, 28 March 1964, pp. 48–9.
59 SE Lee, 'Among the Minors', *Southerly*, 24(2), 1964, p. 133.
60 Flexmore Hudson, 'Slim Volumes', *Australian Book Review*, 3, 7 May 1964, p. 132.
61 *Poetry Magazine*, 2, 1964, pp. 131–7, p. 136.
62 'Two for the Seesaw', *Prospect*, 7(2), 1964, pp. 27–8.
63 Kratzmann, *A Steady Storm*, p. 155.
64 Wallace-Crabbe, 'My Ghost, My Self: The poetry of Gwen Harwood', *Meanjin*, 28(2), 1969, pp. 264–67; Douglas, 'Gwen Harwood: The poet as doppelganger', *Quadrant*, 13(2), 1969, pp. 15–19. Geoffrey Dutton sounded a rare critical note: in a review entitled 'Three Conservatives', he wrote, 'She is the darling of the academics, and one can see why': *ABR*, 7, 9 July 1968, p. 162.
65 Kratzmann, *A Steady Storm*, p. 255.
66 David McCooey, 'A conversation with Rosemary Dobson', *Antipodes*, 10(2), 1996, pp. 107–10, p. 110.
67 *Collected Poems*, p. 324.

CHAPTER SEVEN

Jessica Anderson, 1976

Jessica Anderson: Success delayed

Jessica Anderson was in her forties when her first novel, *An Ordinary Lunacy*, was published in 1963. Over the next fifteen years she wrote four original radio plays and several adaptations of classic novels for the Australian Broadcasting Commission as well as three more novels. It was *Tirra Lirra by the River*, winner of the 1978 Miles Franklin Award, that brought her widespread acclaim. She won the Miles Franklin again two years later for *The Impersonators*. Three further books appeared, the latest, *One of the Wattle Birds*, in 1994, her seventy-eighth year.

She was a 'late starter', as she described herself: 'I have often wondered if I would have done better if I had had an earlier start . . . but I may have done worse.'[1] By her own account, she started late because for a long time she could not afford the leisure to write seriously: 'I had always intended to write a novel,' she told critic Elaine Barry. 'What prompted me was Time's dread chariot, what allowed me were easier financial circumstances.'[2]

In fact, Anderson had earned an income for many years by writing magazine stories and radio plays. The stories were written because she needed the money, and she never signed her own name to them or to her early radio work. She said she wanted 'to make sure that they were ignored', and refused to reveal the pseudonyms she used. 'I began to use my own name when I wrote *An Ordinary Lunacy*, and since then have had the luxury of needing to use no other.'

Anderson's own perception of her professional life made a strict division between writing for money and writing seriously. 'I have never felt myself to be ignored as a writer, or rather, I did not feel UNJUSTLY ignored,' she wrote to me, adding that she felt 'fortunate in the recognition I have had since [*An Ordinary Lunacy*]', and in the support of the Literature Board. Yet this graceful account of the recognition she eventually earned gives no hint of the difficulties she experienced in getting the early novels published. It was not all plain sailing for the erstwhile anonymous magazine writer and radio scriptwriter turned novelist.

The story of Jessica Anderson's becoming a writer, then, falls into two parts, the first concerning her young womanhood and earning a living by writing (about which she has revealed very little), the second concerning her mature years, when writing literary fiction took her through many of the publishing pitfalls that befell an Australian novelist in the 1960s, especially a woman, before she became famous. Fortunately she deposited with her papers in the State Library of New South Wales a wealth of material that makes it possible to identify some of these difficultics and their resolution.

Jessica Anderson, the youngest of four children of educated middle-class parents, was born in rural Queensland in 1916 and educated at Brisbane State High School and the Brisbane Technical College Art School. Though she was an avid reader and 'never doubted that she would be a writer', as a child she loved both to write and to draw, and sensitivity to visual beauty, to shape and form, is evident in all her writing. Her choice of art school may have expressed her desire to be an architect, an impossible ambition for a girl in Brisbane at that time.[3] Yet she did not finish her art studies but at the age of eighteen left home and headed for Sydney. She made her way to Kings Cross, 'the only bohemian centre in the whole of the country' in the 1930s. The adjacent area of Potts Point, with its beautiful old houses divided into apartments and rooms rented by artists, is lovingly described in *Tirra Lirra*. There she met Ross McGill, 'a commercial artist who longed to be a painter', and lived with him for several years before they married. She spared her mother from knowing about this rebellion against the code of proper behaviour for middle-class women.[4]

To leave home and live 'in sin' was a radical move at the time, and among the women writers of this generation not even the rebellious young Dorothy Hewett matches it. Anderson herself accounted for the success of this venture with characteristic dryness: 'Youth, good health, and an optimism bordering on stupidity, had protected me from much damage.'[5]

If her autobiographical tales in *Stories from the Warm Zone* are any guide, her childhood was serene, affectionate and materially secure. Yet the family was somewhat socially isolated: her mother's family would not acknowledge her chosen husband, nor their children, and both mother and father were atheists and pacifists. They were considered strange by their neighbours not only for their political views but because for some time they refused to have the telephone and even gas and electricity connected.

The death of her father when Jessica was sixteen would have been a bitter blow. A good deal older than his wife – he was close to fifty when Jessica, his youngest, was born – he is portrayed in the stories based on her childhood as suffering from emphysema and often ill. A man 'conservative in everything but politics', she described him: 'He was stooped, sick, intelligent, fastidious, humorous, angry.'[6] Her parents' radicalism no doubt offered her early models of intellectual independence,[7] and the combination of such independence with early emotional security could account for her successful rebellion against the rigid social expectations of respectable young women. She once remarked that 'the most personal of all my themes is a resistance to authority,' and in the same interview mentioned in passing the 'restlessness' of women – a combination of themes that appears in her first novel and recurs in others.[8]

It was 1935 when she arrived in Sydney, and the Great Depression still prevailed. The people she got to know were 'poor, but very free. We had a good life.'[9] The first of her various jobs was in a commercial art studio. After a few years she and Ross McGill, now her husband, went to London, where they stayed until the beginning of the war, returning to Sydney in 1939. Jessica wrote stories for newspapers and magazines in both cities, and during the war she worked as a seasonal fruit picker in the Women's Land Army. It was during the postwar years that she started to write for commercial radio, which paid better than stories. Her daughter Laura was born in 1946. She divorced and married again in 1955, Leonard Anderson being the name of her second husband. This marriage, which brought the 'easier financial circumstances' mentioned earlier, ended in the mid 1970s.[10]

In Anderson's own estimation, while her early stories and commercial radio work were formulaic, and 'formulas, once learned, hang on . . . they leave a stain', it was the radio adaptations that taught her 'a sense of structure and an ear for dialogue'.[11] Working with novels by Charles Dickens, Henry James and Martin Boyd served as an excellent literary apprenticeship for the kinds of novels she had begun to write.[12] Her plays, which include an early version of *Tirra Lirra by the River*, deal with themes that recur in the novels: the conditions of women's work, creativity and identity;

crime as a vehicle for probing the human psyche; and the depiction, sometimes satirical and with deft comic touches, of Australian urban (largely Sydney) social life.[13]

Anderson's long-standing admiration for Henry James is evident in her attention to the uses of power, and the power of money. Among her contemporaries, English writers Muriel Spark, Evelyn Waugh and, especially, Henry Green were favourites. Some of these elements of her fiction can be seen in this deft sketch, from her first published novel, of a middle-aged businesswoman contemplating her lawyer son:

> As if she could see through his newspaper, Daisy cocked her head and smiled at him. She herself was quite at home in that world where promises and favours were accepted currency. Negotiation in such currency is tortuous and full of suspense. Daisy had the good nerves, guile and audacity necessary to it. She took pleasure in it, but was pleased that David did not, for though men inhabited this world, its prevailing character was feminine. She saw him taking straighter, grander, and less cluttered paths than hers.[14]

Anderson has said that she felt little affinity with other Australian writers and the documentary fiction that she felt predominated when she began to write seriously. The novels she read seemed to be 'mostly blokey and outback', and 'women were either mates, or martyrs in the kitchen . . .' Her writing, from the beginning, was dramatic, and its setting was the city. She has said that Christina Stead, in writing about Sydney, gave her courage. She also admired Patrick White – both writers too different from herself to be direct influences.[15]

No doubt her apprenticeship in publishing magazine and newspaper stories and commercial radio, undertaken out of financial necessity, taught her the need to be businesslike. Certainly her correspondence with publishers shows a highly professional attitude to writing – her polite but direct questioning of contracts, methods of paying royalties, and marketing strategies. She told an interviewer that she hated the negotiation involved in publishing.

> I think that the writer's position in the publishing world is very unfortunate. They come with their job already done, and they come to a buyer's market, and they're placed in the publishing chain, where all the others, publishers, printers and so on, have to be paid, and most have the protection of unions. The writer is the only negotiable element in the chain, so naturally he's screwed. Almost invariably you have to be highly successful to make any claims on publishers. And that hurts my sense of justice.[16]

Anderson's first novel, *An Ordinary Lunacy*, concerns a Sydney lawyer's fascination with a woman who is charged with the murder of her husband; they begin an affair but when he ends it, the woman commits suicide. It began as a short story, which grew and grew. When finally it was pruned to her satisfaction she decided to approach London publishing houses because, in the early 1960s, she could find no Australian publisher who had issued anything like this book. Other 'dramas of sexual obsession' by Stead and by Elizabeth Harrower had been set – and published – overseas.[17]

An Ordinary Lunacy was published in London by Macmillan and in New York by Scribners, and was 'widely reviewed', but commercially it was not a big success: 'it was a good start, that's all,' said Anderson in an interview.[18] Her assessment is modest. In fact, *An Ordinary Lunacy* was reviewed in the *TLS* and the *Sunday Telegraph*, the *New York Times* and the *New Yorker*. Its polish as a first novel was noted, especially the 'sparkling', 'taut' dialogue. While its intelligence and irony reminded the *TLS* reviewer of EM Forster,[19] its 'witty, urbane, funny, tragic story' about a woman betrayed by her lover reminded Australian critic Nancy Cato of Galsworthy.[20] Two other Australian reviews took opposing views of the novel, one seeing it as 'fundamentally nice', a 'standard bourgeois tale', albeit a complex situation seen from many angles, while the other grouped it with other novels dealing with the 'immoderate inner lives' of characters, commenting astutely on the way Anderson 'comes to the extreme passions of her protagonists by way of the nuances of social response'.[21] Clearly a political difference about the value of 'middle-class' fiction underlay this disagreement, but it suggests that the subtlety of her writing could not be gainsaid.

Despite the success of *An Ordinary Lunacy*, Anderson's second novel, *A Question of Money*, went the rounds of London publishers for over a year without success. Finally it was accepted by Bodley Head on the condition that Collins would distribute it in Australia, but Collins refused.[22] Anderson persisted, trying three more publishers, still without success. For some reason Macmillan, her previous publisher, was the last of the London publishers to look at it, but also refused. In October 1968, more than two years after it was first sent out, she received a reader's report from Curtis Brown's literary agent in Sydney, commenting that criticisms by publishers such as 'it lacks impact' seem nebulous to him. 'This book really has me puzzled – I feel it deserves publication,' he concluded.[23] Yet it never was published. Anderson's later view was that it was rejected because 'sex was new in writing and everything had to be strongly sexual or violent' in the style of James Bond. In this context, readers thought her novel was 'humdrum'. She considered revising it for publication in the late 1980s, when her reputation as a novelist was well established, but did not do so.[24]

While waiting to learn the fate of *A Question of Money* she returned to radio work, and found that the adaptations of James and Dickens for the ABC helped her to overcome her discouragement. She wrote another novel in which, like *An Ordinary Lunacy*, an apparently criminal act is again the focus of personal and sexual conflict. Published as *The Last Man's Head*, this novel involves a large and complex family configuration resulting from divorce and remarriage, which forces incompatible characters into close contact. The protagonist, aptly named Alec Probyn, suspects his wife's manipulative half brother of being capable of violence, and carries out his own investigation with compromising results.

Anderson sent this, her third novel, to Macmillan in London as the editor Alan McLean had invited her to do when he rejected *A Question of Money*.[25] It was instantly accepted, but McLean passed it on ('most unfortunately' in Anderson's view)[26] to George Hardinge, Lord Penshurst, editor of Macmillan's crime list. Anderson queried that decision, insisting that it was not a crime novel as such, but Hardinge would not let it go. The book appeared in 1970, again in both London and New York, but sold slowly, despite some good reviews. This usually happened with hardback crime, Hardinge conceded, although he would not concede to Anderson's apparent suggestion that it should have been published as a general novel.[27]

Reviewers disagreed. 'Not just a crime novel' was the verdict of Martha Lemming in *Australian Book Review*, who characterised it as 'a subtle, sardonic recreation of a man's state of mind, his reactions in a slowly emerging situation, and of his relationships with his fellows'. Cyril Ray in the *Spectator* found echoes of both Simenon and Ivy Compton-Burnett in 'this quite remarkable study of the springs of one kind of crime'.[28]

The exchange between Anderson and Hardinge illustrates her difficulties. As *The Last Man's Head* was being prepared for publication, it appeared that Macmillan had lost both Anderson's author publicity form and the reviews of her first novel.[29] Then Anderson had to return the contract to Hardinge because, she wrote, 'although it is signed it has not been witnessed'.[30] Hardinge assured her that 'contracts are pretty doubtful legal documents anyway . . . In any case this one was signed by Frank Whitehead, Chairman of the Macmillan Group, and I think is therefore pretty sound.'[31] An extraordinary 'reassurance', this, in which you can almost hear the undertone, 'My dear woman, don't worry your pretty head about legal documents.' After publication this exchange between author and publisher continued, mostly in a testy vein. They wrangled about the meaning of various clauses in the contract. Anderson queried the decision of Macmillan her then agent to pay Macmillan her publisher out of *her* half of the first advance from Granada for its proposed paperback edition.[32]

Apparently in response to her queries about the invisibility of *The Last Man's Head* in Australia, Hardinge reported to her the excuses made by Macmillan's Australian agent: he blamed the bookshops but added that that it is 'a great pity that you [the author] are not willing to go in for local promotion', thereby missing out on coverage 'in what is now referred to as the "mass media"'. This, and a later note from Anderson firmly rejecting any suggestion that her novels should be publicised in the *Australian Women's Weekly*,[33] suggest that her drive to be taken seriously as a novelist meant that she shunned publicity in the popular media. No doubt she shared Thea Astley's conviction that to be known as a 'woman's writer' would be the kiss of death,[34] and she was probably right. Hardinge at one stage hastened to reassure her that he was not only a crime specialist but had interests in Macmillan's general list, and to prove this he named two women writers of popular fiction – with whom she would probably *not* have been flattered to be grouped.[35] It was at this time that she contacted a London agent, Peter Janson-Smith, to help her deal with obstreperous publishers.[36] She wrote to him with some enthusiasm about her recent radio plays, although they have never been published.

There was another long delay, this time of five years, between the publication of *The Last Man's Head* and Anderson's next novel *The Commandant* in 1975. She often described this as her favourite book because she so much enjoyed doing the historical research for it. It is set in Moreton Bay penal colony, but is not so much a blood-and-guts tale of the convict system as a story of brutality seen aslant. *The Commandant* is based on the historical personage of Patrick Logan, and most other characters are also based on real persons. Those whose perspectives make up most of the narrative comprise three women, who are at Moreton Bay accompanying the men of their families, as well as a medical officer who is something of a social outcast, and the new commandant, sent from Sydney to take over when Logan's term ends. These characters observe Commandant Logan – his violent death is the mystery at the centre of the book.

Anderson described it wittily – alluding to Elizabeth Gaskell's stories of life in a 1830s English provincial town – as 'almost a case of *Cranford* at Moreton Bay'. She made this comparison with obvious irony, given the brutal context of the actual penal station, but also with justification. She had read Dickens and Mrs Gaskell intensively, in an effort to get the period dialogue right, but beyond such details, there *are* echoes of Cranford as a suffocatingly enclosed social space. And Anderson effectively juxtaposes the gentility of middle-class women's concerns against the brutality of the penal station, just as Gaskell presents the ladies of Cranford as exposed to the dire consequences of laissez-faire capitalism when the local bank fails.

This novel was originally entitled *The Mercy of Her Company*, a reference to the invented character of Frances, Logan's sister-in-law, but Anderson decided eventually on a title that would emphasise not the feminine but the 'equally important masculine' element in it. [37] Nevertheless Frances is the 'main carrier of the story', her author's 'witness and commentator'.[38] Her observations of the penal colony can convey its horror from a sensitive young woman's perspective, which is modified by those of other characters. On her arrival at Moreton Bay she sees from the boat deck a group of labouring convicts and their overseers:

> It was their great number, perhaps, or the clumsiness of their fettered movements that made them appear sub-human, like animals adapted to men's work or goblins from under the hill. She hated herself for her aversion to them, for the recoil of her spirit and the agitation of her heart. She was still standing between Louisa and Henry Cowper. 'Dear God,' she whispered, 'why must they look like that?'
>
> Both turned to look at her. She felt in their attitudes a kind of caution. 'Like what?' asked Henry Cowper.[39]

The manuscript was more or less complete when Anderson arrived in London for an extended stay in April 1974.[40] During this time author and publisher met, after which they addressed one another in letters as 'George' and 'Jessica'. (Previously he had addressed her as 'Mrs Anderson' and had signed himself 'Hardinge of Penshurst'.)[41] It is clear that Anderson regarded *The Commandant* as a serious novel when she suggested that Christina Stead might be asked to read it; she did not want to ask Patrick White, who was known to be writing a 'penal settlement' novel himself (it would appear in 1976 as *A Fringe of Leaves*).[42] Again, however, Macmillan let her down by issuing *The Commandant* with a dust jacket suggestive of a Regency romance.[43] Perhaps this was the inevitable fate of an historical novel with a female perspective, despite the fact that Anderson incorporates into the narrative a social and political context that goes beyond the domestic scene to dramatise the workings of power.

Such misleading marketing meant that Anderson's second and

third novels – one marketed as a crime thriller, the other as a historical romance – more than likely missed their best audiences. She gained a significant advantage in publishing her first three novels with Macmillan London, which ensured the simultaneous appearance of imprints with United States publishers, but neither *The Last Man's Head* nor *The Commandant* was as widely reviewed anywhere as *An Ordinary Lunacy* had been. This was likely because they were seen as genre fiction.

Yet historical novels have always been popular in Australia, where Tom Keneally had recently published *The Chant of Jimmie Blacksmith* (1972), and Thea Astley *A Kindness Cup* (1974). Both these titles by award-winning novelists were widely and positively reviewed, especially Keneally's. But *The Commandant* received only two Australian reviews. Judah Waten, the communist novelist, praised its documentary strength and 'vivid and terrifying pictures', but made no mention of the subtleties of narrative point-of-view.[44]

Jessica Anderson only became well known to Australian readers in 1978, with the publication of *Tirra Lirra by the River*. This novel was an immediate success: readers were captivated by the subject of a woman's life from youth to age, covering most of the twentieth century in Brisbane, Sydney and London, the themes of memory and reconciliation with the past, as well as the Tennysonian echoes of the title.

The focus on a single character, Nora Porteous, lent this novel a more accessible inner dimension than its predecessors. It takes the form of a series of flashbacks as Nora, now old and ill and back in the Brisbane of her youth, searches for the meaning of her past life. Here she describes something very like the movement of the story itself:

> My globe of memory is in free spin, with no obscure side, and although at times in its swelling and spinning it offers the queer

> suggestion that imagination is only memory at one, or two, or twenty, removes, my interest now is in repudiating, or in trying to repudiate, those removes, even if it ends by my finding something only as small as a stone lying on pale grass.[45]

Yet this novel, too, went through a long pre-publication period. It had begun as a prize-winning novella,[46] which she sent to Alan McLean at Macmillans in London in 1971. He advised that although it was beautifully written, it was an awkward length to publish, and so she expanded the English part after a stay in London in 1974. Angus & Robertson returned this version 'without comment'.[47] In November 1975 the radio play version was broadcast on the ABC. The novel was finally placed with Macmillan in Melbourne in 1977,[48] but even then Anderson had to reject firmly their proposal to change the title to 'The Crystal Mirror'.[49] On its appearance in 1978 the novel was widely and enthusiastically reviewed, and was awarded the Miles Franklin prize for that year. More substantial reviews in the literary journals (*Meanjin, Southerly, Westerly, LiNQ*) followed, and the American Penguin paperback in 1984 attracted a range of reviews from the *New York Times Book Review* to *Ms Magazine*.[50]

It had been a long twelve-year haul for Jessica Anderson. Wrangles with publishers, and even a major disappointment like the rejection of *A Question of Money*, are setbacks that may happen to any writer, of course. Like other Australians, Anderson faced a situation where until well into the 1970s Australian publishers were wary of taking on fiction that moved outside the themes of nationalist realism – and publishers in Britain could be offhand in their treatment of 'colonial' writers. Her position as a woman – and a woman with few professional contacts – exacerbated these difficulties. The invaluable archive of Jessica Anderson's professional correspondence reveals attitudes of patriarchal condescension on the part of publishers that it is difficult to imagine, say, Patrick White having to endure.

This archive also provides some insight into her strategies for dealing with the 'enforced domesticity' expected of her generation[51] – or what is today euphemistically called 'balancing work and home life'. She seems to have been one of those writers who develop a scheme for the whole novel (in her case, a group of characters) and who can then work on a small section at a time – a method suited particularly to women who needed, as she did, to set aside a few hours of each day free of her 'first job', the house.[52]

Jessica Anderson was, even more than most women writers, isolated from the Australian literary scene. Because she published abroad, reviewers of her early books frequently expressed surprise and chagrin that they had not known about her previous work. As we have seen, she disliked doing publicity for her novels, especially in the popular media, although some interview-based articles about her appeared in the weekend papers in the early 1990s. She was never a guest at the Adelaide Writers' Week, the premier event of its kind in Australia since the 1960s, although it is highly likely that she was invited.[53] She did hold several Literature Board grants – one for the writing of *The Commandant*, another for *The Impersonators*.[54] A novelist and playwright, she rarely published short pieces in magazines or anthologies, and she seems to have published only two reviews, one of her friend Nancy Phelan's memoir *The Swift Foot of Time*, and other of a novel by Jill Neville, who was also a member of Phelan's circle of friends.

Anderson had met Sydney writer Nancy Phelan in the 1960s at Macmillan parties, but it was only after her second divorce and move to live in Potts Point that they became neighbours and then friends. In her memoir *Writing Round the Edges* Phelan offers some glimpses of Jessica Anderson, who often stayed at her house in the Blue Mountains:

> I admired her guts and liked her humour, her quiet sometimes deadly wit and the surprising larrikin streak that flashed out occasionally. We both enjoyed walking and covered long distances in Sydney and later in the Mountains, talking endlessly of books and writing . . . Jessica was always on deck as a writer; because of her slight stammer she spoke slowly and rather deliberately, choosing her words carefully, explicit and often quietly witty. A word she liked to use was *guarded* . . . In fact, she was guarded herself.[55]

There is plentiful evidence that what held Jessica Anderson back – even after she started writing seriously – was her status as an Australian woman writer in a male-dominated and Anglocentric publishing world. Yet neither financial constraints nor problems with publishers ultimately stifled her, so it is equally important to ask, of her as of her sister writers, what was *enabling* for her development as a writer? It is clear from her professional correspondence and her interviews that, over the long period that preceded her fame, she had cultivated the qualities of character and strategies of survival necessary to sustain enough belief in herself to contend with neglect and condescension, and to go on writing.

Women's negotiations with this second-class rating have a long history, which Anderson evokes in *The Commandant* when Frances, the young woman, is advised: 'You must acquire a manner and refer your intelligence to it, and most of your instincts. That's the way it's done.'[56] Quoting these lines, an interviewer asked the author: 'You are writing here of colonial Australia, but the notion of an acquired self and a submerged real self is the subject of your other novels as well, isn't it?' Anderson replied: 'That is an acute observation. That is true.'[57] The tragedy of her character, Nora, in *Tirra Lirra* is not that she was an unrecognised artist, but that she 'doesn't succeed even in being *conscious* of being an artist'.[58] For Anderson as a writer, learning to tap into her 'submerged real self' was more important than recognition in the literary world. But I would suggest, too, that the acquired self was an effective survival strategy that helped her through the hard times, in the years when her creativity and intellect remained for the most part eclipsed from view.

The eclipse ended with the publication of *Tirra Lirra by the River*. After its success her earlier titles were reprinted and reviewed seriously and favourably in Australia. Her late works – *Stories from the Warm Zone* (1987), *Taking Shelter* (1989) and *One of the Wattle Birds* (1994) – were simultaneously published in Melbourne and New York (a consequence of the Penguin–Viking partnership of the late 1980s), and well reviewed in the USA and the UK.

In 1980, Anderson won the Miles Franklin prize for the second time, and also the Christina Stead Fiction Award, for *The Impersonators* (published in the United States in 1985 as *The Only Daughter*). Here she returned to the situation she had used in *The Last Man's Head* – multiple characters in a family rendered complex by divorce and remarriages. The action stems from the death of the patriarch and includes a love affair between his only daughter and one of his stepsons, and conflict over inheritance. The collection, *Stories from the Warm Zone*, was the *Age* Book of the Year in 1987.

All Anderson's later fiction has contemporary Sydney as its setting, except for the autobiographical 'Stories from the Warm Zone' in the collection of that title. The last two novels have youthful protagonists caught up in sexual confusions (*Taking Shelter*) and dealing with grief (*One of the Wattle Birds*) though in each case an older woman plays a somewhat mysterious and magical presiding role. In this respect, both these novels have an air of Shakespeare's late romances.

During the 1980s fiction publishing in Australia expanded rapidly. There was new interest in Australian fiction, as well as a significant new audience for women writers. In this milieu, from *Tirra Lirra* onwards, Anderson enjoyed the reception she had long deserved, becoming (along with Thea Astley, Kate Grenville, Elizabeth Jolley and others) one of the major female 'voices of the eighties' when, for a brief decade, it seemed that women writers had finally come into their own in Australia.[59] Elaine Barry's full-length study of her novels, *Fabricating the Self*, published in 1992, crowned this period of critical recognition.

Jessica Anderson died in Sydney on 9 July, 2010. *Tirra Lirra by the River* is the best known and most critically valued of her novels, yet it would be a great pity if she were to be remembered as a one-book writer. Each of her novels, as Elaine Barry has pointed out, is an experiment: 'she rarely repeats a note, no matter how successfully sounded.' She has used many genres – crime thriller, historical novel, comedy of manners, female *bildungsroman*, family drama – 'and with each fresh experiment Anderson transcends the expectations of that particular genre.'[60] Yet her preoccupations with the workings of power and strategies of concealment in human relations were constant throughout her career. Intellectually adventurous, emotionally wise and poetically concise, her eight published books constitute a small but precious literary legacy.

Notes

1 This and any quotations otherwise unattributed are quoted with permission from Jessica Anderson's letter to the author, 3 March 2006.

2 Elaine Barry, *Fabricating the Self: The fictions of Jessica Anderson*, UQP, St Lucia, 1992, p. 5.

3 Interview, Jennifer Ellison, *Rooms of their Own*, Penguin, Ringwood, Vic, 1986, p. 45.

4 Interview, Ray Willbanks, *Speaking Volumes*, Penguin, Ringwood, Vic, 1992, p. 17.

5 'Starting too late', *Meanjin*, 62(2), 2003, pp. 209–16, p. 214.

6 'Starting too late', p. 211.

7 Barry, p. 3.

8 Willbanks interview, p. 21.

9 Willbanks interview, p. 17.

10 My thanks to Laura Jones for these details: private communication, 6 July 2010.

11 Barry, p. 4.

12 The adaptations were broadcast on the ABC between 1966 and 1976, roughly the same decade as her own four radio plays were broadcast. See Barry, pp. 4–5.

13 Ruth Blair, 'Jessica Queale Anderson', in *Australian Writers, 1975–2000*, ed. Selina Samuels, *Dictionary of Literary Biography*, vol. 325, Gale, Detroit, 2006.

14 Anderson, *An Ordinary Lunacy* [1963], Penguin, Ringwood, Vic, 1987, p. 30.

15 Ellison, pp. 34–5.

16 Ellison, p. 42.

17 Barry, p. 5.

18 Ellison, p. 32. Barry lists reviews from Australia and New York, but not from London.

19 Reported in 'New Fiction', Martha Lemming, *Australian Book Review*, 10(4), February 1971, p. 70.

20 'Three New Novels', *Australian Book Review*, 2(12), 1963, p. 199.

21 Alan Davies, *Nation*, 2 November 1963, p. 22; HP Heseltine, 'Immoderate Lives: Four new novels', *Meanjin Quarterly*, 22(4), 1963, pp. 422–3.

22 Letter from Bodley Head to JA, 22 September 1967, Jessica Anderson papers, ML MSS 3773.

23 Letter Peter Grose to JA, 28 October 1968. Correspondence relating to *A Question of Money* is held in ML MSS 3773 add-on 2119.

24 Notebook, comments dated 6 May 1987 in ML MSS 3773 add-on 2119.

25 Letter from McLean to Anderson 29 February 1968, in ML MSS 3773 add-on 2119.

26 JA's Note, May 1995, ML MSS 3773 add-on 2040 1.

27 GH to JA, letter 7 October 1970, ML MSS 3773 add-on 2040 1.

28 Lemming, 'New Fiction', p. 70; Ray, 'New Thrillers: Strine crime', *Spectator*, 22 August 1970. No US reviews of this book have been traced.

29 Letter from Hardinge, 3 February 1970, and telegram, 21 March 1970, Jessica Anderson papers, ML MSS 3773.

30 JA to GH, letter 24 March 1970, Jessica Anderson papers, ML MSS 3773.

31 GH to JA, letter 1 April 1970, Jessica Anderson papers, ML MSS 3773.

32 JA to GH, letter [undated ?1972]. Hardinge's letter 19 November 1970 had mentioned that Tess Sacco of the London office had secured an offer from Panther to bring out a paperback edition in the USA, but I have found no further record of such an edition.

33 GH to JA, letter 19 November 1970; JA to John Ross at Macmillan Australia, letter 3 January 1980.

34 Astley interviewed by Ellison, *Rooms of Their Own*, p. 56.

35 GH to JA, letter 14 December 1973. They were Audrey Erskine Lindop and Sarah Gainham, who were both popular writers of crime and romance novels, the former also a movie scriptwriter.

36 Draft letter JA to PJ-S, 30 December 1973, Jessica Anderson papers, ML MSS 3773 add-on 2040.

37 Draft letter to her London agent, 25 March 1974, Jessica Anderson papers, ML MSS 373 add-on 2040.

38 Grenville, Kate and Sue Woolfe, 'Jessica Anderson: *The Commandant*', in *Making Stories: How ten Australian novels were written*, Allen & Unwin, Sydney, 1993, pp.1–32.

39 *The Commandant* [1975], Australian Classics Library, Sydney University Press, 2009, p. 24.
40 She refers to typing the final version herself, in a draft letter to Janson-Smith, 30 December 1973, Jessica Anderson papers, ML MSS 3773.
41 GH to JA, letter 14 June 1974, ML MS3773 add-on 2040.
42 JA to GH, 11 September 1974, ML MS3773 add-on 2040.
43 Barry, p. 6.
44 Judah Waten, 'Working Beasts of Moreton Bay', *Sydney Morning Herald*, 27 December 1975, p. 13; also Olaf Ruhen, 'Drama in the Shadow of Disaster', *Australian*, 6 October 1975, p. 6.
45 *Tirra Lirra by the River*, Macmillan, Melbourne, 1978, p. 140.
46 An early version shared third prize in the Captain Cook Bicentenary competition in 1970: Blair, 'Jessica Queale Anderson', p. 6.
47 JA note, May 1995, Jessica Anderson papers, ML MS3773 add-on 2040 1 (1).
48 In 1971 Macmillan had bought out Sun Books from Geoffrey Dutton and Brian Stonier and expanded its Australian office (AustLit database).
49 JA draft letter to Pamela Reid, 26 August 1977, Jessica Anderson papers, ML MS3773 add-on 2040.
50 See Barry's extensive bibliography in *Fabricating the Self*.
51 Merle Thornton, 'Invisible Women Workers: Feminism, consciousness and the novel', *Overland*, 182, 2006, pp. 36–42.
52 Ellison, *Rooms of Their Own*, pp. 43–4.
53 Ruth Starke, *Writers, Readers & Rebels*, Wakefield Press, Adelaide, 1998.
54 Blair, 'Jessica Queale Anderson'.
55 Phelan, *Writing Round the Edges: A selective memoir*, UQP, St Lucia, 2003, pp. 136 and 153. The stammer no doubt accounted for Anderson's dislike of public appearances.
56 *The Commandant*, p. 12.

57 Willbanks interview, p. 21.

58 Ellison interview, p. 37.

59 Gillian Whitlock, ed., *Eight Voices of the Eighties*, UQP, St Lucia, 1989.

60 Barry, p. 5.

CHAPTER EIGHT

Amy Witting/Joan Levick, 1952

Amy Witting's struggle to say 'I'

Of all the writers in this book, the woman we know as Amy Witting had to wait longest to see her work published in book form. She was fifty-nine years old when her first novel, *The Visit*, appeared in 1977. Although it was well received, another twelve years passed before her second, *I for Isobel*, was published and won her widespread recognition. It was short-listed for the Miles Franklin Prize, and brought invitations to contribute to anthologies and read at writers' festivals as well as enthusiastic reviews.

As a result, the stories she had been writing for many years were published in book form – *Marriages* (1990), *In and Out the Window* (1995), *Faces and Voices* (2000). She was given the Patrick White Award, for writers who have not received adequate recognition, in 1993. The years until her death in 2001 saw the publication, in rapid succession, of four more novels as well as her *Collected Poems*.[1] *The Visit* was republished, and her second Isobel novel, *Isobel on the Way to the Corner Shop*, won the 2000 *Age* Book of the Year Award. She was a writer who published virtually all her life's work during her seventies.

Her own comments vary on the relative invisibility of 'Amy Witting' for most of her life. At times she stressed the lack of opportunity to devote herself more fully to writing, at first because young women like herself were not accorded the privacy and leisure to write, and later because of the demands of her profession as a teacher of French and German. She agreed with the description of herself as '49 per cent writer and 51 per cent teacher'. More often she would blame herself rather than her circumstances, saying that she did not write enough, or rather did not keep enough of what she wrote because 'my critical faculties are higher than my creative faculties'.[2] Memorably, she told Peter Coleman that 'it's not other people's fault, you know. I really didn't produce enough, and I am like Harold Stewart [the poet] in a way. We both had a very long way to go to get to our own little corner.'[3]

The evidence of her writing suggests that she had 'a long way to go to get to her own little corner' not because she was uncertain of her vocation – she had always written stories and poems – but because her formative experiences were so painful that the journey to self-acceptance was long and difficult. Along the way she published a few stories that were much admired, but it took her a long time to make of the Isobel stories a vehicle to work through those early experiences, and find her own voice. The success of *I for Isobel* was a breakthrough that gave her confidence to rework and publish much older material, and released further creative energies in her. It was as if her long struggle to say 'I' as a writer was finally vindicated.

The writer known as Amy Witting was born Joan Austral Fraser on 26 January 1918 (Australia Day, hence her middle name). She grew up in the inner Sydney suburb of Annandale, the middle daughter of three, and was educated at the local Catholic primary school. Her father was a postal worker, and so the family would have struggled to maintain a respectable lower middle-class existence in the Depression years. But the difficulties that accompanied Joan's childhood appear to have been emotional rather than material, as suggested by the recurring family pattern in her stories, where a neurotic mother persecutes a scapegoated child, the father being effectively absent. This victim figure, usually seen by others as unacceptably 'different', develops an inner world that enables her to cling to a belief in her self and to survive. The emotional pattern of rejection, withdrawal and defensiveness is pronounced, and the Isobel stories add Catholicism to the mix, importing a framework of sin and redemption. These patterns are difficult to ignore, and they suggest a connection between the author's life and her art.[4]

Not only the recurrent pattern of relationships, but also the intensity with which incidents such as 'The Birthday Present' are recounted, indicate that the writing draws in autobiographical material. Here is the chilling opening of that story, which begins *I for Isobel*:

> A week before Isobel Callaghan's ninth birthday, her mother said, in a tone of mild regret, 'No birthday presents this year! We have to be very careful about money this year.'
>
> Every year at this time she said this; every year Isobel chose not to believe it. Her mother was just saying that, she told herself, to make the present more of a surprise. Experience told her that there would be no present.[5]

A closer connection between the writing and the life cannot be demonstrated, however. Witting was adamant that she was not a confessional writer and had no desire to revisit her painful past: 'I really was a very disturbed person. I don't like to look back to it,' she told Peter Coleman.[6] Whether overtly autobiographical, like Christina Stead's *The Man Who Loved Children* or almost entirely fictional, like Kate Grenville's *Lilian's Story*, novels exploring the struggles of young women in family relationships were widely read and passionately discussed during the second wave of feminism in the 1970s and 1980s. Witting's long-delayed Isobel stories found a receptive audience, one alert for the truths about female experience that had formerly been silenced. This audience was also inclined to assume that such stories were autobiographical, a tendency Witting, like most of her contemporaries, resisted. What is known about Witting's life comes from a few interviews, and from Yvonne Miels's research on the writer's early journals and unpublished stories as well as the Isobel stories.

As a lonely child shunned by her peers for coming top of the class, for being 'different', Joan Fraser read widely, and wrote poems and stories. At the selective Fort Street Girls' High School she continued to shine, and her exceptional academic abilities won her a coveted Exhibition scholarship to Sydney University. At the age of sixteen she published a poem in the *Sydney Morning Herald*, but was soon dismayed to realise how out of date her poetry was when she read the modernist-inspired experiments of James McAuley and Harold Stewart in the Fort Street Boys' High School magazine. These two young poets became her friends at university, where she took an Arts degree in English, French, German and Latin in 1935–37, and a Diploma of Education in 1939. Having already lost confidence in her poetry, she was now also 'shattered by James Joyce's prose': 'I was so traditional and I couldn't come to grips with what was modern.' Still, admiring Balzac, she turned to writing fiction and worked in her first novel 'which of course was never published'.[7]

Despite the brilliance of the group of poets and wits she joined – McAuley and Stewart, Donald Horne, Alec Hope, Oliver Somerville, Harry Hooton and others – Joan did not really enjoy her undergraduate years, explaining to later enquirers like Peter

Coleman that 'It was a very chauvinist society and girls were dolls and I wasn't . . . It was an extremely sexist society.' She recalled no solidarity with female peers such as Dorothy Auchterlonie or Beverly Tivey.[8] But she wanted to write, and so: 'I hung on, I hung on and I listened, I listened.'[9] She was remembered for her wit, but later dismissed this with the comment: 'I may have made things amusing for other people, but I didn't make them amusing for myself.' In this context she remarked that 'it was necessary to think like a man' and referred to the 'First Boke of Fowle Ayres' circulated at that time by Hope and Somerville: 'it's such a closed society and yet that filth, that dirty river running under the surface, so strange'.[10] There was an element of woman-hatred there, and she had to be careful not to appear too competitive.[11]

Although she was 'not a doll', she did want to be accepted as a woman as well as a mind. This dilemma, and its specific expression in her relationship with James McAuley, recurs in all her comments on her university years. The two young writers were especially close in her Teacher's College year, when she helped him with his master's thesis on symbolist poetry, making translations from French and German poets. Witting later wrote about the relationship in response to the book, *The Devil and James McAuley*, in an article called 'Brotherly Affection'. Such affection, she wrote, was what he offered her, but 'unfortunately I was not in the market for a brother, so we parted when Jim took up with Norma'.[12] In 2001, in response to another book about McAuley, she wrote a 'Posthumous Dialogue' with Jim's ghost in Purgatory. This amounts to an accusation that he had exerted himself to charm her before withdrawing from the sexual side of the relationship, telling her that she lacked 'physical allure', when he realised that her company had become alarmingly important to him. Her revenge, at that late date, was to tell him that 'you overestimated my devotion' when in fact 'I was drifting, too concerned with other problems to worry about romantic entanglements.'[13] The two stories are only superficially at odds with one another, but the theme of deliberate cruelty in sexual affairs recurs in her stories. Nevertheless, she was deeply moved by McAuley's death in 1976: 'I was jolted into serious verse by the death of a poet I associated with at University. I felt death all round me and prose inadequate.'[14]

Armed with the Diploma of Education, Joan Fraser became a teacher in the New South Wales state school system. For the next eight years she was moved from city to country schools and back again, until a longer stint in the far west town of Coonamble allowed her the time to write another novel, and to collect a rich hoard of stories from landladies, shearers and other battlers, stories she could imagine telling along the lines of a Faulkner novel, and would later publish.[15] In 1948, in the northern New South Wales town of Kempsey, she met and married fellow teacher Les Levick. She was now saved from the dread of spinsterhood, as well as having a job she enjoyed and was good at.[16] The final piece of her life to fall into place must have been the discovery when she was thirty-five that she was suffering from tuberculosis. This would explain not only her recurrent ill health but also her emotional volatility, and although it was a life-threatening disease she was fortunately responsive to the streptomycin treatment she received at a sanatorium in the Blue Mountains. She was required to stay there in virtual isolation for five months, and this experience set her to writing again, as well as providing her with the material for her novel *Isobel on the Way to the Corner Shop*, published almost fifty years later.

Returning to Sydney to live, the Levicks bought an old farmhouse at Epping, a newly developed suburb north-west of the city. Their only son was born in 1954, and three years after that Joan returned to teaching, first at nearby Cheltenham Girls' High School, and later in the Modern Languages Department of the selective North Sydney Girls' High School, where she taught until her retirement in the 1970s.

It was during her first unhappy teaching appointment in 1940 that she invented the pen-name that she would use later when she began to publish. Tyrannised by a sadistic headmistress named Amy Wicht, Joan understood that the woman was frustrated and suffering, but that 'you can't give yourself over entirely to your suffering' and take it out on others. She resolved then that she would never be 'unwitting' or unconscious in her dealings with herself and others, no matter what happened.[17] Hence the name 'Amy Witting' signals a moral resolve before she ever began to use it as a pen-name. This account does not, however, explain her retention of the hated teacher's first name, Amy. Miels points out its relationship to the French name, 'Aimée' ('beloved'), and suggests a subliminal link to the recurrent theme of love in her work.[18] The name's closeness to the French word for soul, 'l'âme', might also suggest a darker recognition of affinity with her tormentor.

When she joined the staff at Cheltenham in 1957, Joan Levick had published her first story in *Southerly* the previous year under her new pseudonym. Thea Astley, also a member of staff, a budding writer and another lapsed Catholic, became her friend and encouraged her writing. When they first met, she said in astonishment: 'You can't be Amy Witting!' But Joan Levick was indeed the writer Amy Witting, and would remain Amy Witting for the rest of her writing life.

It was during Witting's time in the sanatorium that a friend suggested she should try her hand at short stories, since she was never able to complete the novels she had been working on ever since university days. She took this advice and the short story became 'the genre in which I feel most at home'.[19] The stories she published between the 1950s and the 1990s, as they appear in the *Faces and Voices* collection, cover situations ranging from country town life to suburban socialising and school encounters. Many deal with male–female relationships across a range of classes and ages, yet her distinctive themes of rejection, shame and resistance lend emotional depth to stories ostensibly about people quite unlike herself, in situations far removed from her own. The stories are realist in style, but not in the fashion of traditional *Bulletin* realism; rather, the details indirectly and subtly convey information about characters and their perceptions. She uses dialogue or small inconspicuous acts to demonstrate the unconscious and often cruel impulses that drive behaviour, incidentally demonstrating how very difficult it is always to be 'witting' and conscious of one's motives.

Her first published story, 'The Strait of Hellespont', in fact climaxes in just such a moment, when a man's teasing remark to his lover unconsciously touches on a deeply wounding experience:

> . . . In the terrible pause his words hung on the air as innocent and unpardonable as a fart and he felt that the room was full of people shocked to silence, while his face began to burn red, as if his grandiose thoughts about love could be read upon it, and they went on looking at each other with a painful, wondering gaze.
>
> Helen began to recover and her face relaxed to a blank politeness. At length she would find a foothold in civility and then she would take command and extricate them from this ridiculous embrace, but the walk back to his boarding house would not be so arduous as the journey to the door.[20]

The story's title, referring to the legendary lovers Hero and Leander, lends a mock heroic dimension to the man's pretensions as a lover, paralleling his embarrassed 'journey' to the door with Leander's swimming the Strait of Hellespont to join his lover.

This first story was accepted for *Southerly* by its editor, the eminent poet Kenneth Slessor, followed the next year by 'A Bottle of

Tears'. Although they never met, he sent a message to Amy Witting through Thea Astley: 'Tell her I would publish any word she ever wrote.' She never forgot this encouragement, although she published only one further story in *Southerly* during his editorship, 'Peppercorn Rental', in 1961. During the 1960s she published two stories in the *Bulletin*, and two in the *New Yorker*.

In 1961, 'The Yellow Dress' appeared in the *Bulletin* (coincidentally in the same August issue as Gwen Harwood's notorious pair of acrostic sonnets) and 'At the Bottom of the Well' in December. This was the year when her university acquaintance Donald Horne became editor of the journal, and announced an end to the long tradition of the *Bulletin* being the major publishing outlet for short stories, because of the poor quality of work submitted.[21] It is likely that he invited her to submit her work, which he knew to be good. Both these stories were incorporated, in revised form, into the early chapters of *I for Isobel*, but had probably had a previous existence in one of the earlier unfinished novels. They offer a perfect illustration of Yvonne Miels's finding, that Witting reworked material from her youthful experience over long periods of time.[22]

Despite publishing relatively few stories during the 1950s and 1960s, Witting's quality was recognised by other writers, who included her work in the annual anthology *Coast to Coast* in 1961 (edited by Cecil Hadgraft), in 1962 (edited by Hal Porter) and in 1970 (edited by Thea Astley). The story that Porter published, 'The Weight of a Man', impressed Patrick White, who asked Witting about techniques of short story writing, a form which he was in the process of trying out (he published his first collection, *The Burnt Ones*, in 1964).[23] He later wrote to congratulate her on 'The Survivors', a novella published in the English journal *Stand* in 1975.[24]

'The Weight of a Man' had been rejected by the *New Yorker*, the leading international publication for short fiction, though in encouraging terms: 'Please try us again,' said their note. Witting then sent 'Goodbye Ady, Goodbye Joe', one of her rural stories, and it was accepted, and published in 1965. The editor had suggested dropping the long ending where focus changed from Joe to other characters, and Witting revised the story accordingly, learning a lot in the process. But she was displeased when a second story, 'The Early Settler', was intrusively revised without consultation, and when the *New Yorker* invited her to write a series of studies of old age, she refused, saying 'Sorry, I didn't have a large talent and I wanted to keep myself available for any ideas that turned up.'[25]

There are several often-told anecdotes about Witting's stories. As well as the *New Yorker* anecdote, there is the famous *Tabloid Story* saga, involving parody, a pseudonym and accusations of obscenity. As Witting told the tale some twenty years later, it all began when Thea Astley's edition of *Coast to Coast* received an insulting review, which singled out Witting's story, 'The Man with the Impediment', as 'Gothic' (presumably because of its incest theme) and inept.[26] The author of this attack was one of the founding editors of the *Tabloid Story* experiment, which made new opportunities for the publication of short fiction by placing a selection of stories as an insert, like a cuckoo's egg, in other magazines.[27] Much of the new fiction was concerned with sex, drugs and rock 'n' roll, and Witting was appalled by a pair of stories by Frank Moorhouse and Michael Wilding that described, in fashionably direct language, the rape of an unconscious woman. She was appalled by the sexism and by the libertarian bullying implied – attitudes all too familiar from her own youth. Under the genderless pseudonym of 'Chris Willoughby', Witting submitted to *Tabloid Story* a parodic story 'in their own idiom, which was a lot easier than they thought'. In 'A Piece of This Puzzle Is Missing' the sex object, the muted girl, speaks back and tells her own story – an allusion to the character muted by sexual trauma in 'The Man with the Impediment'. The four-letter word she utters, which shocks her boyfriend, is 'love'.

When the story was accepted for publication the author confessed that she was in fact Amy Witting, and explained how the story had come to be written. Nevertheless the editors went ahead and printed it and, as luck would have it, the magazine in which that issue of *Tabloid Story* was inserted, in July 1974, was *Education*, the NSW Teachers' Federation journal. The satirical context was lost. Hundreds of angry letters protested against the 'obscenity' of the Amy Witting story, and it was tabled in state parliament. *Education*'s radical editor was interested in the prospect of an obscenity trial – this was a period of activism against censorship laws – but Witting was having none of that.[28] When it was discovered that Amy Witting and the highly respected senior mistress in modern languages at North Sydney Girls' High School, Joan Levick, were one and the same person, the furore died down.[29] Witting must have made her peace with *Tabloid Story*, for she published a second story, 'Report on a Rejected MS' there later in 1974, and in 1975 Michael Wilding published her novella 'Survivors' in *Stand*, when he edited the 'Australian new writing' issue.

Witting thought of the short story as 'the bystander's genre', not springing from personal experience but based on 'collectable' ideas, from news items or other people's conversations. Yet reading her collected stories, *Faces and Voices*, it becomes clear that her distinctive themes recur, lending tension to story ideas that are sometimes so slight as to be little more than anecdotes. In the preface to this volume she suggested that 'it may be the balance between the intrusion of the outside world and the inner world of the writer that makes the great short stories so memorable.' This is surely the case with her own best stories. Chekhov was her mentor.[30] Like her friend Thea Astley, she represented the short story genre as a demanding art, where the gap between good and bad is greater than in other forms of writing.

One explanation for the delayed recognition of her achievement may be the perennial problem of the genre – that short stories disappear into the literary wallpaper, especially in Australian publishing. Collections of short stories are rarely published unless the writer has already established a name as a novelist. Witting herself took a more optimistic position on this when she wrote that in the 1990s the literary scene, no longer haunted by the elusive Great Australian Novel, 'is so much expanded that there is room for the oddball and the small talent, the narrator of episodes and celebrator of moments, whether in prose or verse. It is good to have lived to see that transformation'.[31]

Twenty years earlier she had felt that she should attempt the novel form. When she was awaiting the publication of her first novel, *The Visit*, in 1977, she wrote to a former student: 'It is not a very ambitious effort. I was rather tentative, using a new form . . . [but] a necessary undertaking, I think, for a prose writer.'[32] Witting wrote this novel while on long service leave from teaching. It is set in a fictional country town in northern New South Wales, based on her experience of Kempsey. It concerns a group of teachers and other professionals of the town who meet in a play-reading group and are engaged in a production of Beckett's *Endgame*. At the same time the librarian, a single mother with a sixteen-year old son, is asked to help a biographer find out about a poet named Fitzallen who lived briefly in the town some forty years before and wrote poetry about its river, including some love poems. Uncovering the identity of his mystery lover becomes one strand of the plot, and the literary references expand the novel's range, but the central dilemmas explored are those of the two main female characters. Their uncertain love lives are resolved in a benignly comic manner, with a marriage and a pregnancy.[33]

When *The Visit* appeared in 1977 it was quite well received, but the review that really pleased Witting was Barry Oakley's, when he compared her to Chekhov.[34] This was a particular triumph because Chekhov was her hero, and she had argued with her editor at Nelson, the redoubtable Beatrice Davis, about her use of dialogue which, she felt, needed to be illogical, as in Chekhov, where 'everybody talks about two things at once and harks back and so on'.[35] Davis was Thea Astley's editor, and Astley had followed her from Angus & Robertson to Nelson in 1974, which may account for Witting's decision to submit the manuscript to Nelson.

Witting's relationship with Davis, unlike Astley's, was not a happy one. She felt pressured by the editor to come up with the Great Australian Novel, but Davis hated her second novel, *I for Isobel*: 'No mother has ever behaved so badly!' she insisted.[36] It is not clear exactly what happened to this manuscript at Nelson. Witting said later that it was accepted and then 'unaccepted' the following year, 1980.[37] But that was the year when Nelson London reconsidered its Australian publishing program and decided to cut back on general publishing because the company had lost money on novels and poetry, and soon after this Davis lost her job there.[38] This commercial decision might well have been a factor in the company's rejection of *I for Isobel*.

After the Nelson rejection Witting rewrote and submitted the novel elsewhere, in vain. She tried University of Queensland Press and Macmillan. She had an agent, who 'forgot about it', forcing the author to retrieve the manuscript from her office.[39]

A second factor that might have influenced the fate of *I for Isobel* concerns the literary community. *The Visit* was proofread with the help of Anne Robson, Witting's old friend from North Sydney Girls' High, then Lady Kerr, and it was launched by her husband, Sir John Kerr, the governor-general.[40] Since Kerr's dismissal of the Whitlam Labor government in November 1975, he had been vilified by most of the arts community. Witting's choice of Sir John to launch her book was a gesture of loyalty to their friendship, but it could well have influenced people against her. Patrick White, for instance, in his memoir *Flaws in the Glass*, refers scornfully to Amy Witting (without naming her) as 'a woman writer whose work and character I had always respected, till her continued loyalty to . . . Anne Kerr became difficult to understand as history was made and the dramatis personae came out in their true colours.'[41]

In the end, Witting rewrote the book as *she* wanted – and put it away in a drawer.[42] There it stayed for almost a decade, until she asked a former student to take it to Curtis Brown in London for her in 1987. They passed it on to Curtis Brown in Sydney, who loved the book and sold it to Penguin Australia, and it was launched on its successful journey into print.[43]

During the 1980s, before *Isobel* finally saw the light of day, Witting published poetry, almost exclusively.[44] Fitzallen's poems in *The Visit* were of course hers, but the real return to her first love happened in 'a moment of illumination', as she told Yvonne Miels, when

> I saw myself as a 'real' poet – that was in 1980, in the archives at Augsburg, where I was studying the life of a friend who spent four years there in a Displaced Persons camp. I came across the Ricarda Huch poem which I translated then and there as 'The Street of Pain', giving up research for poetry with relief.[45]

This poem appeared in her self-published collection *Travel Diary* in 1985. Throughout the 1980s Witting's poems appeared regularly in *Quadrant*, where Vivian Smith was poetry editor. In the early 1990s *Overland*, under Barrett Reid's editorship, was her main outlet, until Angus & Robertson published the collection, *Beauty is the Straw*, in 1991, and Penguin brought out her *Collected Poems* in 1998.

Witting's poetry displays a delight in the beauty of the world, which rarely shows in her fiction, and pleasure in word-spinning, which does. Both those qualities are evident in the short poem 'Riddle', which also evokes her early love of Gerard Manley Hopkins' poetry in its use of alliteration and compound words:

Glass glinting spearsharp atop the guardwall,
shards strewn spiteful in fool's footsteps,
river of ripples flowing among friends,
despair dressed brightly in bold disguise,
foil fierce to pierce excess of pity,
silver key for springing the stubborn lock.
What am I?

I am laughter.[46]

What is most striking about this poem to a reader familiar with her fiction is the swift series of transitions from cruelty to warmth to defensiveness to release. This is certainly characteristic of her best known novel.

I for Isobel was published in Australia by Penguin in 1989 to great acclaim. It received good reviews in the *New York Times Book Review* and the *New Yorker* (whose reviewer said she was 'like Jean Rhys, but has more starch, or vinegar'[47]). It won the Fellowship of Australian Writers Barbara Ramsden Award, and was hot favourite for the Miles Franklin that year, although the prize went to Tom Flood's *Oceana Fine*. Eminent younger writers Helen Garner and Janette Turner Hospital both told Witting how deeply and painfully they identified with Isobel's struggle to speak out as a woman, and to redeem her tormented past.[48]

It was a narrative ahead of its time. As Witting told an interviewer:

> I think child abuse was just coming into focus, people were just beginning to see the permanent damage that can be done emotionally in a domestic situation. The letters I've had from people in their 60s and 70s who said they'd wept Isobel's 'artesian tears'. Also there were people who didn't want to accept that, who didn't want sacred motherhood to be attacked.[49]

The manner of her writing, however, ensures that *Isobel* stands out in a regiment of other child abuse stories. One reviewer, singling out 'her outrageous comedy, grounded often in black passion', characterised Witting as 'this sophisticated, individual writer, intense yet ice-cool, her apparent simplicity masking subtle technique'.[50]

With the Isobel figure, Witting's characteristically restrained irony and subtle humour are released into a degree of savagery that makes these stories especially memorable. Here, for example, is a passage from the final chapter of *I for Isobel*, where the girl wakes in the morning in a strange man's bed. She wanders across the room, naked, to inspect his bookshelf and the following dialogue takes place between Isobel and her self and the man.

> "Now I wonder,' he said vaguely, not wondering, "about girls like you. I wonder why you do things like this."
>
> What does he mean, 'things like this'? There's only one thing like this.
>
> That's the question, though. The one with the hundred inadequate answers.
>
> There's the connection with love – the dubious connection.
>
> You do it because you can. Two ways to do it and our Isobel would get it wrong.
>
> You like to join the human race at the only level you can manage.
>
> There is a deeper reason, but it has no words. It is a landscape, an

unlighted desert strewn with epic lumber, dead machines, stopped clocks. All my own work. Call it INERTIA.

Wouldn't he gape if you said it was a religious rite – perform it often enough and the god might descend.

"I might wonder why you do things like this. But I don't think I would have asked."

Who said that?

You did, and in a tone you didn't know you could use, detached and easy.

It was the book. There was no doubt about it, the calm she felt flowed into her from the solid little faded book in her hand. She read the title, *Words of the Saints*. Mysterious.

A feeling of freedom, of stepping out of chains.

He said, "It doesn't mean much to you physically, that's obvious."

Oh. He had caught on to that. Even on that level, you can't really join the human race.

She said, "Is that a real question? I mean, do you want to know the answer?"

"I would hardly have asked if I didn't." But he sounded shaken, defensive.

"You might have wanted me to know that you disapproved of me."

The bedsprings squawked. To be accused of disapproval was a keen thrust.

You're not yourself, Isobel. You're somebody a whole lot smarter.

And that was a reason for leaving him alone; if she was smarter than he was, she could afford to.[51]

Amy Witting's emergence as an acclaimed writer may be seen as a triumphant synthesis of her practice of the short story as a vehicle for other people's stories, and her need to understand and transform into art her own experience of rejection, as a child and as a young woman. *I for Isobel* married the art of the short story to the narrative of self-acceptance suggested by the book's title: Isobel survives her abusive mother and alienation from her peers, finally to emerge as a writer. The novel is presented in the form of five stories, one the length of a novella, which are bound together by recurring themes of rejection and resistance, finally resolved in Isobel's realisation that writing can heal rather than harm. The economy and intensity of the short story form enhances the narrative, so that the girl's suffering is rendered without sentimentality, and the forward narrative movement is fuelled by her desire to restore the unknown part of herself that has been buried under her defences.

Critic Peter Craven is one of the few to have explored the form of this novel. He called it a 'poetic novel' comparable to Joyce's *Portrait of the Artist as a Young Man*, structured on 'a set of scenes which get their continuity from the vision within them'. Locating it historically, he wrote that '*I for Isobel* burst onto the Australian literary world like a coda to a lost tradition,' one made up of voices marginalised and sometimes silenced in the 'wasteland of Australian publishing in the 40s and 50s', a tradition made up largely of the 'quieter and subtler voices, which were liable to be the voices of women'.[52]

Like other women novelists of her generation, Amy Witting's approach to questions of sexuality and sexual politics displeased commercial editors and publishers. Yet it did not sit well, either, with the new writing promoted by the young male writers such as Moorhouse and Wilding. Her *Tabloid Story* experience of 1974, like Elizabeth Jolley's encounter with Outback Press, graphically demonstrated that. In these respects, writing from a distinctively critical female point of view – unlike Thea Astley's decision to write from a male perspective – was a disadvantage right up until around 1980. Witting's work published in the 1960s and 1970s was too early for feminism, and then she all but missed the 'women writers' bus of the 1980s.

The gaps and silences in Witting's publishing record are mostly explicable in terms of her own self-criticism and diffidence about sending her work out into the world uninvited. Behind this lack of confidence lies the long journey she had to make to reach her own corner of the literary world. She did not seek its centre stage, and her professional identity was as much as a teacher as a writer. Beyond these personal factors, however, was the problem of her chosen genre, the short story, which had few local outlets for publication and even fewer opportunities for serious critical appreciation. Yet when she eventually tackled the genre of the novel, making a strong start with *The Visit*, the rejection of her second novel marked a crucial failure on the part of Australian publishers to take on this story of an evil mother and an awkward, isolated young woman. The appearance of *I for Isobel*, already delayed by some forty years until Witting was ready to complete the book, was then delayed by another decade. If it had not appeared at all, Witting would be known in literary circles as a good poet and a fine short story writer. But she would not have had the chance to make the wide and lasting impression she made with her portrait of the artist as a young woman.

The delayed publication of her best novel from 1980 until 1989 had a profound effect on Witting's literary reputation, for it was during the 1980s that the 'decade of the women' brought to prominence a new group of women writers, several of them of Witting's own vintage – Jessica Anderson, Elizabeth Jolley and Olga Masters (who published her first novel in 1982). Missing out on this women writers' revival of the 1980s, Witting was not included in any of the significant interview collections by Guiffre, Baker and Ellison, or in *Eight Voices of the Eighties*. Further down the track, her work has received no sustained critical attention, apart from reviews and a doctoral thesis,[53] and her name is left out of recent compendia such as the *Macquarie PEN Anthology of Australian Literature* and the *Cambridge History of Australian Literature*, both published in 2009.

I believe her work is neglected today partly because she missed the decade of the women and partly because she writes uncompromisingly about characters who, by virtue of their age or oddness, are misfits in a world that has little time for such women. Yet *I for Isobel* and the four novels, three story collections and two volumes of poetry that followed it constitute a significant contribution to the tradition of Australian women's writing – all of it published after Witting turned seventy.

Notes

1 The four novels were: *A Change in the Lighting* (1994), *Maria's War* (1998), *Isobel on the Way to the Corner Shop* (1999) and *After Cynthia* (2001).

2 Ian Hicks, 'Understated writer honoured', *Sydney Morning Herald*, 20 November 1993, p. 7.

3 Peter Coleman, Interview with Amy Witting, 1992, National Library of Australia Oral History TRC 2864, Transcript p. 44. Stewart was a contemporary at Sydney University, a close friend of James McAuley and co-conspirator in the Ern Malley hoax of 1944. Witting seems here to allude here to Stewart's journey towards self-acceptance as a homosexual man, and his expatriate life in Japan.

4 As suggested by Yvonne Miels, 'The Net Under the Tightrope: The poetry and prose of Amy Witting', unpublished PhD thesis, Flinders University, 1997, pp. 12–14. The present chapter is much indebted to Miels's ground-breaking work.

5 *I for Isobel*, Penguin, Ringwood, Vic, 1989, p. 1.

6 Coleman interview, transcript, p. 49.

7 Coleman interview, transcript, pp. 5–7.

8 Dorothy Auchterlonie Green, poet and critic (see Chapter 5); Beverly Tivey became a film and book reviewer.

9 Coleman interview, transcript, p. 9.

10 Coleman interview, transcript, p. 11.

11 Cassandra Pybus, *The Devil and James McAuley*, UQP, St Lucia, 1999, pp. 10–11.

12 Witting, 'Brotherly Affection', *Australian*, 14 August 1999, n.p. (sourced Factiva Inc, March 2010). Refers to Norma Abernathy, whom McAuley married in 1942.

13 Witting, 'Posthumous Dialogue concerning certain errors in Michael Ackland's *Damaged Men*', *Quadrant*, 45(11), November 2001, pp. 37–9.

14 AW to Sabina Flanagan, 27 February 1977. Thanks to the recipient for letting me have a copy of this letter.

15 Coleman interview, transcript, p.8.

16 In her first miserable teaching appointment, at Riverside domestic science (that is, non-academic girls') high school in Sydney, 'I thought I was going to be a spinster and I was going to have a job I hated and I was simply not going to give in': Coleman interview, transcript p. 20.

17 Coleman interview, transcript, pp. 18–20.

18 Miels, 'The Net Under the Tightrope', p. 11.

19 Witting, 'Preface', *Faces and Voices: Collected Stories*, Penguin Viking, Ringwood, Vic, 2000, pp. xi–xii.

20 *Faces and Voices*, p. 48.

21 Miels, 'The Net Under the Tightrope', p. 25.

22 Miels, p. 33.

23 Miels, p. 25.

24 Letter to AW, 7 July 1975: Witting papers, ML MSS 5303, ML 13/89, State Library of NSW. Cited in Yvonne Miels, 'Amy Witting', *Australian Writers 1975–2000*, ed. Selina Samuels, *Dictionary of Literary Biography*, vol. 325, Gale, Detroit, 2006.

25 Coleman interview, transcript, pp. 23–4.

26 Brian Kiernan, 'A glut of sameness', *Australian*, 21 November 1970, p. 22.

27 Michael Wilding, 'The *Tabloid Story* Story' in *The Tabloid Story Pocketbook*, ed. Wilding, Wild & Woolley, Sydney, 1978, pp. 295–316. Elizabeth Jolley published an early story in a *Tabloid Story* insert in the rock music magazine *Loose Licks* in 1976 (see Chapter 9).

28 Coleman interview, transcript, pp. 27–9.

29 Janette Turner Hospital, 'A Writer Comes in from the Cold', *Sydney Morning Herald*, 14 October 1989, p. 80.

30 Witting, 'Preface', *Faces and Voices*.

31 Witting, 'Surviving', *Southerly*, 57(3), 1997, pp. 235–7.

32 AW to Sabina Flanagan, 27 February 1977. Thanks to the recipient for letting me have a copy of this letter.

33 *The Visit*, Nelson, Melbourne, 1977.

34 Oakley, 'Rituals of the Heartland', *National Times*, 5 December 1977, p. 57.

35 Coleman interview, transcript, pp. 16–17.

36 Witting, 'Surviving'.

37 Hospital, 'A Writer Comes in from the Cold'.

38 Jacqueline Kent, *A Certain Style: Beatrice Davis, a literary life*, Penguin, Ringwood, Vic, 2001, pp. 283–5.

39 Coleman interview, transcript, p. 34.

40 Coleman interview, transcript, pp. 31–2.

41 *Flaws in the Glass*, Cape, London, 1981, p. 230. Witting identifies herself as this woman in the Coleman interview.

42 Coleman interview, transcript, pp. 34–5.

43 Coleman interview, transcript, pp.43–4.

44 During this ten-year gap in her publication of fiction, only one story appeared: 'The Rescue', in *Quadrant* in 1983. This was the year that Peter Coleman, along with Robin Marsden, became editor, so I surmise that he asked her for a story.

45 AM letter to YM, 30 November 1994. Quoted in Miels, 'The Net Under the Tightrope', p. 35.

46 Witting, *Collected Poems*, Penguin, Ringwood, Vic, 1998, p. 66.

47 Anon, *New Yorker*, 23 July 1990, p. 88.

48 Coleman interview, transcript, pp. 44–5.

49 Jason Steger, 'A is for Amy', *The Age*, 26 August 2000, p. 3.

50 Verna Coleman, 'Portrait of the Artist as a Young Girl', *Quadrant*, 34(1–2), 1990, pp. 110–11.

51 *I for Isobel*, pp. 132–3.

52 'Peter Craven looks at the career of Amy Witting and reviews her latest book, *In and Out the Window*', *Australian Book Review*, 174, September 1995, pp. 40–42.

53 Miels, 'The Net Under the Tightrope'.

CHAPTER NINE

Elizabeth Jolley, 1979

Elizabeth Jolley: An outsider comes in from the cold

For sheer drama, Elizabeth Jolley's literary success story is unmatched in the annals of Australian literature.

Born in 1923 in Birmingham, Jolley emigrated to Australia with her husband in 1959. For many years she sent out stories and novels in a steady stream, but few appeared in print until her first book of short stories in 1976. She then published nine novels in rapid succession and another book of stories: ten books in as many years. Over the years from 1990 to 2001, six more novels and several other titles appeared. She won many literary awards, including the Miles Franklin Award in 1986 and a Literature Board Senior Fellowship. Her books were regularly published in New York and London as well as in Australia, and translated into other languages. On her death in 2007 she was hailed as one of the great originals of Australian literature.

At first glance, a major writer seemed to have sprung fully formed onto the national and international literary scene. Yet the most extraordinary thing about Elizabeth Jolley gaining recognition as a published writer is the immensely long apprenticeship that she served before any of these books appeared. Her search for publishers went on longer and involved more manuscripts in circulation than any other we know of. In fact, she had been writing seriously since the early 1950s. Her early manuscripts included 'The Feast of Life', which was transmuted some forty years later into the trilogy of *My Father's Moon*, *Cabin Fever* and *The Georges' Wife*. The trilogy, for Nobel laureate JM Coetzee as for many other readers, 'stands out as the most ambitious and most accomplished work in Elizabeth Jolley's oeuvre'.[1]

For all the intervening years Jolley had kept this and other manuscripts in a trunk, which accompanied her and her family when they emigrated from Glasgow to Perth. During her first fifteen years in Australia she submitted six novel-length manuscripts – versions of these early works and new ones – and five variant collections of short stories to thirteen different publishers in Australia and England, without success. In a single year she received thirty-nine rejection slips.[2] Her first success with a novel came when *Palomino* won a prize for an unpublished manuscript in 1974, but even so that book did not appear in print until 1980, when she was fifty-seven years old.

It was her short stories that eventually rewarded her persistence. Beginning in 1965, some found places in Australian magazines and anthologies. Then the BBC World Service broadcast several, which later made up her first published collection and part of her second. In 1975 she entered four radio play scripts in the ABC Soundstage competition, which she developed from unpublished short stories based on monologues or dialogues. These successes were followed by others, later published in *Off the Air: Nine plays for radio by Elizabeth Jolley*.[3] At the time radio was an important publishing outlet for short story and play writers, and it provided Jolley with vital training in the use of dialogue and understanding how to shape her stories along a 'climactic curve'.[4]

She published short story and radio play versions of several stories, including 'Woman in a Lampshade', a story with the hallmark qualities of her early published work. Here the protagonist, a writer called Jasmine Tredwell, has brought a young male hitchhiker, rescued from the cold and rain, back to her farm:

> Jasmine felt safe in the lamplight. And she felt safe in the lampshade, pretty too. She was not a pretty woman, she never pretended to be. But the lampshade, when she put it on, made her feel pretty, softly so, and feminine. It was the colour of ripe peaches and made of soft pleats of silk . . . To wear the lampshade suggested the dangerous and the exotic while still sheltered under a cosy domesticity . . .
>
> 'Are you awake?' she asked the young man later that night. He was buried under a heap of old fur coats and several spoiled pages . . .
>
> 'Young man, could you move over a bit, my typewriter's falling off my knee, it's giving me the most awful cramp. Also, I'm getting a pain in my back. Ah! That's better. No, no further or you'll fall out . . .'
>
> He drew the coats closer and made no sound.[5]

Absurd humour with sinister undertones teeters on the edge of sexual innuendo as Jasmine, wearing the pink lampshade, tapping away on her typewriter in bed, insists on telling the young man about the problems posed by the story she is writing, about two lesbians and a hotel clerk. Suggesting 'the dangerous and the exotic while still sheltered under a cosy domesticity', Jolley's stock in trade in these early stories, was a profoundly unfamiliar combination of elements in 1960s Australian fiction. It is hardly surprising, though regrettable, that her fiction did not readily find a hearing among publishers and editors. She later relished reporting their rude remarks, such as 'too menopausal' (Richard Walsh of *Pol* magazine), too many capital letters (James McAuley of *Quadrant*), sentimental and twee (Beatrice Davis at Angus & Robertson), and even (this one not attributed) that the author was clearly disturbed and should seek professional help immediately.[6] But at the time such comments must have cut deep, and she admitted that many times during this long period of rejections she was very despondent.[7]

Jolley also suffered from the lack of contacts with other writers and the literary world in general. In her study of Jolley's career Barbara Milech points out the particular isolation experienced by Western Australian writers, especially before the 1970s: for Elizabeth this was exacerbated by her being a migrant.[8] Even the local literary world was for many years a closed book to her. Her husband Leonard Jolley had been appointed university librarian at the University of Western Australia, but she had to forge her own connections with the academic community through what used to be known as the 'wives' club'. Here she made some good friends but resented being subjected to a 'wardrobe makeover' involving a perm, a brassiere and new dress and shoes – not her style at all: she leaned more towards sandals and caftans.[9] Isolated at home with young children, she broke with the expected practice of married women at the time, and took a number of paid jobs – as a nurse (for which she was trained), 'a door-to-door salesman (failed), and a flying domestic'.[10] She later told interviewers that she took these jobs in order to earn money to pay for the typing and postage of her manuscripts, but employment also gave her a degree of psychological and financial independence, a space that she could claim for herself, outside the demands of husband, children and housekeeping.

For her literary education, however, she was indebted to her husband, who had a degree in classical and modern literature.

Although Elizabeth had been educated at a Quaker boarding school and there were always books and music in the home of her English schoolteacher father and Viennese mother, her further formal education had been limited to her nursing training during World War II. As Elizabeth's biographer Brian Dibble makes clear, Leonard's wide knowledge of modernist literature was a crucial resource when she began seriously to write – and also a major element of his attraction for her. During the long and traumatic lead-up to their marriage (for Leonard was already married when they met) and in their early years together in Scotland, they habitually talked books and theatre, sometimes wrote stories together, and Leonard would read and comment on her journals.[11]

The initial years in Western Australia were crowded with new experiences, some happy, some distressing, but eventually Elizabeth returned to her writing.[12] What she needed at this stage in her life was a circle of people outside the family, who would understand and support her literary ambitions without being close enough to exert demands on her.

A fortuitous meeting in 1974 with Ian Templeman, the founder of the Fremantle Arts Centre, and his invitation to teach there brought Elizabeth Jolley into contact with a whole new community of people who cared about writing, welcomed her and appreciated what she had to offer.[13] She taught classes 'for the enjoyment of literature and the art of writing'[14] in Fremantle and also at country community centres and in prisons. From 1978 she also taught creative writing at WAIT (now Curtin University) where Tim Winton was one of her students, and where she established friendships with, among others, Brian Dibble and Barbara Milech, whose research on her life and writing have provided crucial resources for later Jolley readers.

Something of what Fremantle Arts Centre meant to her is expressed in her memory of feeling elated and excited going into the building itself, for 'If people are going towards something they want to do very much a secret intangible excitement is generated and perhaps this is a part of the magic.' It was also because of the Arts Centre that she experienced the 'long journeys into the wheat [country]', 'far away places' that she would otherwise never have seen – and so, she wrote, she was able to incorporate into her fiction a character who pushes a dead body down a well and another who loses his sense of direction in unending paddocks.[15]

Teaching gave her the opportunity to explore her own and others' writing techniques, but also to reflect on her own processes of composition. The effort of clarification that teaching requires no doubt helped her to imagine her readers as she reworked and polished her stories, a process she described in an interview. 'When I'm first writing,' she said, 'I'm reader and writer. And then in subsequent writings I rearrange and craft, and think, what will a reader make of this?'[16] Perhaps most important of all, teaching 'created her first audience, and it gave her an opportunity to develop the persona she would use as a writer'.[17] The pleasures of teaching as performance are suggested in her story, 'The Performance', where a husband tells of listening to his wife, a teacher, in the bathroom:

> She's already preparing her next class, her next informal lecture. She talks it out aloud to herself in the shower and in front of the mirror. I hear her, her voice joyful, eager, laughing, telling, talking to her class, talking to herself.
>
> "I want you to listen to Beethoven," she says . . . "I want you to listen to the music and note down your private thoughts, and then suddenly a woman darts across the road, she stumbles on the pavement and falls and the contents of her handbag spill . . . Now write, and while the piano goes on playing Beethoven, write everything as it scatters from the handbag. Write!"[18]

Significantly, the wife's pleasure and excitement are observed by the husband who, not being a part of these new experiences, feels as if he is merely 'on the edge of her performance'. Jolley's biographer observes that the time of writing this story was fraught for her, as Leonard's arthritis made him more difficult to live with and she worried about 'the starvation of family life'.[19]

Yet finding a new circle of people who could advise her and open up new experiences to feed into her writing must have lessened Elizabeth's dependence on Leonard's judgment and given her a firmer sense of her own powers. Her husband declined to be involved in her new activities, and she saw her writing as 'the beginning of a new way of life for us'.[20] Having more congenial paid work, she no longer had to indulge in protective self-mockery about being a 'flying domestic' or 'failed salesman'. Their children were grown up, and when Leonard retired in 1979 she no longer had to ferry him to the university and back every day. By 1980 she was freer than she had ever been, the balance of her marriage appears to have stabilised, and she was ready to turn the corner into the broad and busy avenue of her public career.

Writers' Week in Adelaide in March 1980 and the launch of Jolley's second book of stories, *The Travelling Entertainer*, marked the end of her isolation from the literary scene and ushered in her miraculous publishing decade. It was on this occasion that she met Caroline Lurie, who became her literary agent and helped to launch her brilliant career. Writers' Week gave Elizabeth a taste of the wider literary world that she was about to join.[21] Among other Australian guests, several of whom would soon be reviewing her books, she probably met Dorothy Hewett, Tom Shapcott, Judith Rodriguez, Jean Bedford, Laurie Clancy, Christopher Koch, and chair of the Literature Board Bob Brissenden. She could have heard a panel of speakers on the position of women writers in cultures reluctant to accept them as voices of authority, where

Dorothy Hewett nevertheless objected to the 'ghetto' mentality that would cast her always as a 'woman writer' rather than a citizen of the world.[22] But Elizabeth was by no means converted to an activist stance on this issue.

A few years later, when she was famous enough to be interviewed by journalists, Elizabeth enjoyed a little gentle feminist-baiting, insisting, for example, that she was unable to settle down to write whenever there were household tasks left undone or she was needed by a member of her family[23] – though in truth by the mid 1980s the children were adults and the only family member constantly in need of her attention was her husband. Jolley's compassion for social outsiders, a constant in her writing, did not lead her in the direction of cultural politics, feminist or otherwise. Unlike her contemporaries, the poets Dorothy Hewett and Rosemary Dobson, she did not participate in women's publishing enterprises such as Sisters, although she did contribute to the feminist anthologies *Stories of Her Life* (Outback Press, 1979) and *Frictions* (Sybylla Cooperative Press, 1982). Unlike Hewett or Thea Astley she did not relish mocking patriarchal attitudes, and she resisted the suggestion that the difficulties she had experienced had anything to do with her being a woman.[24] Nevertheless 1980, which marked the beginning of a decade of success for her, also became known as the decade of the women, when numbers of women writers of her generation and younger dominated the Australian literary scene.[25]

The shape of Elizabeth Jolley's career, according to Barbara Milech's analysis, shows how important to her growing success were developments in the national literary institutional infrastructure through the 1980s. The Fremantle Arts Centre was brought into being because of Commonwealth grants for regional arts, and its outreach program provided Jolley with teaching opportunities. Its publishing arm, supported by grants from the Literature Board of the Australia Council, brought out five of her early books. Most of Jolley's first seven books, in fact, were published with Literature Board subsidies, and she was awarded one of the Board's Senior Fellowships in 1984. Delys Bird's account of her radio broadcasting career notes that the revival of ABC radio drama in the 1970s from which she benefited was also prompted by the new levels of government support for the arts.[26]

In a 1986 interview after Jolley won the Miles Franklin prize for *The Well*, she was asked if she was concerned about her long overdue recognition. She answered: 'No, it doesn't worry me at all. I'm rather glad it's come, but I was writing for many years before my work was acceptable because I was writing about things that were not acceptable in Australia, in literature. And things have changed a lot. The climate of acceptance has changed a lot, and that has been very fortunate for me.'[27]

The view that the world was not yet ready for her kind of writing – a view Jolley encouraged by comments like this and supported with the kind of horror stories about editors' comments quoted earlier – does not wholly account for her long, slow battle to be published. Barbara Milech convincingly demonstrates that Jolley learned 'a canny determination not only to write in her own way but also to find access to the literary infrastructure of a particular time and place'. Yet there was a significant confluence between that expansion of the 'literary infrastructure' and the liberalisation of attitudes, especially in sexual matters, in the early 1970s. Jolley's interest in unconventional sexual and erotic encounters seemed to belong to this movement of liberalisation, yet her way of treating emotional states and relationships did not. The new Australian writing of the 1970s, of the kind represented by the work of Frank Moorhouse with its focus on urban youth in sexual and social rebellion, offered no obvious place for a writer whose characters were usually middle-aged or old, denizens of the suburbs rather than the inner city, not rebels against restriction but social outcasts or misfits, pursuing and usually failing to establish connection with others. Among her younger mostly male contemporaries the pathos of her stories could easily seem sentimental.

Nevertheless, connections with literary radicals were important in her early publishing career. In 1976 her story 'Hilda's Wedding' was published by *Tabloid Story*, an innovative venture for publishing short fiction as an insert in regular magazines (where Amy Witting had published two years earlier). The brainchild of Frank Moorhouse, Michael Wilding and Carmel Kelly, its agenda included combating the censorship of sexual material as well as promoting experimental short fiction.[28] Jolley's work fulfilled both criteria, but she might have been surprised to find her first published story appearing in *Tabloid Story* number 22, an insert in a rock magazine called *Loose Licks: A Bi-monthly Review of Music, Media, Drugs and Lifestyles*. This was a far cry from the BBC World Service, where her stories had so far been broadcast, although those stories were just as anarchic and darkly funny as 'Hilda's Wedding'.[29] Judging from what she had written, the editors 'imagined her as some groovy young thing in her twenties, not a woman past fifty . . . whose husband Leonard was the University Librarian . . . [who] could send his staff searching (in vain) for information about *Loose Licks*'.[30]

Another radical publishing venture of the 1970s, Outback Press, took up her first novel, *Palomino*. Outback had been responsible for two pioneering anthologies of women's poetry (*Mother I'm Rooted*, 1975) and stories (*Stories of her Life*, 1979, in which Jolley's story 'Winter Nelis' appeared). It was established in Melbourne in 1973 by a group of young men including Morry Schwartz and Alfred Milgrom, just in time to benefit from the Whitlam government's new literature grants, aimed at creating an Australian publishing industry. Outback Press was quickly awarded five publishing subsidies, worth $5000.[31] It saw itself 'in the new tradition of small presses, aiming for a young, thinking market . . . relying on offset printing, eye-grabbing graphics and unconventional typography. The new journalism is one of our strong things'.[32]

These stylistic features suited the unconventional nature of Jolley's writing, and were shared by the new Fremantle Arts Centre Press, which published her first book, *Five Acre Virgin and other stories*, in 1976. No doubt it looked rather different from the first book Elizabeth had envisaged when she vowed that she would never publish her own work.[33] Professionally produced, it was nevertheless unlike commercially published books of fiction: it featured line drawings by a local artist, Sue Grey-Smith, who also designed the book. The jacket description of the author as 'half English and three-quarters Viennese' was refreshingly insouciant. The author's photo shows a strong-featured woman with short hair and glasses, wearing an embroidered Indian shirt of the kind favoured by students and hippies in the 1970s. She is caught mid-speech, and while one hand holds a coffee mug, the other gestures eloquently with long, bony fingers. The relaxed style of the times was also evident in the inclusion of an 'Author's Note', describing the provenance of the stories, written since Jolley's arrival in Australia, and her method of starting with 'one little picture, a few words, an idea so slender it hardly matters and then, suddenly, I am exploring human feelings and reasons'.

In contrast, her third collection of stories, *Woman in a Lampshade*, published by Penguin Australia in 1983, had no such personal touches or individualised design. Nevertheless it represented a new dimension of success for the writer to see this and *Mr Scobie's Riddle* published under the Penguin Australia imprint in the same year, with a vastly increased readership.

Small independent presses, vital though they were in the 1970s, could rarely compete in terms of distribution and reviews. Jolley's first books attracted only two or three reviews apiece, although when her fourth, *The Newspaper of Claremont Street*, appeared under the Fremantle Arts Centre Press imprint in 1981, there were at least a dozen.[34] As her titles began to accumulate there were several important critical evaluations published in the early 1980s by Tom Shapcott, Laurie Clancy, Andrew Reimer and Helen Garner. Even so, breaking into the world of commercial publishing did not guarantee that all Jolley's books would be accepted, and Fremantle Arts Centre Press stepped in to publish several titles that were deemed too strange for the commercial presses – *Milk and Honey* in 1984 and *The Sugar Mother* in 1988.[35]

Outback Press's success as an independent publisher was shorter-lived than that of Fremantle Arts Centre Press. Elizabeth's experience in publishing *Palomino* with Outback was not a happy one. Her manuscript was accepted in May 1977, and in March 1978 she met the publisher at Adelaide Writers' Week, to her great joy. But the book did not appear until 1980, and even then – to add insult to injury – the press went broke before it had sent out any but review copies. She received no royalties, and a court case had to be instigated before she could regain the rights and have the book republished by University of Queensland Press.[36]

Palomino concerns a love affair between two women, a subject almost never treated in an Australian novel before. Even more unusually, the lovers are separated in age by thirty years, and the older woman, Laura, was once in love with the mother of the younger one, Andrea. A further potentially shocking aspect of the story is that Andrea is infatuated with her younger brother, and is pregnant by him during the time that the love between her and Laura develops. Despite the potential melodrama of this situation, the novel is tender and lyrical, incorporating the sensations of the transition from winter through spring into the heat of summer on Laura's isolated farm as her loneliness is assuaged and intimacy grows, only to become oppressive. The presence of the feckless Mr Murphy and his intrusive wife and ragged children counteracts the lyricism and suggests Laura's dependence and vulnerability. Without the anarchic humour of her 1980s novels like *Mr Scobie's Riddle* and *Miss Peabody's Inheritance*, in *Palomino* the rhythms of the narrative are slow and repetitive, and the structure is complex, the main story enfolded around revelations of the past and future of this inevitably doomed relationship.

Jolley had been working on this novel for a long time, and would re-work it again at the behest of her publisher.[37] An earlier version had been summarily rejected by Angus & Robertson in 1963, as 'a dull and melancholy work', 'merely neurotic – not life like',[38] and the following note by Jolley, probably an unsent response to these comments, expressed scorn for those who misunderstood what she was saying:

> It is true I am interested in the psychology of lonely women. Most people if they read this book will relate the situation and the events to the Author. This is natural but it is narrow and conventional. A greater mind can see the relationship of Laura and Eva as something far wider and deeper and far reaching into the lives of people. It is a predicament existing and yet non existent because such feelings are crushed in the superficial trivial details which crowd up most people's lives . . .
>
> I love the relationship I might have created between these two had not Eva been swept along in a suburban canal of the shallow and the superficial. I love the tenderness and the nobility and the depths of feeling and I love the possibilities.
>
> This writing will be lost among the small minded men and women brought up in safe rigid rules which prevent them for ever from reaching any heights or depths of feeling about anything.[39]

Clearly, she was anxious that the lesbian love story not be seen as sensational, but as principally a meditation on loneliness, love and friendship.

By the time the book was published some seventeen years after this note was written, few readers were shocked and many, exposed to new ideas about sexual and social liberation, were intrigued. They not only questioned those 'safe rigid rules' that Jolley also scorned, but also understood that, as one reviewer put it, 'society at once publicly condemns, outlaws and sensationalises' such relationships.[40] Some responses even suggested disappointment that the relationship was too obviously headed for failure.[41] The 'personal is political' idea, so crucial to both women's and gay liberation in the 1970s and 1980s, also fed into the expectation that writers would confidently admit to drawing on their own experiences of unconventional relationships, but Elizabeth Jolley did not share this view, and she continued to resist readers' desire to 'relate the situation and the events to the Author', as she put it in her 1963 note on the text.

The process of editing the manuscript seems to have caused a good deal of heartache. Elizabeth's later comments on the three-year delay suggest that Outback was worried about negative reactions to the lesbian theme in general.[42] However, the manuscript versions, and Jolley's draft notes addressed to Alfred Milgrom, suggest that he had asked her for various kinds of clarification, both to the structure and about the characters' relationships, and that she took this to be a request to simplify. In the published version, rather than conventional chapters, the narrative is presented in seven unevenly sized parts, the central three of which comprise an account of earlier episodes in Laura's life, in the form of letters left for Andrea to read in her absence. Jolley's notes mention having condensed these sections. The following note refers to the section entitled 'The Cardboard Diary', which deals with Laura's love for Andrea's mother, Eva, many years previously:

> I hope the relationship which is unacceptable in society and in Eva's life (which represents a section of society) will be more believable to a reader. Laura longs to love etc. I hope I have made this longing clearer and I hope I have made its impossibility clear. I think this section must make a little block between the two halves of the book . . . but of course I don't want to 'block off' possible readers![43]

It sounds as if, rather than simplifying, she had to make the unrequited nature of this earlier love convincing to a young man at Outback Press in the 1970s.

As so few copies of this edition of the novel were published, initial reviews were rare, but two were highly positive. Thomas Shapcott's substantial review in *Westerly* set the novel in the context of Jolley's short stories and their distinctive 'psychic world', using the ambiguities of predator and victim in the lesbian story 'Grasshoppers' to introduce *Palomino*. His discussion of the novel took into account the dangers of the youth/age 'ritual of infatuation', noting Jolley's evocation of *Death in Venice*, as well as the 'warmly celebrative' presentation of the sexual relationship and the resolution 'towards growth rather than decay'.[44] Nancy Keesing, reviewing the novel with Beverly Farmer's treatment of a lesbian relationship in *Alone*, offered some reflections on the time lag between the practice of taboo behaviours and their social acceptance (she mentioned abortion as well as same-sex relationships). She had little to say about the novel, expressing doubt about Andrea's 'excessive background' – her infatuation with her brother – and a conviction that this relationship between a 'real' and a 'temporary' lesbian was doomed. Nevertheless she opened her review with the firm opinion that '*Palomino* establishes Elizabeth Jolley as absolutely one of the best writers of fiction in this country.'[45]

These appreciative reviews suggest the importance for a writer to be known to other writers. Shapcott recalls that he had met

Jolley in 1979 when he was writer in residence at Curtin, although he had begun a correspondence with her earlier, after the appearance of her first book.[46] Among Keesing's correspondence is a letter from Jolley in December 1980. Referring to their having met at a Fremantle Writers Weekend, she thanked Keesing for permission to use her poems in teaching, and described *Palomino* having been 'ignored by the *West Australian*' and called a 'dismal failure' in the *Weekend Australian* – but in *Cleo* 'someone called Brenda Little has given a different picture of the book', for which she felt grateful.[47]

Most important of all for Elizabeth Jolley was having her books placed with reliable publishers, and here Caroline Lurie's work as her agent from 1980 was crucial. Jolley was Lurie's first author though she soon added other eminent names to her list, including Jessica Anderson, Kate Grenville and Tim Winton. Inexperienced as an agent she might have been, but her years of working in the publishing industry in London and Melbourne had shown her that authors who had an agent were treated differently from others. Her knowledge of Australian publishing meant that she could take advantage of new opportunities for her client. As well, Lurie was an Englishwoman who had come to Australia with her husband.[48] She and Elizabeth Jolley had much in common and became friends, despite their difference in age, and Lurie later edited two collections of Jolley's occasional prose, *Central Mischief* (1992) and *Learning to Dance* (2006).

Within a very few years Elizabeth Jolley was winning prizes and being inundated with requests for interviews and invitations to writers' festivals. Her readership was large and appreciative. Success fed success. After those long years of rejection slips and suburban isolation in a new country, Jolley's journey in from the cold was enabled by her literary agent, her teaching colleagues, her students and her writer friends, as well as her own courage and persistence.

Her successes were also enabled by the growth of literary

infrastructure in Australia, government funded grants and prizes, and other enterprises – literary awards and associated judging panels, writers' associations and festivals, increased media interest in literature, writers' residencies and creative writing programs in schools and universities, more Australian works appearing on syllabi, with related scholarly interest at conferences and in journals. When Jolley's career is placed in the context of this new energy and investment in regional and community arts, of school and university interest in Australian writing and writers, and of extensive Australian-based publishing, it can be read, as Barbara Milech suggests, as a 'micro-history of cultural politics in Australia' during this period[49] as well as a fascinating story in its own right.

Notes

1 JM Coetzee, 'Jolley's Moon Shines Bright', *Age*, 17 May 2008, A2, p. 16.

2 Brian Dibble, *Doing Life: A biography of Elizabeth Jolley*, University of Western Australia Press, Perth, 2008, p. 184. This chapter is deeply indebted to Dibble's biography, and also to the work of Barbara Milech.

3 Delys Bird, 'Introduction', Elizabeth Jolley, *Off the Air: Nine plays for radio*, Penguin Ringwood, Vic, 1995, pp. xx–xxi.

4 Jolley, quoted in Bird, pp. xxi–xxii.

5 Jolley, *Woman in a Lampshade*, Penguin, Ringwood, Vic, 1983, pp. 138–9.

6 Dibble, *Doing Life*, p. 184.

7 Interview, Jennifer Ellison, *Rooms of their Own*, Penguin, Ringwood, Vic, 1986, pp. 178–9.

8 Milech, 'The Shape of a Writing Career', Introduction to *Elizabeth Jolley Bibliography*, <john.curtin.edu.au/jolley/bibliography_introduction1.html>, accessed 15 April 2009.

9 Dibble, pp. 147–8.

10 This self-description appeared on the cover of her first book, *Five Acre Virgin*, Fremantle Arts Centre Press, 1976, and was repeated in later books.
11 Dibble, pp. 122, 131.
12 Dibble, pp. 145–7.
13 Dibble, pp. 169–71.
14 Wording from *Five Acre Virgin* cover, 1976.
15 'The Fremantle Arts Centre Press and Regional Publishing – Personal Views', *Westerly*, 31(1), 1986, pp. 83–4.
16 Ellison, p. 181.
17 Dibble, p. 170.
18 *The Travelling Entertainer*, Fremantle Arts Centre Press, 1979, pp. 6–7. Jolley used to use music in this way in her own classes: Dibble, p. 170; Tim Winton, 'Remembering Elizabeth Jolley', *Westerly*, 52, 2007, pp. 27–34.
19 Dibble, p. 186.
20 Dibble, p. 203.
21 She had also attended in 1978 with a FACP contingent: Dibble, pp. 180–1.
22 Later published as 'Isis in Search', *New Poetry*, 28, 1, 1980, pp. 49–56, p.50.
23 As reported in Jolley, *Central Mischief*, ed. Caroline Lurie, Penguin Viking, Ringwood, Vic, 1992, pp. 9–10 and 23–4.
24 Ellison p. 188.
25 See Gillian Whitlock, ed., *Eight Voices of the Eighties*, UQP, St Lucia, 1990.
26 Milech, 'The Shape of a Writing Career', *Bibliography*; Bird, Introduction, *Off the Air*, pp. xvii–xviii.
27 ABC Radio National, quoted in ABC obituary transcript 2007.
28 Michael Wilding, 'The *Tabloid Story* Story', *The Tabloid Story Pocketbook*, ed. Wilding, Wild & Woolley, Sydney, 1978, pp. 295–316; also Austlit database, 'Tabloid Story'.

29 BBC World Service broadcasts from 1968 to 1975: Milech bibliography.

30 Lucy Frost, 'Remembering Elizabeth Jolley', *Westerly*, 52, 2007, pp. 24–6. Jolley's persistence with this story, seeking publication in shorter and longer versions over more than ten years, is detailed by Barbara Milech in 'The Shape of a Writing Career'.

31 James Button, 'The art of the deal', *Age*, 21 March 2004, <www.theage.com.au/articles/2004/03/21>, accessed 9 February 2006.

32 Quoted by Morry Schwartz, 'Case Study: Inner-urban and outback', *Paper Empires: A History of the Book in Australia, 1946–2005*, eds Craig Munro and Robyn Sheahan-Bright, UQP, St Lucia, 2006, p. 64.

33 Quoted by Milech, 'The Shape of a Writing Career'.

34 By this time FACP had itself achieved national recognition for publishing Albert Facey's award-winning memoir, *A Fortunate Life*.

35 She asked Tom Shapcott for a report on *Milk and Honey*, which her agent disliked. He strongly recommended it to FACP, and was thrilled when it won an award: Tom Shapcott, personal communication, 8 February 2006.

36 Dibble, p. 184. A rescue of sorts was effected by former Outback partner Alfred Milgrom, who published the novel from his London-based Melbourne House (also dated 1980).

37 The typescript of *Palomino* is headed by a handwritten note, 'Mark 1978. Rewritten from 1960–63–73'. Jolley papers, Mitchell Library, MSS 4880, box 5, item 2.

38 Quoted in Delys Bird, 'Now for the real thing: Elizabeth Jolley's Manuscripts', in Bird and Walker, eds, *Elizabeth Jolley, New Critical Essays*, Collins/Angus & Robertson, North Ryde, NSW, 1991, p. 170.

39 Jolley, note on 'The Cardboard Diary', 1963, Jolley papers, ML MSS 4880, box 4, item 3, notebook; also printed on a card published by the State Library of NSW.

40 Carol Treloar, 'Not What it Seems', *Advertiser*, 13 December 1980, p. 25.

41 Greg Baxter, 'Palomino needs to gallop', *Weekend Australian*, 18–19 October 1980, p. 20.

42 See 'An interview with Elizabeth Jolley', *Scripsi*, 4 (1), 1986, pp. 256–7.

43 'Notes to Mr Alfred Milgrom', Jolley papers, ML MSS 4880, box 5, item 2, p. 1.

44 'Five Acre Hell,' *Westerly*, 4, December 1980, pp. 73–5.

45 'Female friendships', *Australian Book Review*, March 1981, pp. 34–5.

46 Email to the author, 8 February 2006.

47 Jolley to Keesing, 9/12/1980, Keesing papers, MLMSS 2828 add-on 1772, MLK3937. 'Dismal failure' was her interpretation of the review that said 'the emotional wrenchings become tiresome, the outcome obvious': see note 41 above.

48 Barry Oakley, 'Elizabeth Jolley's Guardian Agent', *Weekend Australian*, 17–18 December 1988, p. 7.

49 Milech, 'The Shape of a Writing Career'.

Epilogue

Major changes in arts funding and the associated expansion of literary infrastructure, and growing interest in Australian literature from the mid 1960s onwards benefited all Australian writers. But, especially for the nine women who are the subject of this book, better conditions for writing and publishing were matched by more opportunities to make contact with other writers, and with their readers. The isolation that is so often the theme of their stories melted away.

These nine lives have demonstrated many common features of women's early careers even today. They had to battle with the demons of under-confidence, were torn by conflicting duties to their writing and to their families, and were often isolated or alienated from the literary community. For each one, the particulars of editors' responses to the work they submitted, and reviewers' responses to their published work, strongly suggest that a double standard was frequently applied to women. Yet, looking at them together also brings out the differences of circumstance and temperament which ensured that each woman dealt in her own way with these common difficulties.

In each case, the woman writer's return to publication after periods of silence resembles the nine lives of the legendary cat. If these women seem to us today extraordinarily stoical in the face of the trials and tribulations of their profession, it may be that something about the model of womanhood they were given formed their subjectivities in this way. Something – a mask or a persona – allowed them to deal, unaided, with the demands of marriage and motherhood at the same time as they wrote. Something enabled them to weather disappointments and obscurity and still go on writing. They had few illusions about where they stood as women. Women were to be decorative, charming, but not to have ideas. As Thea Astley said: 'I grew up believing that women weren't really people, and didn't matter in the scheme of things. You've got to remember my age. Men didn't listen to women when they expressed an opinion.'[1]

Astley's way around this perception of having been 'spiritually neutered' by social expectations was to write from a male point of view – a practice that left her, in her fifties, trying to figure out how to write in a female voice. Yet she adapted to this change, and kept on writing 'because I get amused by things, little things that happen, and I want to put them down, and I hope other people might be amused, or interested, or charmed, or revolted, or whatever'.[2] Comparable reinventions of their writing strategies occur in several of these nine lives: Gwen Harwood's proliferation of poetic personae, Rosemary Dobson's engagement with the visual arts, Jessica Anderson's experiments with various genres. Dorothy Hewett pursued a multi-stranded literary career as poet, fiction writer and ultimately dramatist. Elizabeth Jolley eventually found her way around the literary world so that she could call upon a range of contacts and publishers. For others, it was a case of having several careers: Dorothy Green was a poet, scholar, journalist and teacher, Amy Witting a writer and teacher. While critics tend to see Judith Wright as a poet first and last, she herself set high value on her historical work, and regarded her political work for conservation and Aboriginal rights as an absolute necessity. This capacity for reinvention, this flexibility and range, ensured that each writer herself managed nine lives or so.

Nine lives, nine women of the same generation establishing literary careers that eventually brought them recognition as major artists of their time, significant actors in the creation of Australian cultural life. I hope that this book will inspire readers to return to the works themselves, to read them again, or perhaps for the first time, and enter into the worlds they create.

Notes

1 Astley in Jennifer Ellison, *Rooms of their Own*, Penguin Australia, Ringwood, Vic, 1986, p. 56.

2 Astley in *Rooms of their Own*, p. 67.

Acknowledgments

The research for *Nine Lives* was made possible by an Australian Research Council Discovery grant. This book was published with the assistance of a grant from the Australian Academy of the Humanities.

I am grateful for the unstinting help I received from the librarians responsible for the following collections: Manuscripts at the National Library of Australia, the Fryer Library at the University of Queensland, Special Collections at Melbourne University Library, the Mitchell Library at the State Library of NSW and the Manuscripts Collection at the Australian Defence Force Academy. Special Collections librarians at Flinders University and the University of Adelaide were a constant source of help. I would like to record special thanks to the creators and compilers of the AustLit database, in particular Kerry Kilner and Carol Hetherington at the University of Queensland.

For their generous permission to quote from published and unpublished materials I thank the authors and their literary executors: Rosemary Dobson and Robert and Lissant Bolton, the late

Jessica Anderson and Laura Jones, Ed Gregson, Kate Lilley, John Harwood, Meredith McKinney and Patricia Clarke, Andrew Green, Margaret Connolly & Associates, Caroline Lurie and Jenny Darling & Associates.

For photographs of the authors reproduced here I thank Robert Bolton, Kate Lilley, Laura Jones, Meredith McKinney, John Harwood, Margaret Connolly & Associates, the Fryer Library, the Fremantle Arts Centre Press and the Scots PGC College, Warwick.

Some material from the Introduction was published in a different form in my article 'Generations Lost and Found: Reading women writers together' in *Manifesting Literary Feminisms*, edited by Margaret Henderson and Ann Vickery, a special issue of *Australian Literary Studies*, 24 (3–4), 2009.

I am grateful to Rosemary Dobson for sharing her recollections of her early years in Sydney, and to Ed Gregson for talking to me about his mother, Thea Astley. My thanks go to Robert Phiddian, Director of the Flinders Humanities Research Centre, for his support for the project from the beginning, and to Tully Barnett for her work as research assistant in its early stages. I thank Kate Llewellyn for the title, and Tom Shapcott for leads on Elizabeth Jolley's *Palomino*. I am grateful to Jacqueline Kent for her wise and good-humoured editing, and to Nikola Lusk, my editor at UQP, for looking after this book so well.

Thanks to all those colleagues who offered insights and ideas in response to papers on this material, and especially to those who generously read and commented on individual chapters – Debra Adelaide, Delys Bird, Patricia Clarke, Paul Genoni, Susan Lever, Kate Lilley, Willa McDonald, Yvonne Miels, Barbara Milech, Nicole Moore, Brigid Rooney, Ann Vickery. I thank Elizabeth Webby for her encouragement over a long time. As always, my love and gratitude go to Susan Magarey, who read everything, more than once, and endlessly discussed these writers and their work with me.

Extracts from the following poems are taken from *A Human Pattern: Selected Poems* © Judith Wright 1990, published by ETT Imprint, Sydney, 1996: 'The Company of Lovers' (p. 2), 'South of My Days' (p. 11), 'Woman to Man' (p. 20), 'For Precision' (p. 73), 'Sanctuary' (p. 82). Reproduced with permission by ETT Imprint. Extracts from the following poems are taken from *Collected Poems 1942–1970* © Judith Wright 1971, published by Angus & Robertson, North Ryde, NSW, 1971: 'Waiting' (p. 9) , 'Dust' (p. 23), 'The Maker' (p. 32). Reproduced with permission by HarperCollins. Extracts from *A Descant for Gossips* © Thea Astley 1960, published by Angus & Robertson, Sydney, 1960; *The Well Dressed Explorer* © Thea Astley 1962, published by Angus & Robertson, Sydney, 1962; and *The Slow Natives* © Thea Astley 1965, published by Angus & Robertson, Sydney, 1965. Reproduced with permission by Curtis Brown (Australia). Extracts from the following poems are taken from *Selected Poems* © Rosemary Dobson 1973, published by Angus & Robertson, Sydney, 1973: 'The Bystander' (p. 56), 'Young Girl at a Window' (p. 4), 'The Missal' (p. 74), 'The Birth (2)' (p. 89), 'Cock Crow' (p. 100), 'Annunciations' (p. 95); 'Divining Colander' © Rosemary Dobson 2006 is taken from *Australian Book Review*, 282, June–July 2006, p. 54. Reproduced with permission by Curtis Brown (Australia). 'Alter Ego' is taken from *Gwen Harwood: Selected Poems* © Gwen Harwood, published by Angus & Robertson, North Ryde, NSW, 1990. Reproduced with permission by Penguin Group (Australia). Extracts from *I is for Isobel* © Amy Witting 1989, published by Penguin, Ringwood, Vic, 1989; *Collected Poems* © Amy Witting 1998, published by Penguin, Ringwood, Vic, 1998; and *Faces and Voices* © Amy Witting 2000, published by Penguin Viking, Ringwood, Vic, 2000. Reproduced with permission by Penguin Group (Australia). Extract from *Woman in a Lampshade* © Elizabeth Jolley 1983, published by Penguin, Ringwood, Vic, 1983. Reproduced with permission by Penguin Group (Australia).

Select Bibliography

Primary Sources

Includes only those books by the nine writers discussed in the text

Anderson, Jessica, papers, State Library of NSW, ML MSS 3773 and ML MSS 3773 add-on 2040.

—— *An Ordinary Lunacy*, Macmillan, London, 1963.

—— *The Last Man's Head*, Macmillan, London, 1970.

—— *The Commandant*, Macmillan, London, 1975.

—— *Tirra Lirra by the River*, Macmillan, Melbourne, 1978.

—— 'Starting too late', *Meanjin*, 62(2), 2003, pp. 209–16.

Astley, Thea, papers, University of Queensland Fryer Library, UQFL 97.

—— *Meanjin* Archive, Melbourne University Library Special Collections.

—— *Girl with a Monkey*, Angus & Robertson, Sydney, 1958.

—— *A Descant for Gossips*, Angus & Robertson, Sydney, 1960.

—— *The Well Dressed Explorer*, Angus & Robertson, Sydney, 1962.

—— *The Slow Natives*, Angus & Robertson, Sydney, 1965.

—— ed., *Coast to Coast*, Angus & Robertson, Sydney, 1970.

—— and Vida Horn, 'Barjai Days: Hello Laurie, Hello Barrie', *Overland*, 142, 1996, p. 36.

Dobson, Rosemary, papers, National Library of Australia, MS4955.

—— *In a Convex Mirror: Poems*, Dymocks, Sydney, 1944.

—— *The Ship of Ice: With other poems*, Angus & Robertson, Sydney, 1948.

—— *Child with a Cockatoo: With other poems*, Angus & Robertson, Sydney, 1955.

—— *Cock Crow: Poems*, Angus & Robertson, Sydney, 1965.

—— *Focus on Ray Crooke*, UQP, St Lucia, 1971.

—— *A World of Difference: Australian poetry and painting in the 1940s*, 3rd Blaiklock Lecture, Wentworth Press, Sydney, 1973.

—— *Selected Poems*, Angus & Robertson, Sydney, 1973.

—— 'Australian Poets in Profile: 2. Rosemary Dobson', *Southerly*, 40(1), 1980, pp. 3–10.

—— 'Starting out', *Australian Book Review*, 161, June 1994, pp. 55–6.

Green, Dorothy, papers, Australian Defence Force Academy Archives, MS20.

—— papers, National Library of Australia, NLA MS 5678.

—— *Meanjin* Archive, Melbourne University Library Special Collections.

Auchterlonie, Dorothy, *Kaleidoscope*, Viking Press, Sydney, 1940.

—— *The Dolphin*, ANU Press, Canberra, 1967.

Green, Dorothy, ed., *Australian Poetry 1968*, Angus & Robertson, Sydney, 1968.

—— *Ulysses Bound: Henry Handel Richardson and her fiction*, ANU Press, Canberra, 1973.

—— *The Music of Love: Critical essays on literature and life*, Penguin, Ringwood, Vic, 1984.

—— *Writer, Reader, Critic*, Primavera Press, Sydney, 1990.

Harwood, Gwen, *Meanjin* Archive, Melbourne University Library Special Collections.
—— *Poems*, Angus & Robertson, Sydney, 1963.
—— *Poems Volume 2*, Angus & Robertson, Sydney, 1968.
—— 'Lamplit Presences', *Southerly*, 40(3), 1980, pp. 247–54.
—— 'Words and Music', *Southerly*, 46(4), 1986, pp. 367–76.
—— 'Time Beyond Reason', in *Gwen Harwood*, ed. Robert Sellick, CRNLE, Adelaide, 1987, pp. 13–21.
—— *Blessed City: The letters of Gwen Harwood to Thomas Riddell, January–September 1943*, ed. Alison Hoddinott, Angus & Robertson, Sydney, 1990.
—— *A Steady Storm of Correspondence: Selected letters of Gwen Harwood 1943–1995*, ed. Gregory Kratzmann, UQP, St Lucia, 2001.
—— *Gwen Harwood: Collected Poems*, eds Alison Hoddinott and Gregory Kratzmann, UQP, St Lucia, 2003.

Hewett, Dorothy, papers, National Library of Australia, MS 6184.
—— *Meanjin* Archive, Melbourne University Library Special Collections.
—— *Bobbin Up: A novel*, Australasian Book Society, Melbourne, 1959.
—— and Merv Lilley, *What About the People!* National Council of Realist Writers, Sydney, 1962.
—— *Windmill Country*, *Overland* in conjunction with Peter Leyden Publishing, Melbourne, 1968.
—— 'Excess of Love: The irreconcilable in Katharine Susannah Prichard', *Overland*, 43, 1969, pp. 27–31.
—— 'Creating Heroines in Australian plays', *Hecate*, 5(2), 1979, pp. 73–9.
—— 'Shirts, Prams and Tomato Sauce: The All-Australian Theatre', *Contemporary Australian Drama*, ed. Peter Holloway, Currency Press, Sydney, 1981, pp. 77–87.
—— *Wild Card: An Autobiography 1923–1958*, McPhee Gribble, Melbourne, 1990.

—— *Dorothy Hewett: Collected Poems 1940–1995*, ed. William de Grono, Fremantle Arts Centre Press, Perth, 1995.
—— 'Excerpt from "The Empty Room', an autobiography in progress', *Overland*, 160, 2000, pp. 4–10.
—— *The Gipsy Dancer & Early Poems*, ed. Christine Alexander, with others, Juvenilia Press, Sydney, 2009.

Jolley, Elizabeth, papers, State Library of NSW, MLMSS 4880.
—— *Five Acre Virgin*, Fremantle Arts Centre Press, 1976.
—— *The Travelling Entertainer*, Fremantle Arts Centre Press, 1979.
—— *Palomino*, Outback Press, Collingwood, Vic, 1980.
—— *Woman in a Lampshade*, Penguin, Ringwood, Vic, 1983.
—— 'An Interview with Elizabeth Jolley', *Scripsi*, 4(1), 1986, pp. 245–64.
—— 'The Fremantle Arts Centre Press and Regional Publishing – Personal Views', *Westerly*, 31(1), 1986, pp. 83–4.
—— *Central Mischief*, ed. Caroline Lurie, Penguin Viking, Ringwood, Vic, 1992.
—— *Off the Air: Nine plays for radio*, ed. Delys Bird, Penguin, Ringwood, Vic, 1995.

Witting, Amy, papers, State Library of NSW, MLMSS 5303, ML 13/89.
—— *The Visit*, Nelson, Melbourne, 1977.
—— *I for Isobel*, Penguin, Ringwood, Vic, 1989.
—— *Collected Poems*, Penguin, Ringwood, Vic, 1998.
—— *Faces and Voices: Collected Stories*, Penguin Viking, Ringwood, Vic, 2000.
—— 'Surviving', *Southerly*, 57(3), 1997, pp. 235–7.
—— 'Brotherly Affection', *Australian*, 14 August 1999.
—— 'Posthumous Dialogue Concerning Certain Errors in Michael Ackland's *Damaged Men*', *Quadrant*, 45(11), November 2001, pp. 37–9.

Wright, Judith, papers, National Library of Australia, MS 5781.
—— *Meanjin* archive, Melbourne University Library Special Collections.
—— *The Moving Image*, Meanjin Press, Melbourne, 1946.
—— *Woman to Man*, Angus & Robertson, Sydney, 1949.
—— *The Gateway*, Angus & Robertson, Sydney, 1953.
—— *The Two Fires*, Angus & Robertson, Sydney, 1955.
—— *Five Senses: Selected poems*, Angus & Robertson, Sydney, 1963.
—— *Preoccupations in Australian Poetry*, OUP, Melbourne, 1965.
—— *The Nature of Love*, Sun Books, Melbourne, 1966.
—— *Collected Poems 1942–1970*, Angus & Robertson, Sydney, 1971.
—— *Because I Was Invited*, OUP, Melbourne, 1975.
—— *A Human Pattern: Selected Poems*, ETT Imprint, Sydney, 1996.
—— *Half a Lifetime*, ed. Patricia Clarke, Text Publishing, Melbourne, 2001.
—— *The Equal Heart and Mind: Letters between Judith Wright and Jack McKinney*, eds Patricia Clarke and Meredith McKinney, UQP, St Lucia, 2004.
—— *With Love & Fury: Selected letters of Judith Wright*, eds Patricia Clarke and Meredith McKinney, National Library of Australia, Canberra, 2006.
—— *Portrait of a Friendship: The letters of Barbara Blackman and Judith Wright, 1950–2000*, ed. Bryony Cosgrove, The Miegunyah Press, Melbourne, 2007.

Secondary Sources

Atherton, Cassandra, *Flashing Eyes and Floating Hair: A reading of Gwen Harwood's pseudonymous poetry*, Australian Scholarly Publishing, Melbourne, 2006.
Ayres, Marie-Louise, '"Me" is not a stable reality: Negotiations of identity in the poetry of Dorothy Auchterlonie, Rosemary Dobson, Dorothy Hewett and JS Harry', unpublished PhD thesis, ANU, Canberra, 1994.
—— 'Rosemary Dobson', *Australian Writers 1915–1950*, ed. Selina

Samuels, *Dictionary of Literary Biography*, vol. 260, 2002, pp. 99–105.

Baker, Candida, *Yacker 3: Australian writers talk about their work*, Pan, Sydney, 1989.

Barry, Elaine, *Fabricating the Self: The fictions of Jessica Anderson*, UQP, St Lucia, 1992.

Bird, Delys and Brenda Walker, eds, *Elizabeth Jolley, New Critical Essays*, Collins/Angus & Robertson, North Ryde, NSW, 1991.

Blackman, Barbara, 'Brisbane in the Forties: My "Barjai" days', *Meanjin*, 54(3), 1995, pp. 531–41.

Blair, Ruth, 'Jessica Queale Anderson', in *Australian Writers 1975–2000*, ed. Selina Samuels, *Dictionary of Literary Biography*, vol. 325, Gale, Detroit, 2006, accessed through *Literature Resource Center*, Gale, Flinders University Library, 14 September 2008.

Bode, Katherine, 'Along Gender Lines: Reassessing relationships between Australian novels, gender and genre from 1930 to 2006', *Australian Literary Studies*, 24(3–4), 2009, pp. 79–95.

Bolton, Alec, 'Angus & Robertson in the 1950s: Publishing in an age of innocence', *Publishing Studies*, 1 Spring 1995, pp. 12–20.

Bourdieu, Pierre, *The Field of Cultural Production*, Polity, Cambridge, UK, 1993.

Brady, Veronica, *South of My Days, A biography of Judith Wright*, Angus & Robertson, Sydney, 1998.

Brissenden, RF, 'The poetry of Judith Wright', in *Critical Essays on Judith Wright*, ed. AK Thomson, Jacaranda Press, Brisbane, 1968.

Brooks, David and Brenda Walker, eds, *Poetry and Gender*, UQP, St Lucia, 1989.

Buckridge, Patrick, 'Clearing a Space for Australian Literature, 1940–1965', in *The Oxford Literary History of Australia*, eds Bruce Bennett and Jennifer Strauss, OUP, Melbourne, 1998, pp. 169–92.

Burrows, JF, 'Chalk and Cheese', *Southerly*, 23(4), 1963, pp. 276–80.

Campbell, Richard, 'Dorothy Green, 1915–1991', *LiNQ*, 18(2), 1991, pp. 110–11.

Carter, David, 'Publishing, patronage and cultural politics: Institutional changes in the field of Australian literature from 1950', *The Cambridge History of Australian Literature*, ed. Peter Pierce, CUP, Melbourne, 2009, pp. 360–90.

Coleman, Peter, Interview with Amy Witting, 1992, National Library of Australia Oral History, TRC 2864.

Couper, JM, 'The Novels of Thea Astley', *Meanjin*, 26(3), 1967, pp. 332–7.

Davidson, Jim, *Sideways from the page: The Meanjin interviews*, Fontana, Sydney, 1983.

De Berg, Hazel, Interview with Thea Astley, 1964, National Library of Australia, TRC 1/102.

—— Interview with Dorothy Hewett, 1973, National Library of Australia, Oral History Collection 658, 2/26.

Dibble, Brian, *Doing Life: A biography of Elizabeth Jolley*, University of WA Press, Perth, 2008.

Digby, Jenny, *A Woman's Voice: Conversations with Australian poets*, UQP, St Lucia, 1996.

Douglas, Dennis, 'Gwen Harwood: The Poet as Doppelganger', *Quadrant*, 13(2), 1969, pp. 15–19.

Dunlevy, Maurice, 'Dorothy Green the Woman', *Canberra Times*, 30 December 1967.

DuPlessis, Rachel Blau, *Blue Studios: Poetry and its cultural work*, University of Alabama Press, Tuscaloosa, AL, 2006.

Ellison, Jennifer, *Rooms of their Own*, Penguin, Ringwood, Vic, 1986.

Grant, Jane, *Kylie Tennant: A life*, National Library of Australia, Canberra, 2006.

Grenville, Kate and Sue Woolfe, 'Jessica Anderson: *The Commandant*', *Making Stories: How ten Australian novels were written*, Allen & Unwin, Sydney, 1993, pp.1–32.

Hatherell, William, *The Third Metropolis*, UQP, St Lucia, 2007.

Heseltine, HP, *The Most Glittering Prize: The Miles Franklin Literary Award*

1957–1998, Australian Defence Force Academy, School of Literature and Communication and Permanent Press, Canberra, ACT, 2001.

Hoddinott, Alison, *Gwen Harwood: The real and the imagined world*, Angus & Robertson, Sydney, 1991.

Hooton, Joy, 'Rosemary Dobson: A life of making poetry', in Hooton, ed., *Rosemary Dobson: A celebration*, National Library of Australia, Canberra, 2000.

Hope, AD, *Australian Poets 1950–1962*, Melbourne University Press, Parkville, Vic, 1963.

—— 'Rosemary Dobson: Portrait in a Mirror', *Quadrant*, 16(4), 1972, pp. 10–14.

—— *AD Hope: Selected poetry and prose*, ed. David Brooks, Halstead, Sydney, 2000.

Hospital, Janette Turner, 'A Writer Comes in from the Cold', *Sydney Morning Herald*, 14 October 1989, p. 80.

James, Neil and Elizabeth Webby, 'Canon around the hub: Angus & Robertson and the post-war literary canon', *Southerly*, 57(3), 1997, pp. 51–66.

Kent, Jacqueline, *A Certain Style: Beatrice Davis, a literary life*, Penguin, Ringwood, Vic, 2001.

Kinross-Smith, Graeme, 'The intricate, devised, hearing of sight: A profile of Rosemary Dobson', *Westerly*, 3, September 1974, pp. 55–63.

McCooey, David, 'A conversation with Rosemary Dobson', *Antipodes*, 10(2), 1996, pp. 107–10.

McDonald, Willa, *Warrior for Peace: Dorothy Auchterlonie Green*, Australian Scholarly Publishing, Melbourne, 2009.

McKernan, Susan, *A Question of Commitment: Australian literature in the twenty years after the war*, Allen & Unwin, Sydney, 1989.

McLaren, John, *Writing in Hope and Fear*, Cambridge University Press, Melbourne, 1995.

Marr, David, *Patrick White: A life*, Vintage, Sydney, 1992.

—— ed. *Patrick White: Letters*, Random House, Sydney, 1994.

Miels, Yvonne, 'The Net Under the Tightrope: The poetry and prose of Amy Witting', unpublished PhD thesis, Flinders University, Adelaide, 1997.

—— 'Amy Witting', *Australian Writers 1975–2000*, ed. Selina Samuels, *Dictionary of Literary Biography*, vol. 325, Gale, Detroit, 2006.

Milech, Barbara, 'The Shape of a Writing Career', Introduction to *Elizabeth Jolley Bibliography*, <http://john.curtin.edu.au/jolley/bibliography_introduction1.html>, accessed 15 April 2009.

Modjeska, Drusilla, *Exiles at Home: Australian women writers 1925–1945*, Sirius/Angus & Robertson, Sydney, 1981.

Moody, David, 'The Poems of Gwen Harwood', *Meanjin*, 22(4), 1963, pp. 418–21.

Moore, Nicole, 'Dorothy Hewett', *Companion to Australian Literature*, eds Nicholas Birns and Rebecca McNeer, Boydell and Brewer/University of Rochester Press, New York, 2007, pp. 321–34.

Munro, Craig and Robyn Sheahan-Bright, eds, *Paper Empires: A history of the book in Australia 1946–2005*, UQP, St Lucia, 2006.

Oakley, Barry, 'Elizabeth Jolley's Guardian Agent', *Weekend Australian*, 17–18 December 1988.

Phelan, Nancy, *Writing Round the Edges: A selective memoir*, UQP, St Lucia, 2003.

Rooney, Brigid, *Literary Activists*, UQP, St Lucia, 2009.

Sheridan, Susan, with Barbara Baird, Kate Borrett and Lyndall Ryan, *Who Was That Woman? The* Australian Women's Weekly *in the postwar years*, UNSW Press, Sydney, 2002.

—— 'Cold War, Home Front: Australian women writers and artists in the 1950s', *Australian Literary Studies*, 20(3), 2002, pp. 155–66.

—— 'Thea Astley: A woman among the satirists of postwar modernity', *Australian Feminist Studies*, 29(3), 2003, pp. 261–71.

—— 'Violence, Irony and Reading Relations: Thea Astley's *Drylands*', in *Thea Astley's Fictional Worlds*, Cambridge Scholars Press, Newcastle-upon-Tyne, 2006, pp. 164–75.

—— and Paul Genoni, eds, *Thea Astley's Fictional Worlds*, Cambridge Scholars Press, Newcastle-upon-Tyne, 2006.

—— 'Gentlemen's Agreements: *Southerly*'s first editors', *Southerly*, 67(1 & 2), 2007, pp. 333–47.

—— 'Suburban Sonnets: "Mrs Harwood", Miriam Stone and domestic modernity', *Australian Literary Studies*, 23(2), 2007, pp. 140–52.

—— '*Australian Letters* and Postwar Modernity', *Australian Literary Studies*, 23(3), 2008, pp. 264–78.

—— 'Dorothy Hewett's Paths to *The Chapel Perilous*', *Westerly*, 54, July 2009, pp. 170–88.

Strauss, Jennifer, *Boundary Conditions: The poetry of Gwen Harwood*, UQP, St Lucia, 1992.

—— *Judith Wright*, OUP, Melbourne, 1995.

—— 'Gwen Harwood', *Australian Writers 1950–1975*, ed. Selina Samuels, *Dictionary of Literary Biography*, vol. 289, Gale Research, Detroit, 2004, pp. 107–13.

Thompson, John, 'Poetry in Australia: Rosemary Dobson', *Southerly*, 28(3), 1968, p. 204.

Tranter, John, 'Rosemary Dobson in conversation with John Tranter', 2004, pp. 1–2, <www.austlit.edu.au>, accessed 5 January 2006.

Trigg, Stephanie, *Gwen Harwood*, Oxford Australian Writers, OUP, Melbourne, 1994.

Vickery, Ann, *Stressing the Modern: Cultural politics in Australian women's poetry*, Salt, Cambridge, UK, 2007.

Walker, Shirley, *The Poetry of Judith Wright*, Edward Arnold, Melbourne, 1980.

Walker, Suzanne, Interview with Thea Astley, 1974, National Library of Australia Transcript, TRC 275.

Wallace-Crabbe, Chris, 'My Ghost, My Self: The poetry of Gwen Harwood', *Meanjin*, 28(2), 1969, pp. 264–67.

—— 'Poetry and Modernism', *Oxford Literary History of Australia*, eds Bruce Bennett and Jennifer Strauss, OUP, Melbourne, 1998, pp. 217–35.

Whitlock, Gillian, ed., *Eight Voices of the Eighties*, UQP, St Lucia, 1989.

Wilding, Michael, 'The *Tabloid Story* Story' in *The Tabloid Story Pocketbook*, ed. Michael Wilding, Wild & Woolley, Sydney, 1978, pp. 295–316.

Willbanks, Ray, 'Thea Astley in America', *Antipodes*, 2(2), 1988, pp. 107–8.

—— *Speaking Volumes*, Penguin, Ringwood, Vic, 1992.

Williams, Barbara, *In Other Words: Interviews with Australian poets*, Rodopi, Amsterdam, 1998.

Woolf, Virginia, *A Room of One's Own*, Hogarth Press, London, 1928.

Index